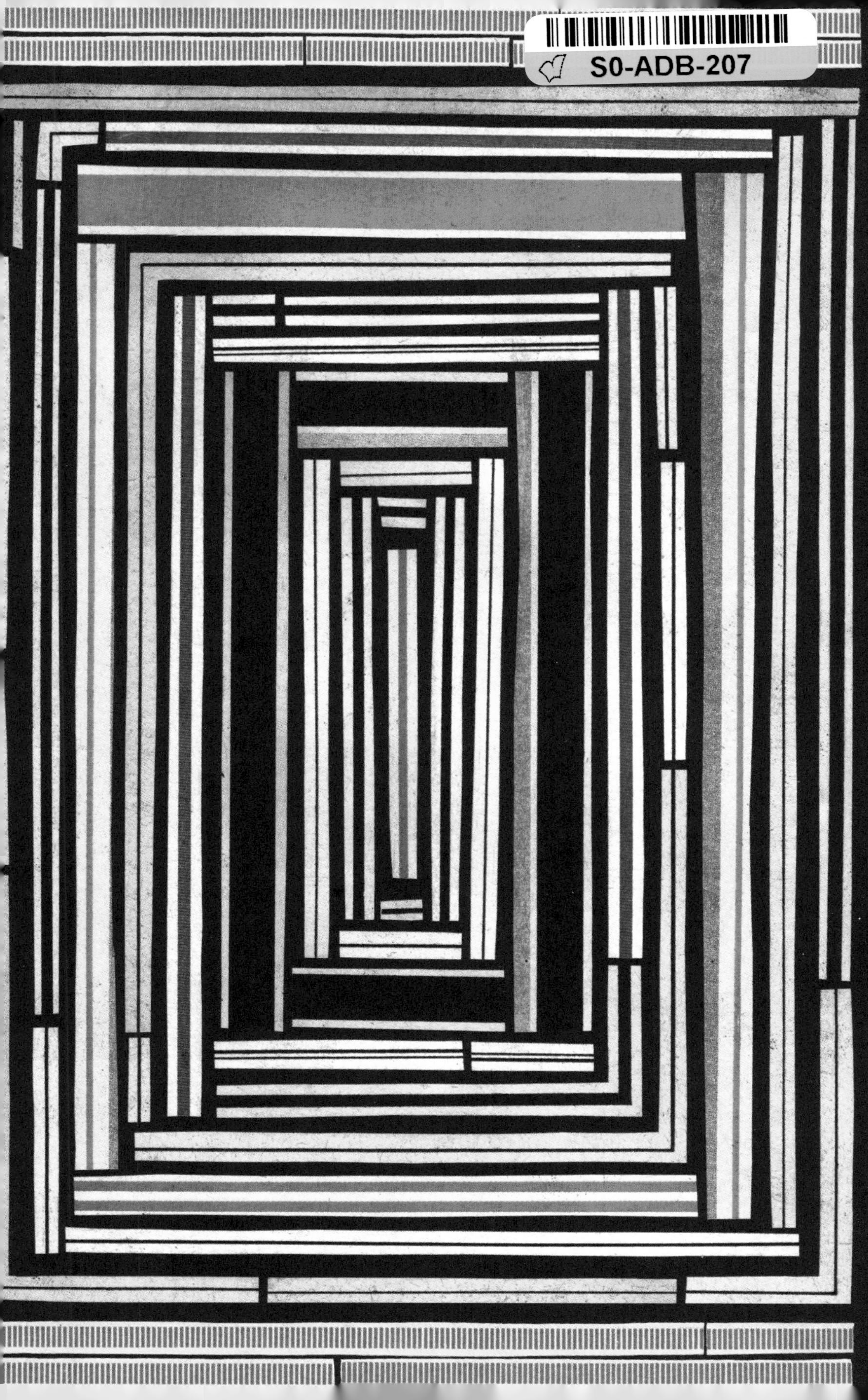

MY MOST SECRET DESIRE

Production: Ian Topple, Jeremy Morris, Rebecca Rosen, Chris Oliveros,
and Tom Devlin.
Publisher: Chris Oliveros.
Publicity: Peggy Burns and Jamie Quail.

Originally published by Drawn & Quarterly in a different form in 1995.
New hardcover edition: April 2006.
Printed in Singapore.

Drawn & Quarterly
Post Office Box 48056
Montreal, Quebec
Canada H2V 4S8
www.drawnandquarterly.com

Library and Archives Canada Cataloguing in Publication
Doucet, Julie, 1965-
My Most Secret Desire / Julie Doucet.
ISBN 1-896597-95-5
I. Title. PN6733.D68M8 2006   741.5'971   C2005-906362-9

Drawn & Quarterly acknowledges the financial support of the Government
of Canada through the Book Publishing Industry Development Program (BPIDP)
and the Canada Council for the Arts for our publishing activities.

Distributed in the USA and abroad by:
Farrar, Straus and Giroux
19 Union Square West
New York, NY 10003
Orders: 888.330.8477

Distributed in Canada by:
Raincoast Books
9050 Shaughnessy Street
Vancouver, BC V6P 6E5
Orders: 800.663.5714

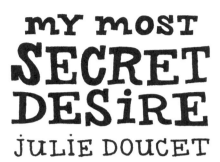

MY MOST SECRET DESIRE

JULIE DOUCET

DRAWN & QUARTERLY
MONTRÉAL

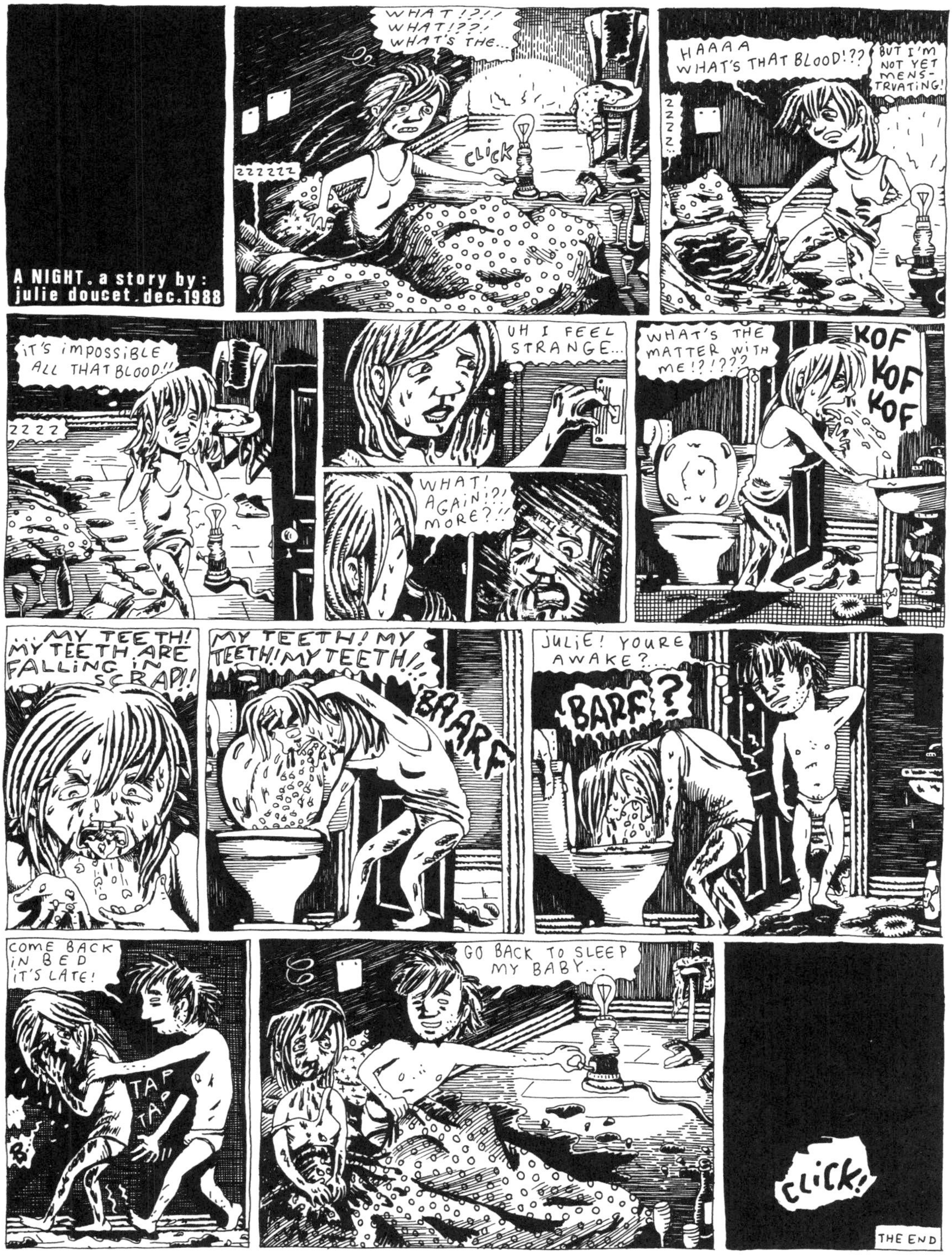
A NIGHT. a story by: julie doucet. dec. 1988
WHAT!?!! WHAT!??! WHAT'S THE...
ZZZZZZ
CLICK
HAAAA WHAT'S THAT BLOOD!??
BUT I'M NOT YET MENS-TRUATING!
ZZZZ
IT'S IMPOSSIBLE ALL THAT BLOOD!!
ZZZZ
UH I FEEL STRANGE...
WHAT! AGAIN!?! MORE?!!
WHAT'S THE MATTER WITH ME!?!???
KOF KOF KOF
...MY TEETH! MY TEETH ARE FALLING IN SCRAP!!
MY TEETH! MY TEETH! MY TEETH!!
BAARF
JULIE! YOURE AWAKE?...
BARF
?
COME BACK IN BED IT'S LATE!
TAP TAP
GO BACK TO SLEEP MY BABY...
CLICK!
THE END

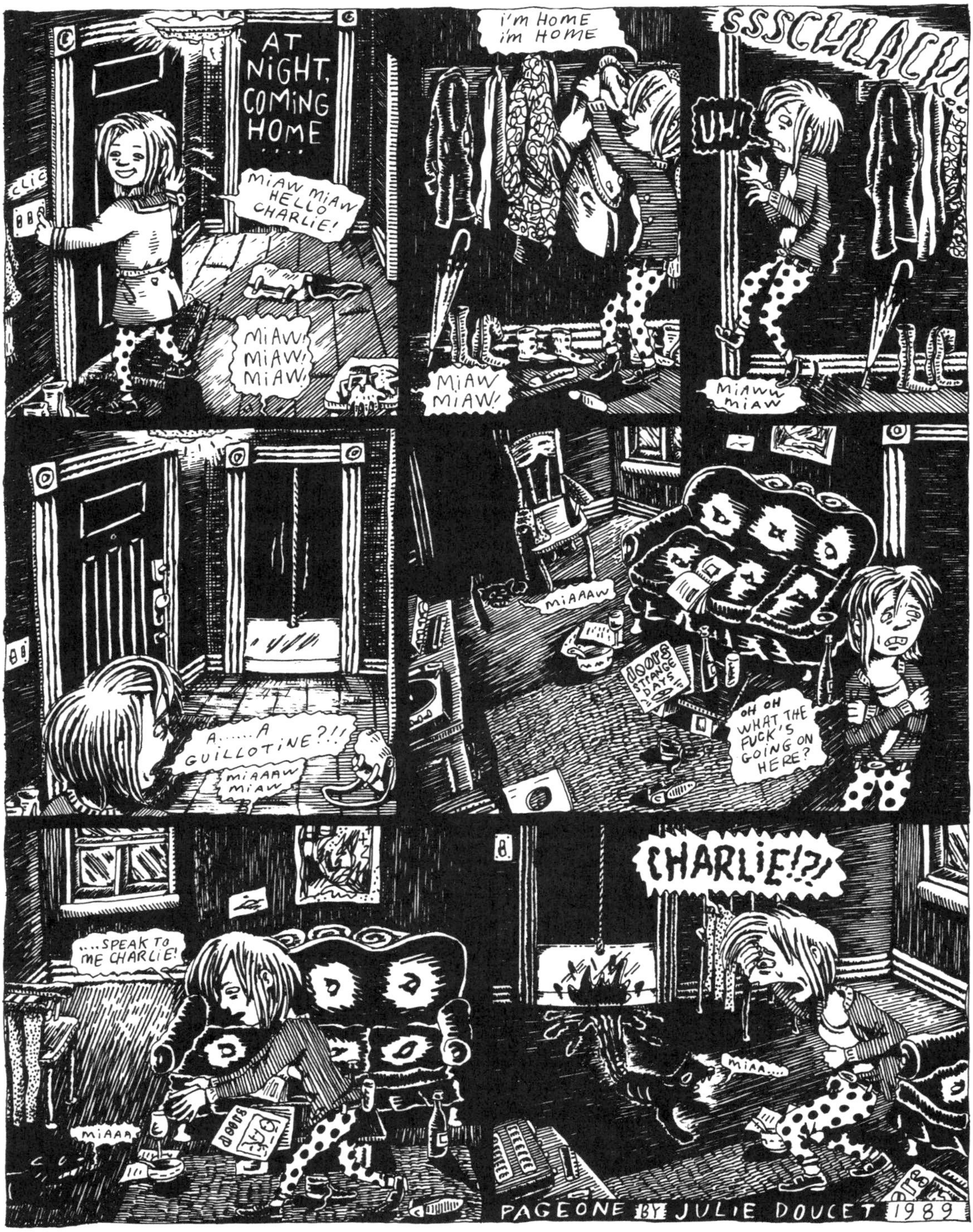
AT NIGHT, COMING HOME ....
CLIC
MIAW MIAW HELLO CHARLIE!
MIAW! MIAW! MIAW!
i'm HOME i'm HOME
MIAW MIAW!
SSSCHLACK
UH!
MIAWW MIAW
A...... A GUILLOTINE?!!
MIAAAW MIAW
MIAAAW
DOORS STRANGE DAYS
OH OH WHAT THE FUCK'S GOING ON HERE?
...SPEAK TO ME CHARLIE!
MIAAA
CHARLIE!?!
MIAA....
PAGEONE BY JULIE DOUCET 1989

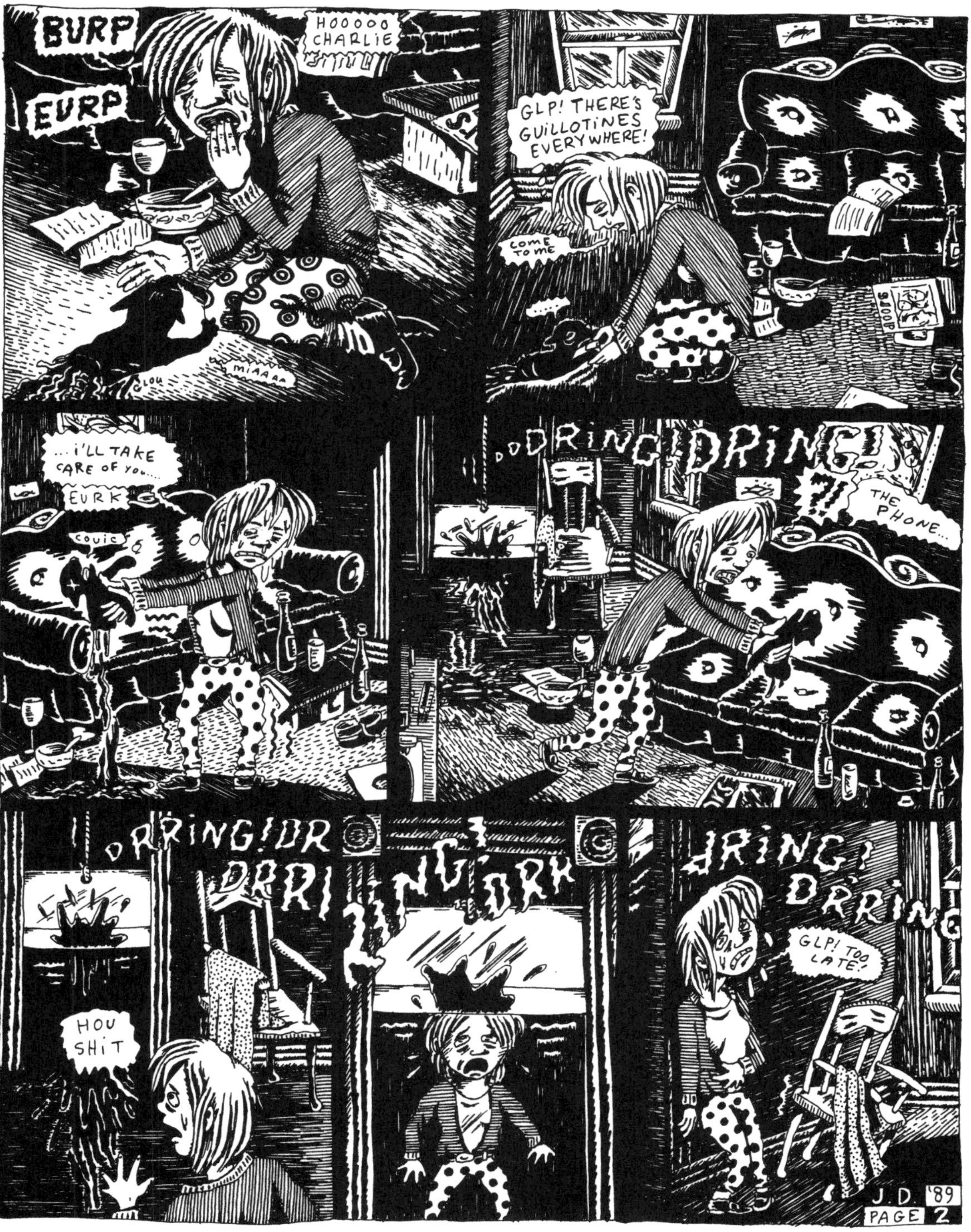
BURP
EVRP
HOOOOO CHARLIE
CLOU
MIAAAAA
GLP! THERE'S GUILLOTINES EVERYWHERE!
COME TO ME
...I'LL TAKE CARE OF YOU...
EURK
COUIC
DDDRING! DRRING!
?!
THE PHONE...
DRRING! DR
DRRING! DRR
HOU SHIT
DRING! DRRING
GLP! TOO LATE!
J.D. '89
PAGE 2

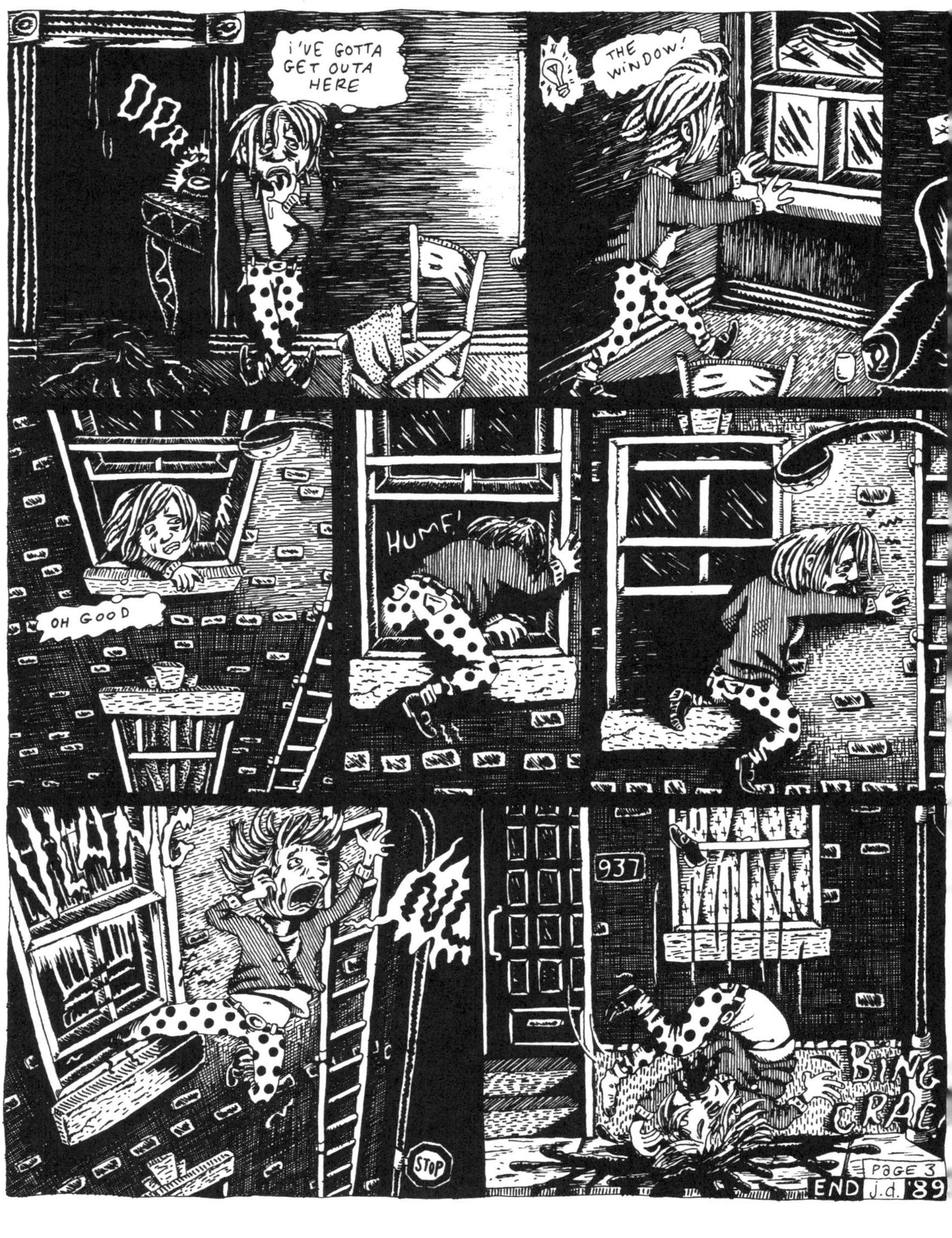

DRR
I'VE GOTTA GET OUTA HERE
THE WINDOW!
OH GOOD
HUMF!
937
STOP
BING
CRA
PAGE 3
END j.d. '89

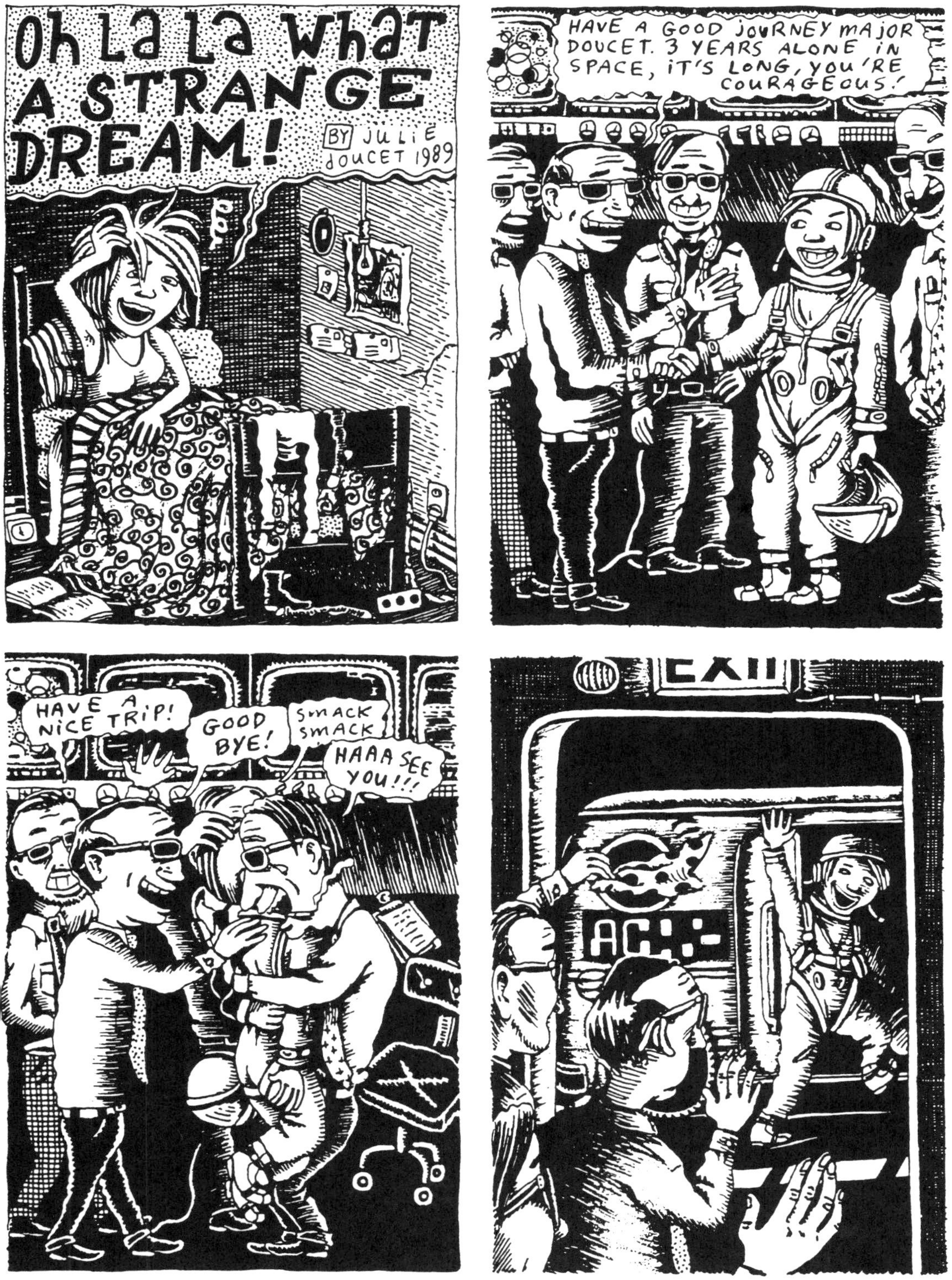
Oh La La What A Strange Dream!
By Julie Doucet 1989
HAVE A GOOD JOURNEY MAJOR DOUCET. 3 YEARS ALONE IN SPACE, IT'S LONG, YOU'RE COURAGEOUS!
HAVE A NICE TRIP!
GOOD BYE!
SMACK SMACK
HAAA SEE YOU!!!

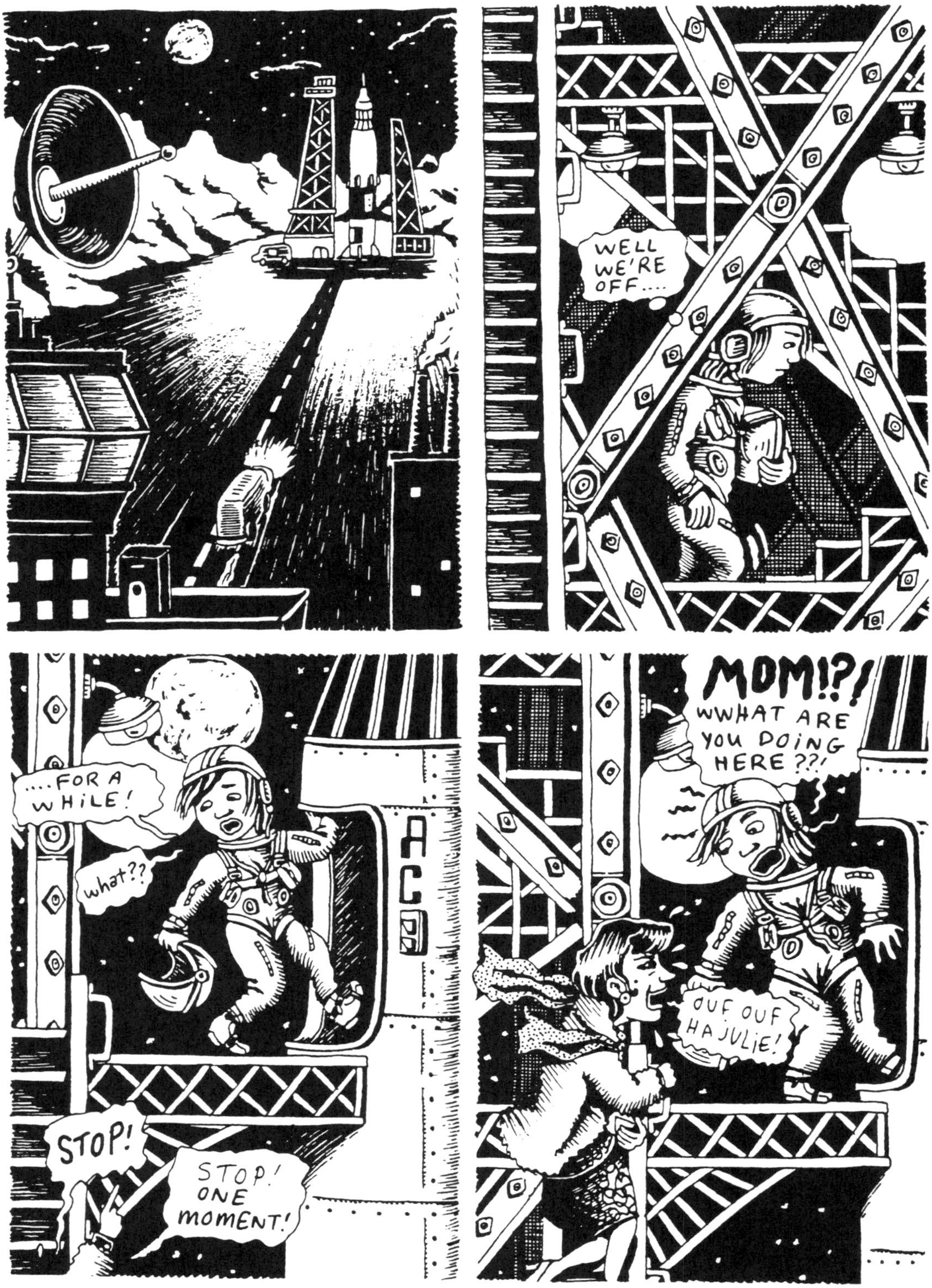
WELL WE'RE OFF....
....FOR A WHILE!
what??
STOP!
STOP! ONE MOMENT!
MOM!?!
WWHAT ARE YOU DOING HERE??!
OUF OUF HA JULIE!

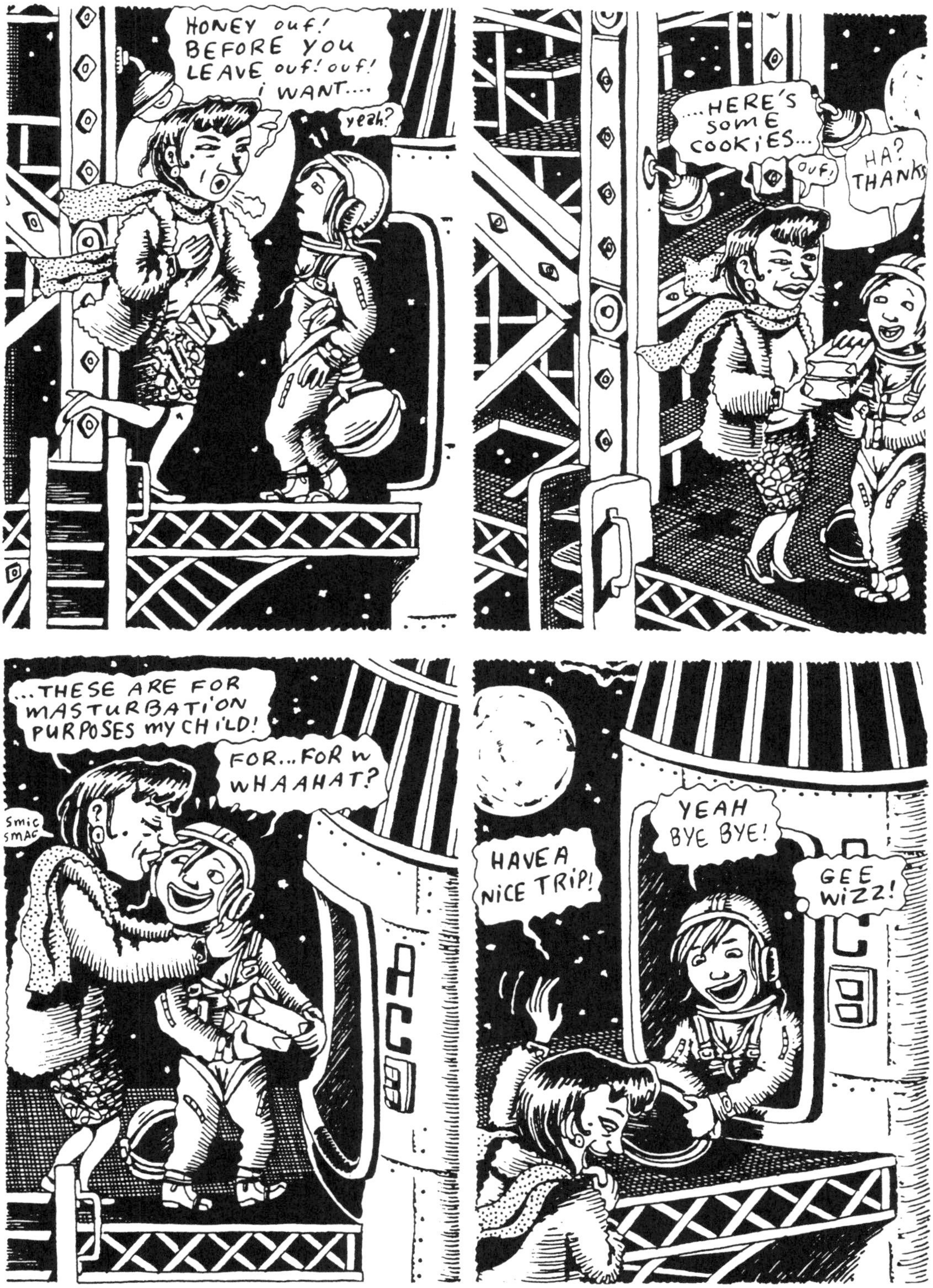
HONEY ouf! BEFORE YOU LEAVE ouf! ouf! i WANT....
yeah?
....HERE'S some COOKiES...
ouf!
HA? THANKS
...THESE ARE FOR MASTURBATiON PURPOSES my CHiLD!
smic smac
?
FOR... FOR W WHAAAHAT?
HAVE A NiCE TRiP!
YEAH BYE BYE!
GEE WiZZ!

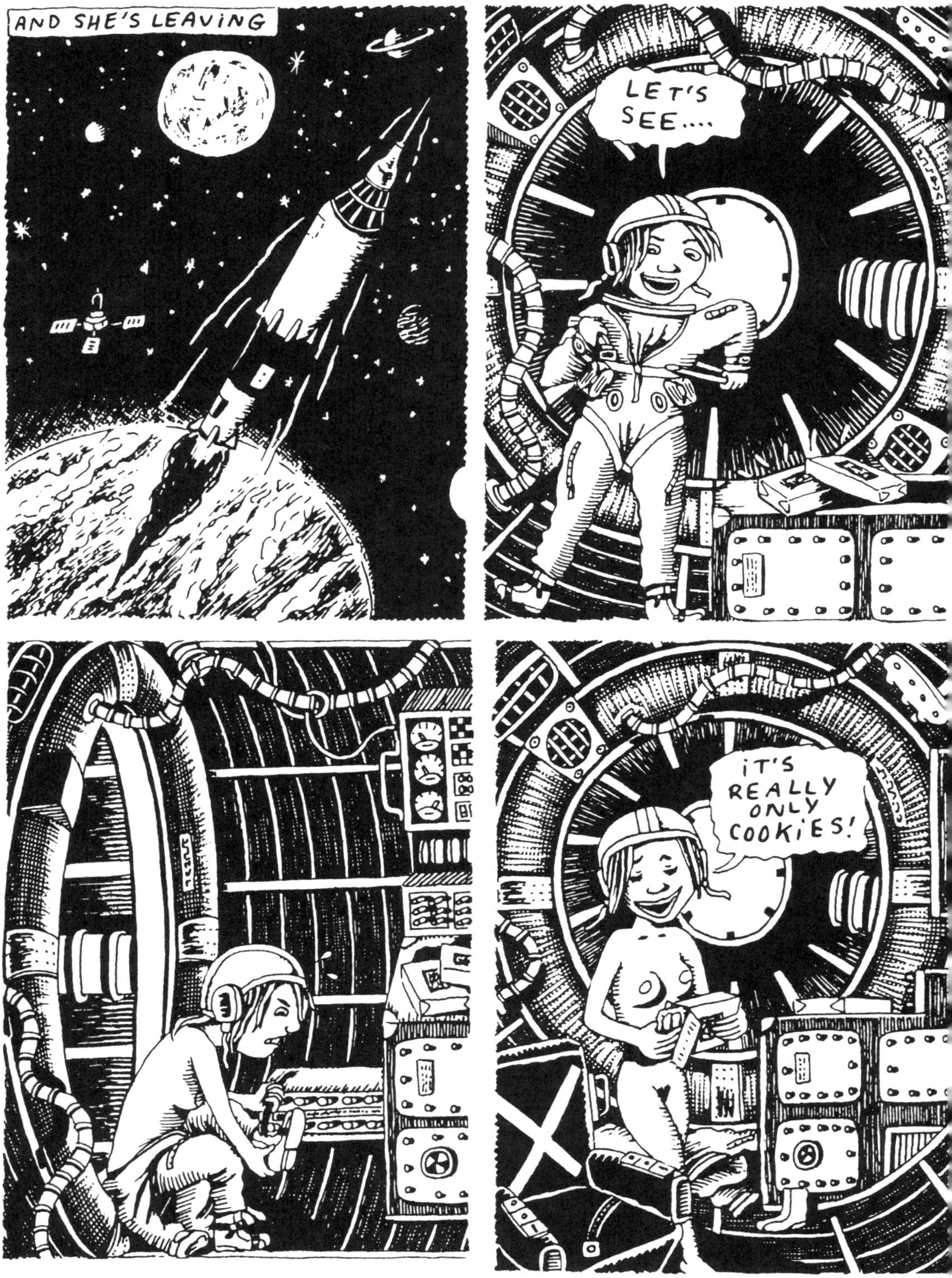
AND SHE'S LEAVING
LET'S SEE....
IT'S REALLY ONLY COOKIES!

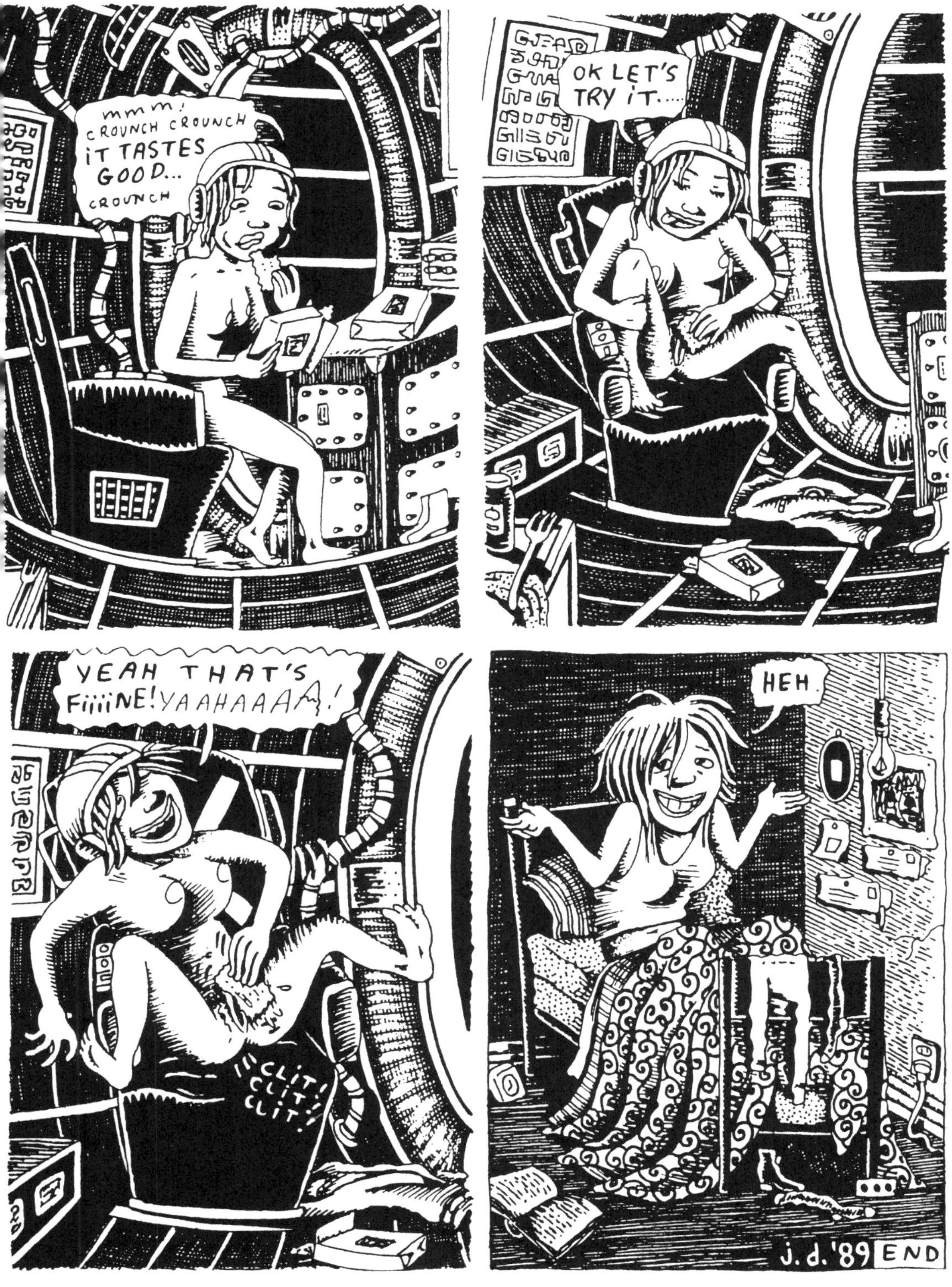
mmm! CROUNCH CROUNCH iT TASTES GOOD... CROUNCH
OK LET'S TRY iT.....
YEAH THAT'S FiiiiNE! YAAHAAAA!
CLIT! CLIT! CLIT!
HEH.
j. d. '89
END

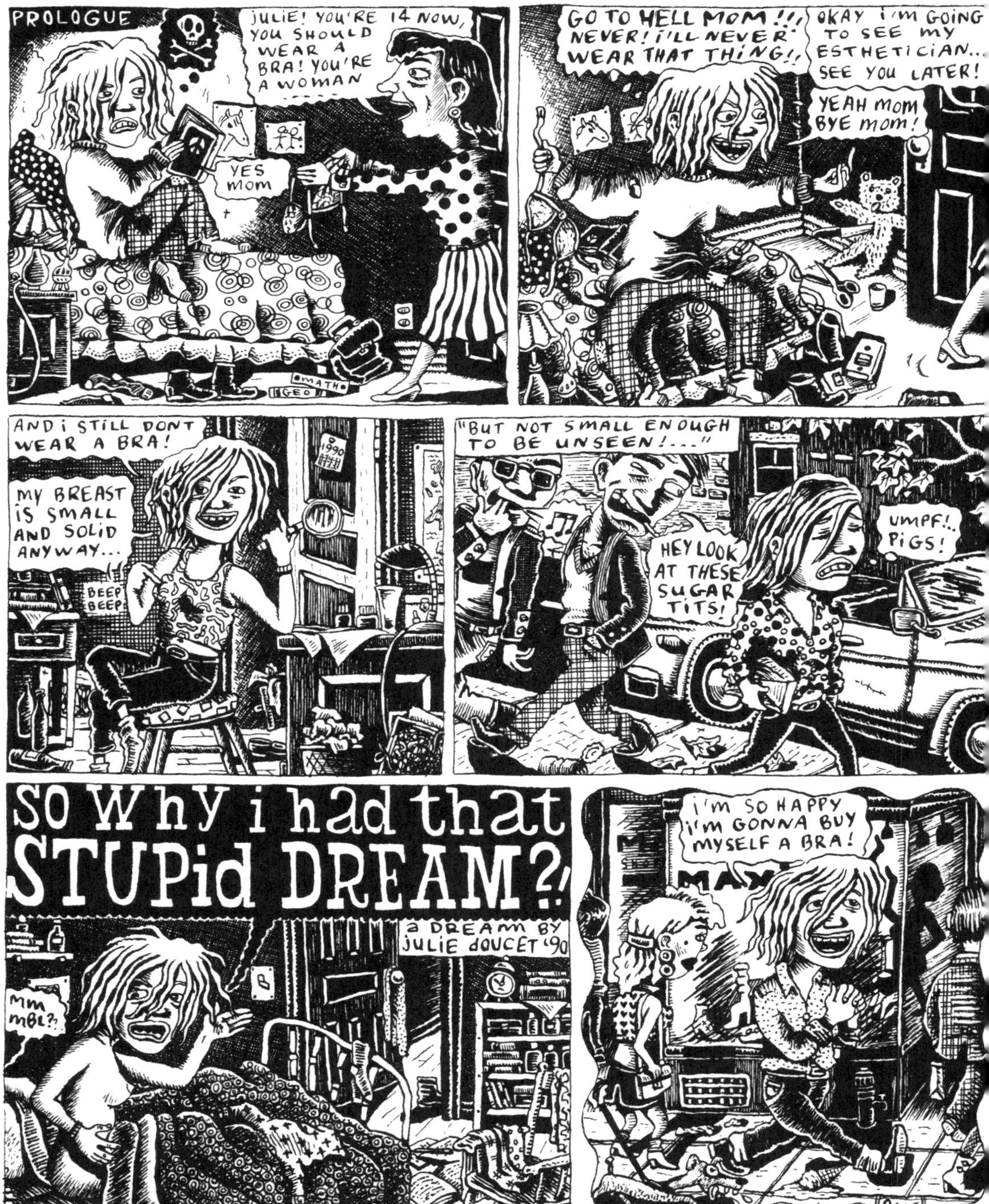
PROLOGUE
JULIE! YOU'RE 14 NOW, YOU SHOULD WEAR A BRA! YOU'RE A WOMAN
YES MOM
MATH
GEO
GO TO HELL MOM!!! NEVER! I'LL NEVER WEAR THAT THING!!
OKAY I'M GOING TO SEE MY ESTHETICIAN... SEE YOU LATER!
YEAH MOM BYE MOM!
AND I STILL DONT WEAR A BRA!
MY BREAST IS SMALL AND SOLID ANYWAY...
BEEP BEEP
1990
"BUT NOT SMALL ENOUGH TO BE UNSEEN!..."
HEY LOOK AT THESE SUGAR TITS!
UMPF!.. PIGS!
SO WHY I HAD THAT STUPID DREAM?!
A DREAM BY JULIE DOUCET '90
MM MBL?!
I'M SO HAPPY I'M GONNA BUY MYSELF A BRA!
MAX
ONE

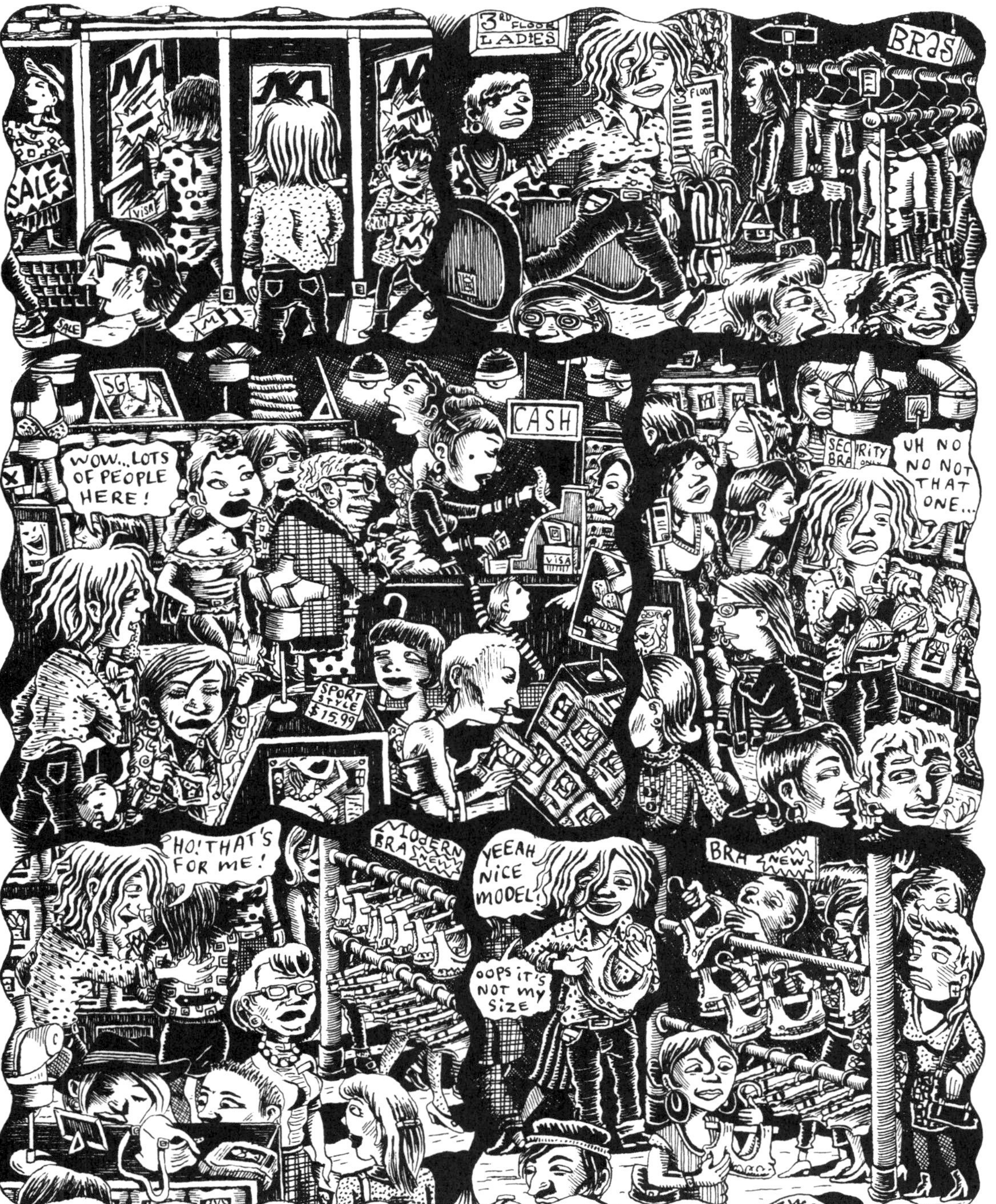
SALE
3RD FLOOR LADIES
BRAS
SG
CASH
WOW...LOTS OF PEOPLE HERE!
SECURITY ONLY
UH NO NO NOT THAT ONE...
SPORT STYLE $15.99
HO! THAT'S FOR ME!
MODERN BRA NEW
YEEAH NICE MODEL!
OOPS IT'S NOT MY SIZE
BRA NEW
TWO

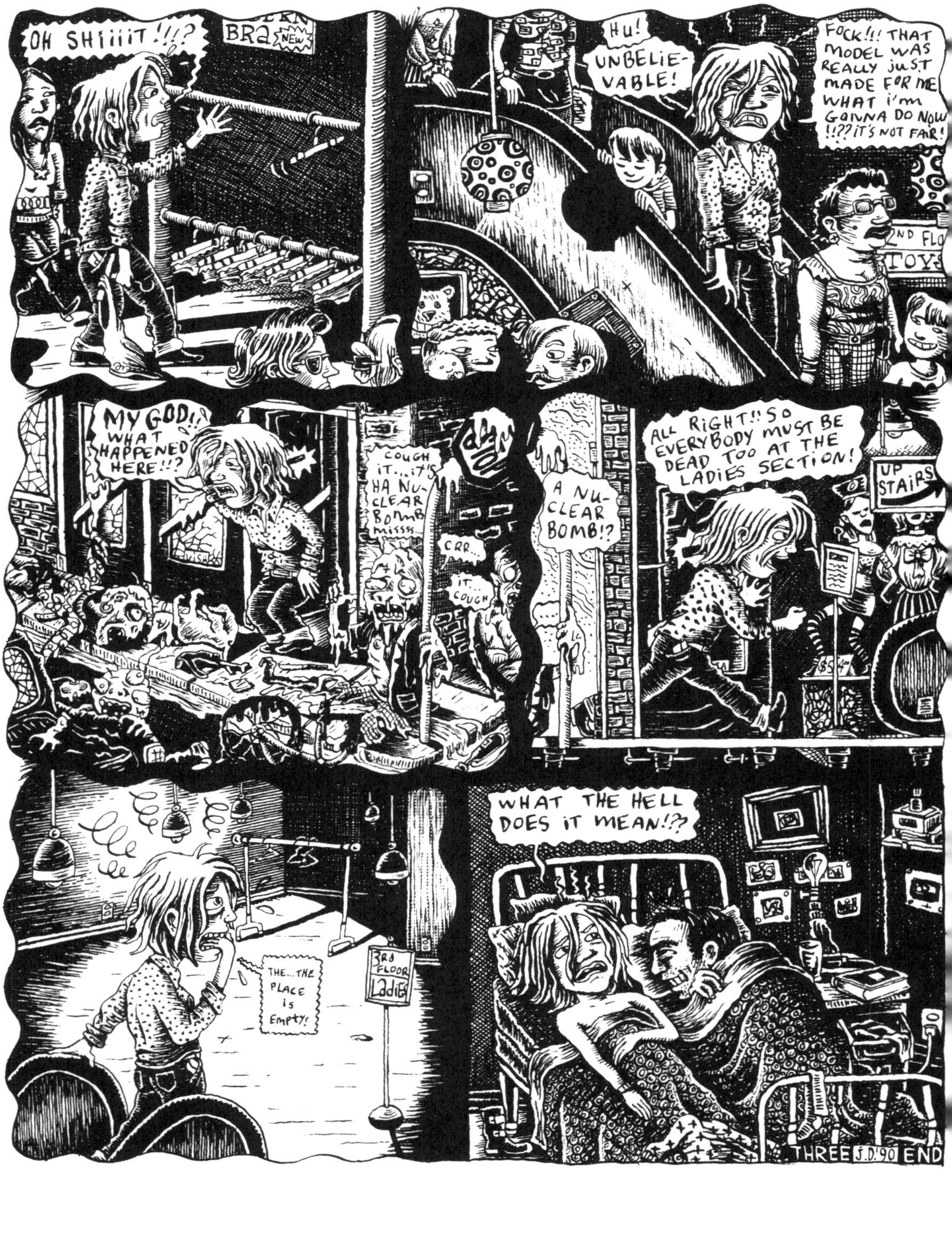

OH SHIiiiT!!!?
BRA NEW
HU! UNBELIE-VABLE!
FUCK!!! THAT MODEL WAS REALLY JUST MADE FOR ME WHAT I'M GONNA DO NOW!!?? IT'S NOT FAIR!
2ND FLO
TOYS
MY GOD!! WHAT HAPPENED HERE!!?
COUGH IT...IT'S HA NU-CLEAR BOMB MISSSS...
CRR...
IT... COUGH
A NU-CLEAR BOMB!?
ALL RIGHT!! SO EVERYBODY MUST BE DEAD TOO AT THE LADIES SECTION!
UP STAIRS
THE...THE PLACE IS EMPTY!
3RD FLOOR LADIES
WHAT THE HELL DOES IT MEAN!?
THREE J.D.'90 END

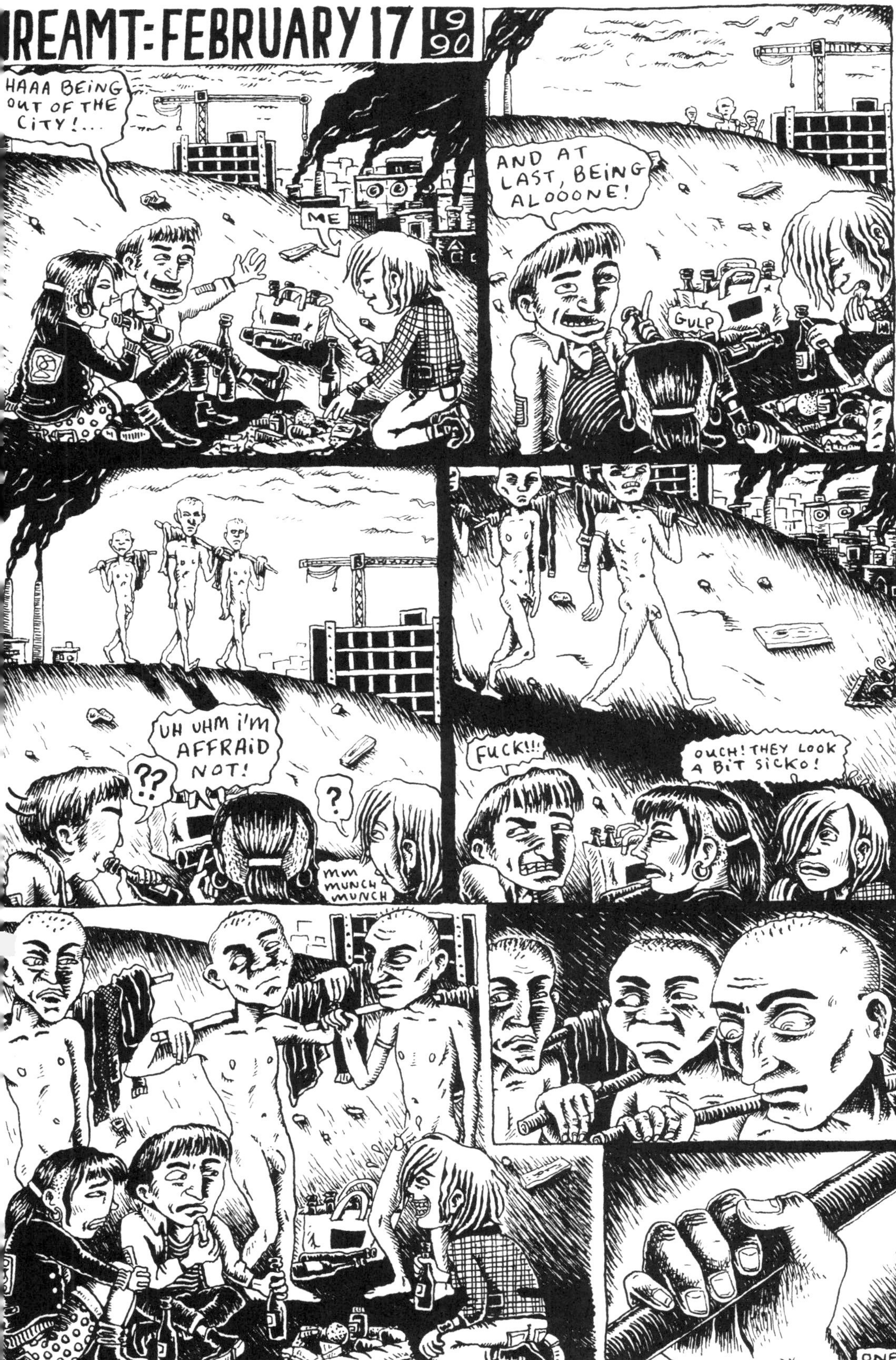
REAMT: FEBRUARY 17 1990
HAAA BEING OUT OF THE CITY!...
ME
AND AT LAST, BEING ALOOONE!
GULP
??
UH UHM I'M AFFRAID NOT!
?
MM MUNCH MUNCH
FUCK!!!
OUCH! THEY LOOK A BIT SICKO!
ONE

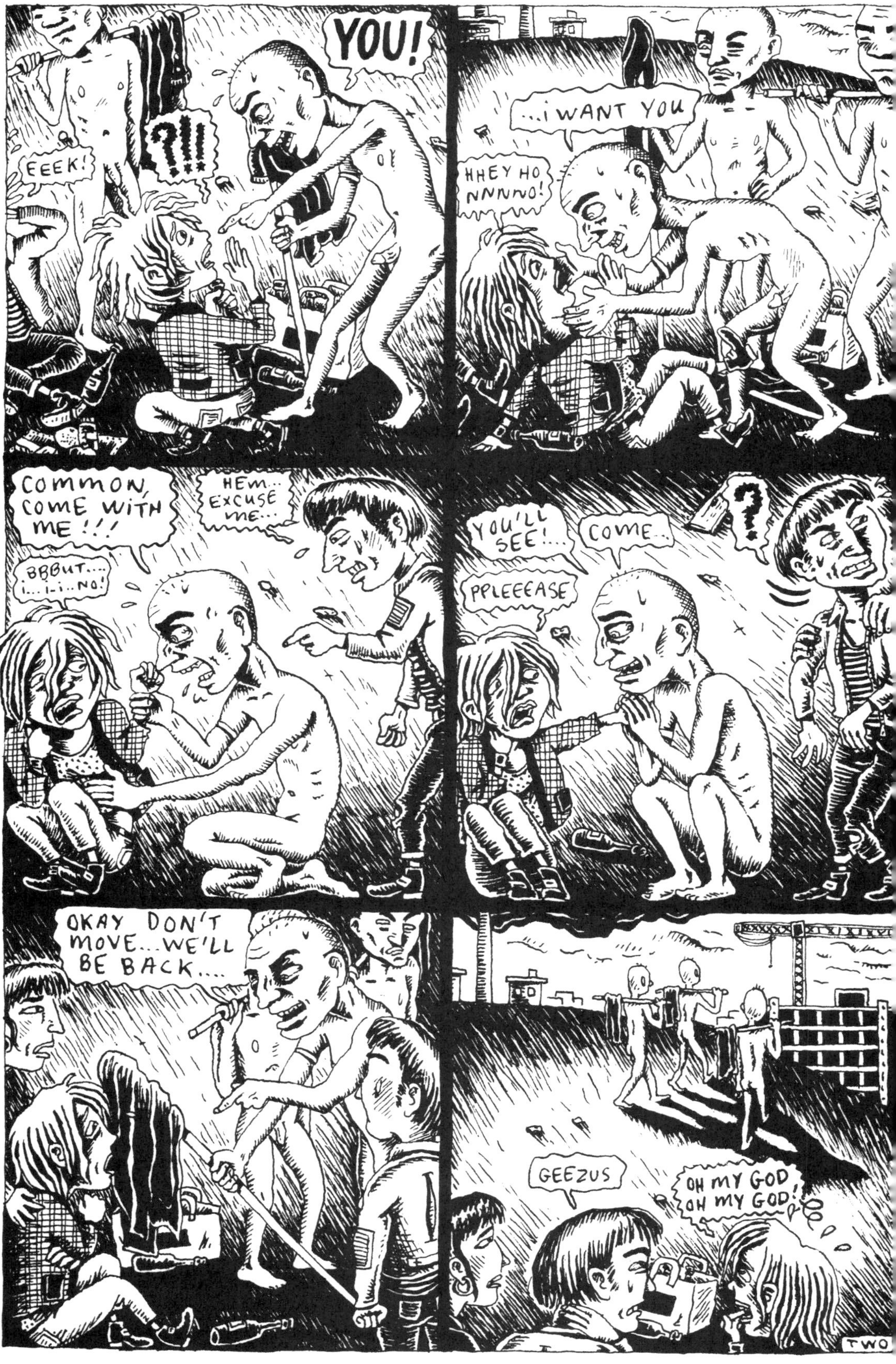
YOU!
?!!
EEEK!
...I WANT YOU
HHEY HO NNNNO!
COMMON, COME WITH ME!!!
HEM... EXCUSE ME...
BBBUT.... I... I-I.. NO!
YOU'LL SEE!...
COME...
?
PPLEEEASE
OKAY DON'T MOVE...WE'LL BE BACK....
GEEZUS
OH MY GOD, OH MY GOD!
TWO

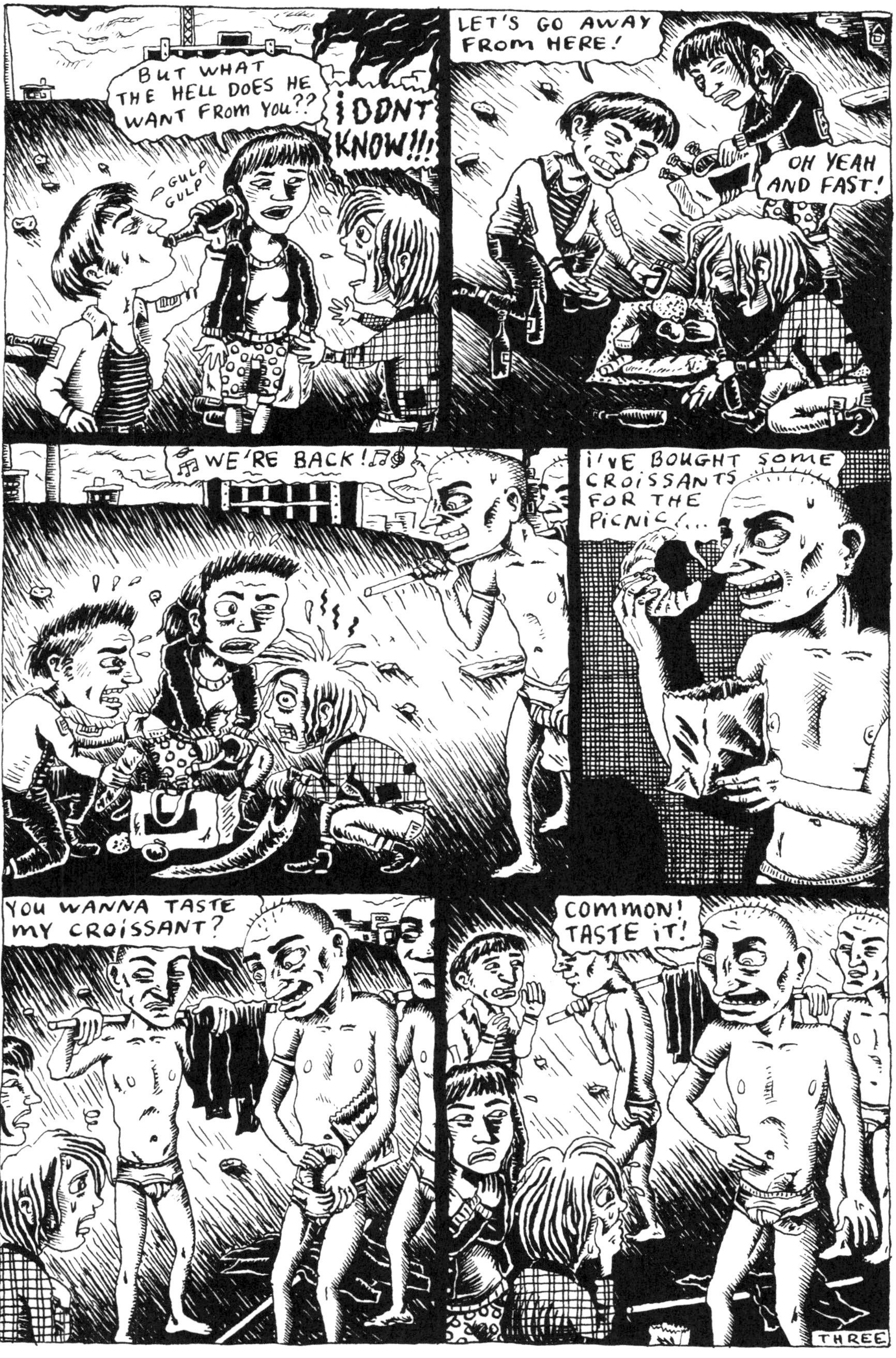
BUT WHAT THE HELL DOES HE WANT FROM YOU??
GULP GULP
¡DONT KNOW!!!
LET'S GO AWAY FROM HERE!
OH YEAH AND FAST!
WE'RE BACK!
I'VE BOUGHT SOME CROISSANTS FOR THE PICNIC!...
YOU WANNA TASTE MY CROISSANT?
COMMON! TASTE IT!

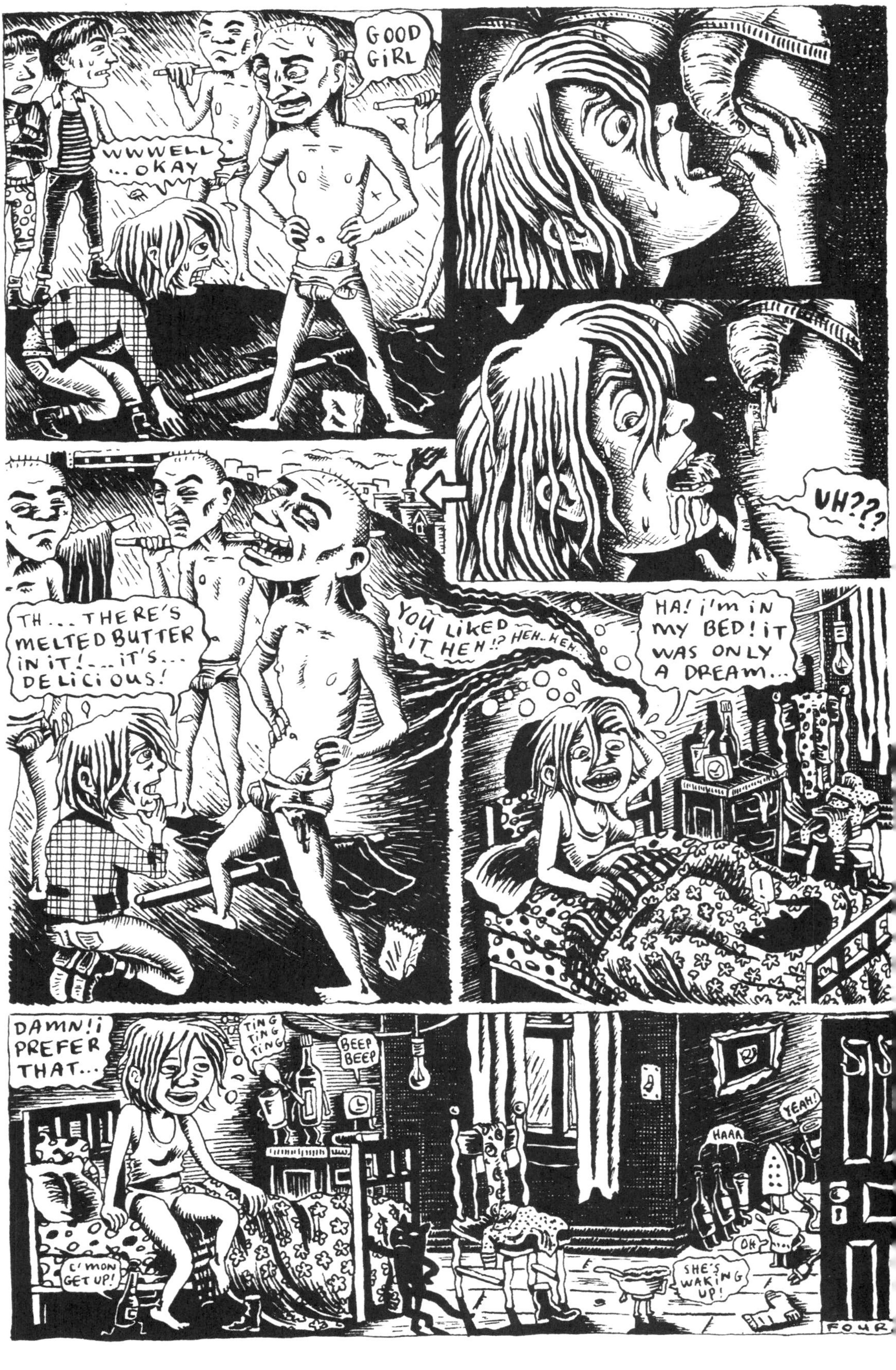
GOOD GIRL
WWWELL ...OKAY
UH???
TH... THERE'S MELTED BUTTER IN IT!... IT'S... DELICIOUS!
YOU LIKED IT HEH!? HEH.. HEH..
HA! i'm IN MY BED! IT WAS ONLY A DREAM...
DAMN! i PREFER THAT...
TING TING TING
BEEP BEEP
C'MON GET UP!
HAAA
YEAH!
OK
SHE'S WAKING UP!
FOUR

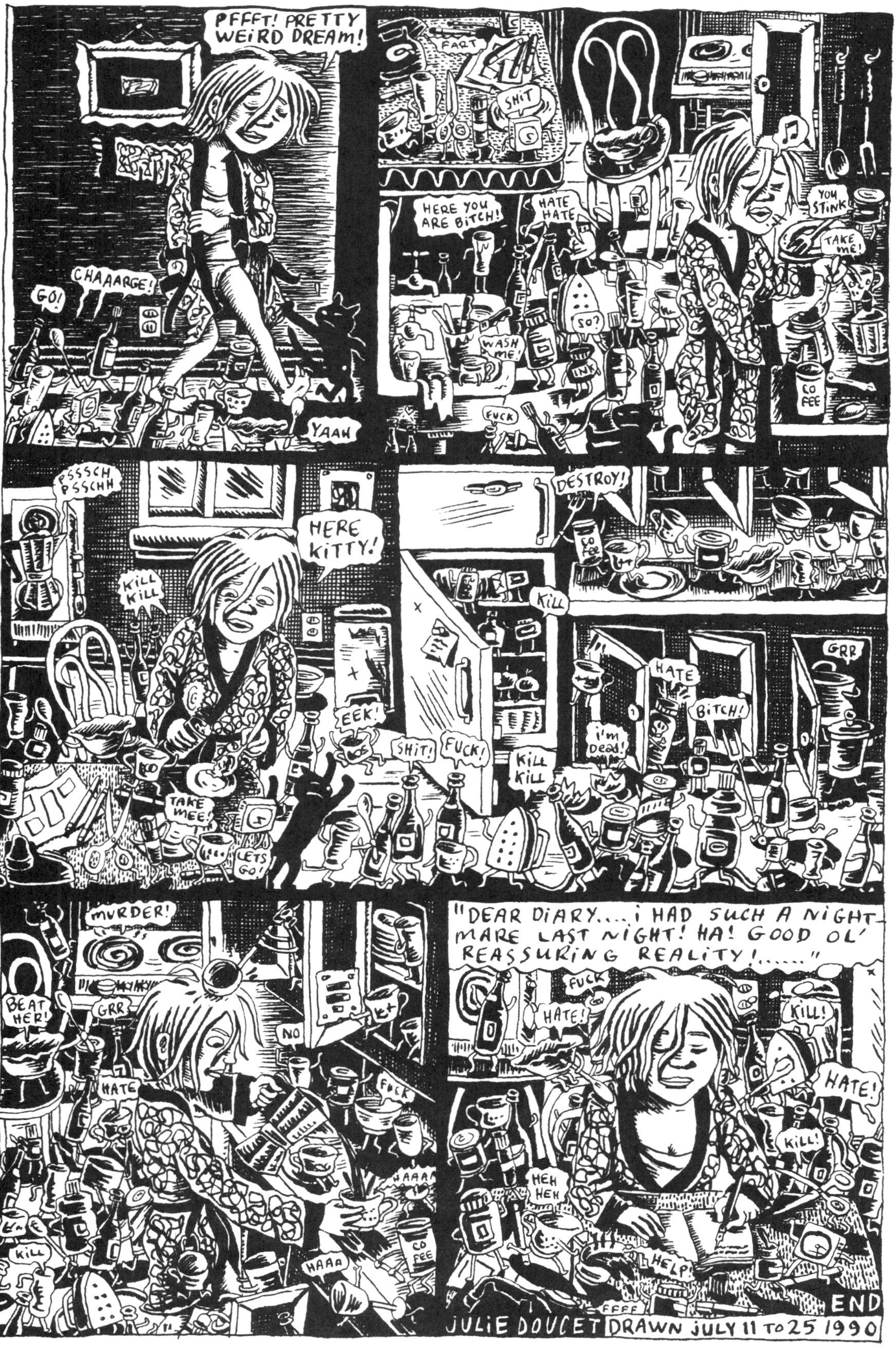
PFFFT! PRETTY WEIRD DREAM!
CHAAARGE!
GO!
YAAH
FART
SHIT
HERE YOU ARE BITCH!
HATE HATE
YOU STINK
TAKE ME!
SO?
WASH ME!
INK
CO FEE
FUCK
PSSSCH PSSSCHH
HERE KITTY!
KILL KILL
EEK!
SHIT!
FUCK!
TAKE MEE!
LETS GO!
DESTROY!
CO FEE
KILL
KILL KILL
HATE
BITCH!
I'M DEAD!
GRR
MURDER!
BEAT HER!
GRR
NO
HATE
FUCK
HAAAA
KILL
CO FEE
HAAA
"DEAR DIARY.... I HAD SUCH A NIGHTMARE LAST NIGHT! HA! GOOD OL' REASSURING REALITY!....."
FUCK
HATE!
KILL!
HATE!
KILL!
HEH HEH
HELP
FFFF
END
JULIE DOUCET
DRAWN JULY 11 TO 25 1990

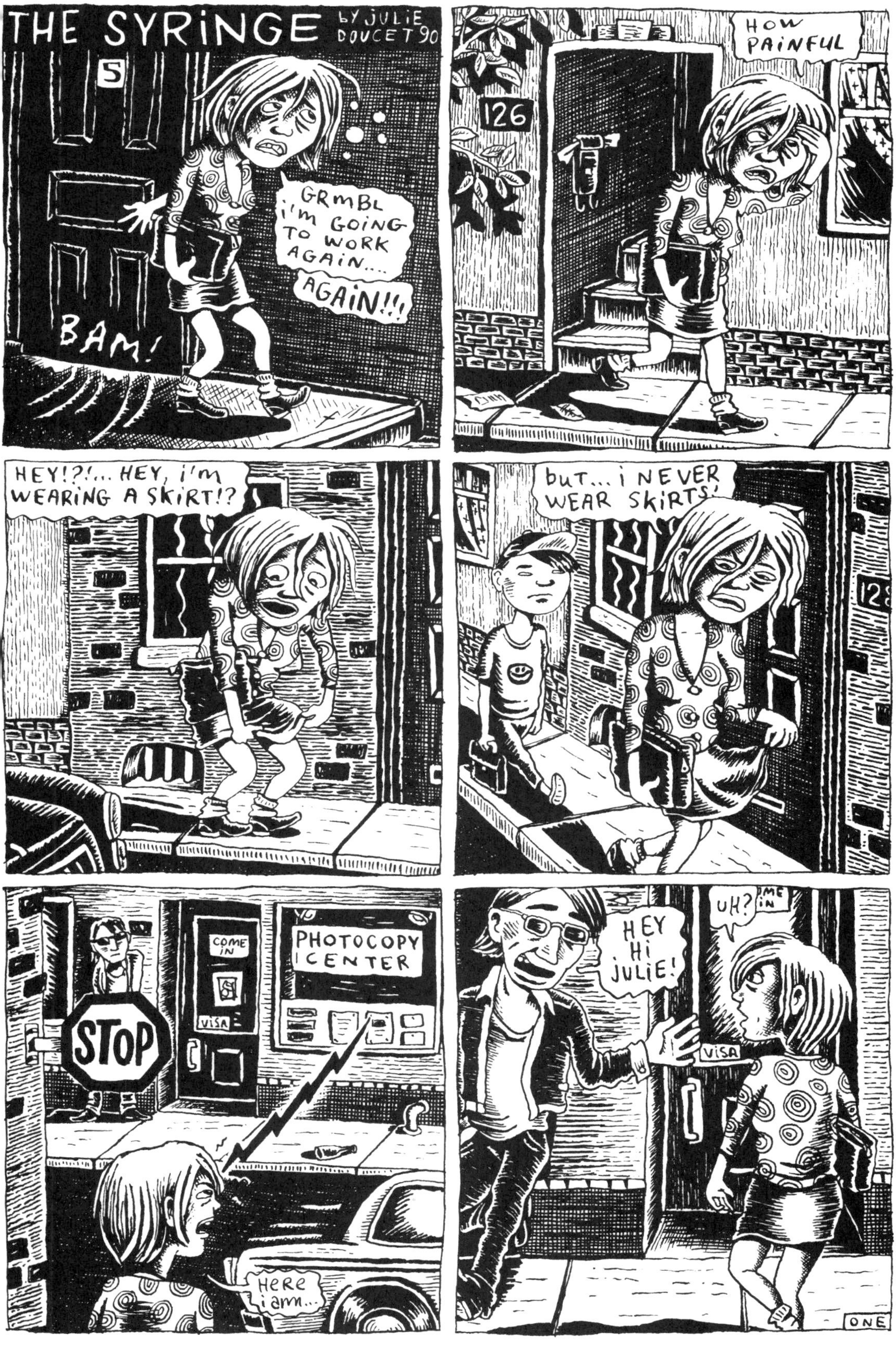
THE SYRiNGE by JULiE DOUCET '90
5
GRMBL i'm GOING TO WORK AGAiN....
AGAiN!!!
BAM!
126
HOW PAiNFUL
HEY!?!... HEY, i'm WEARiNG A SKiRT!?
but... i NEVER WEAR SKiRTS!
COME iN
PHOTOCOPY CENTER
STOP
ViSA
Here i am...
HEY Hi JULiE!
UH?
ViSA
ONE

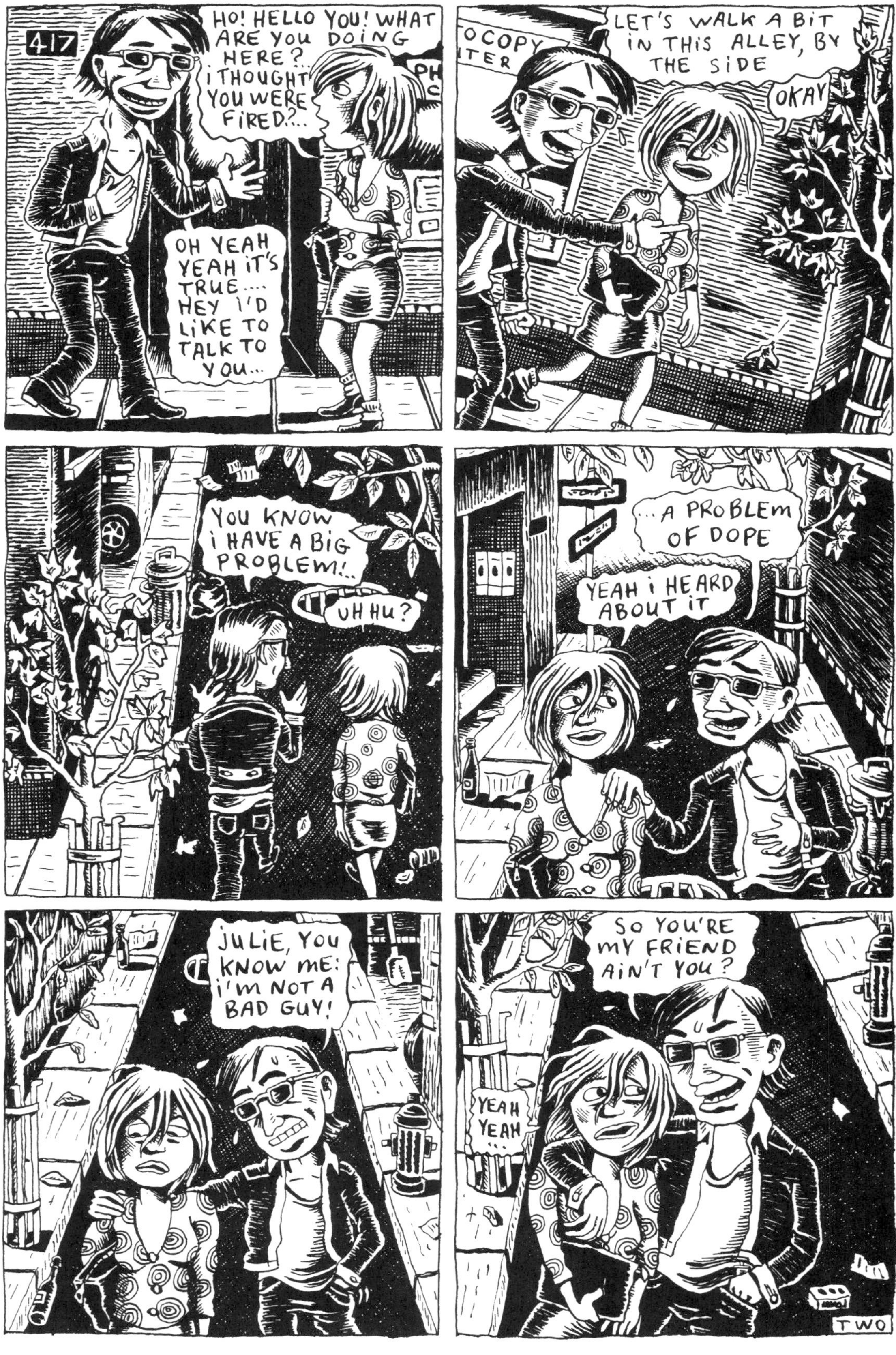
417
HO! HELLO YOU! WHAT ARE YOU DOING HERE?.. I THOUGHT YOU WERE FIRED?...
OH YEAH YEAH IT'S TRUE.... HEY I'D LIKE TO TALK TO YOU...
LET'S WALK A BIT IN THIS ALLEY, BY THE SIDE
OKAY
YOU KNOW I HAVE A BIG PROBLEM!..
UH HU?
...A PROBLEM OF DOPE
YEAH I HEARD ABOUT IT
JULIE, YOU KNOW ME: I'M NOT A BAD GUY!
SO YOU'RE MY FRIEND AIN'T YOU?
YEAH YEAH ...
TWO

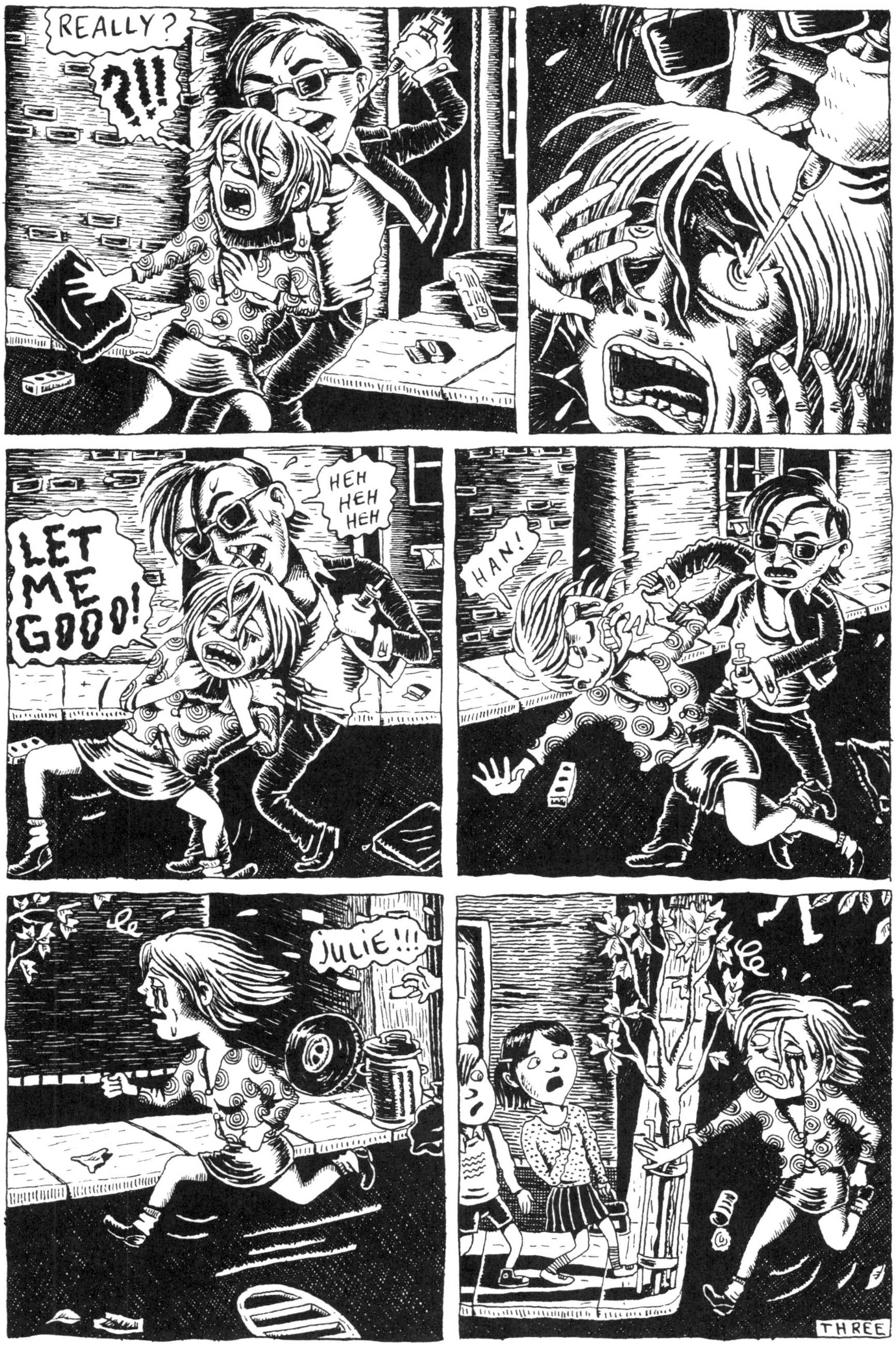
REALLY?
?!!
HEH HEH HEH
LET ME GOOO!
HAN!
JULIE!!!
THREE

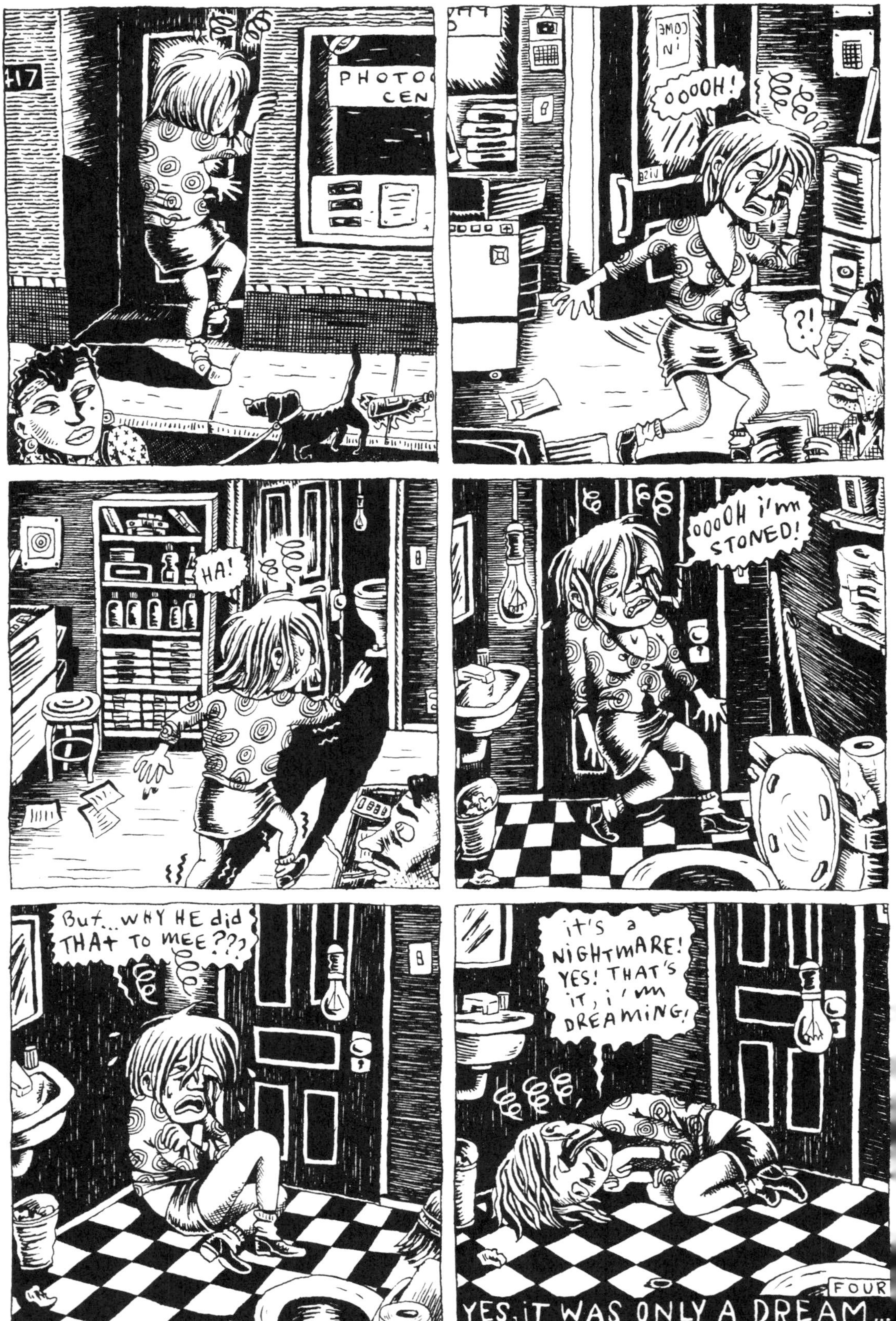
417
OOOOH!
?!
HA!
OOOOH i'm STONED!
But... WHY HE did THAT TO MEE???
it's a NIGHTMARE! YES! THAT'S iT, i'm DREAMING!
FOUR
YES, iT WAS ONLY A DREAM...
DREAMT MAY 26 1989 END AND DRAWN SEPT. 1990.

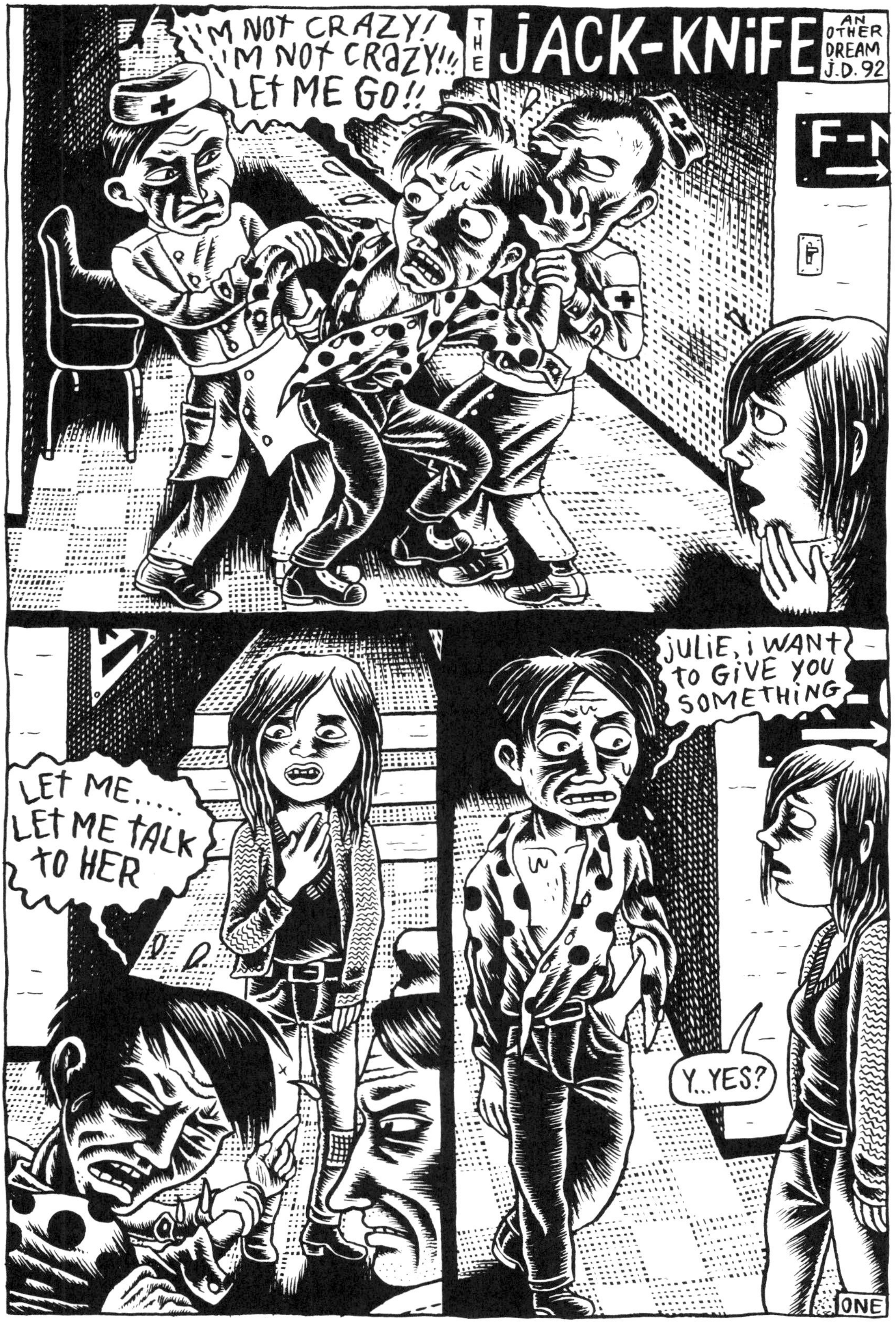
THE JACK-KNIFE
ANOTHER DREAM J.D. 92
I'M NOT CRAZY! I'M NOT CRAZY!!! LET ME GO!!
F-N
LET ME..... LET ME TALK TO HER
JULIE, I WANT TO GIVE YOU SOMETHING
Y..YES?
ONE

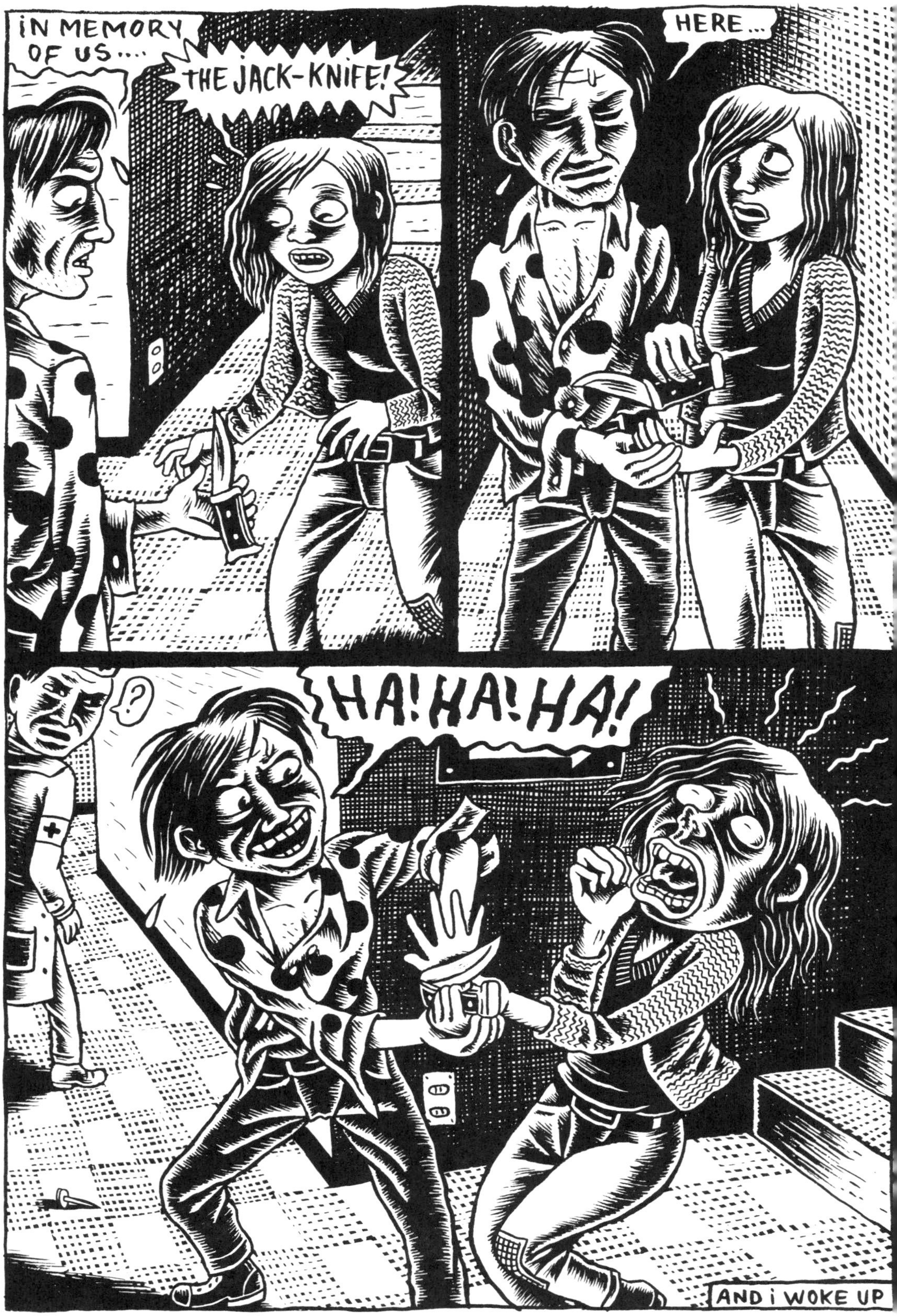

iN MEMORY OF US....
THE JACK-KNIFE!
HERE...
?
HA!HA!HA!
AND i WOKE UP

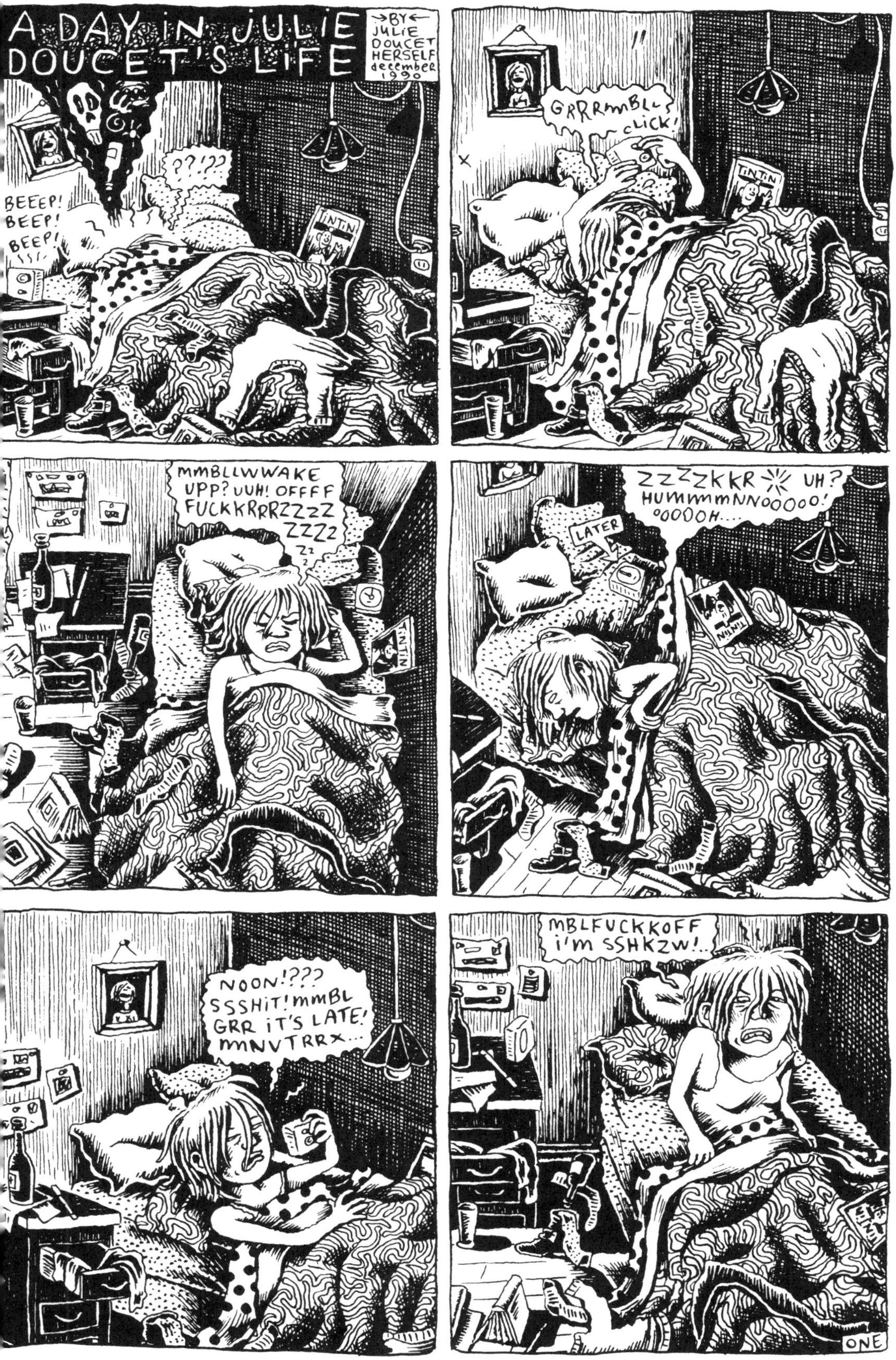
A DAY IN JULIE DOUCET'S LIFE
→BY← JULIE DOUCET HERSELF december 1990
BEEEP! BEEP! BEEP!
??!??
TINTIN
GRRRMBL CLICK!
MMBLLWWAKE UPP? UUH! OFFFF FUCKKRRRZZZZ ZZZZ Zz z
LATER
ZZZZKKR UH? HUMMMMNNOOOOO! OOOOOH...
NOON!??? SSSHIT! MMBL GRR IT'S LATE! MMNVTRRX...
MBLFUCKKOFF I'M SSHKZW!
ONE

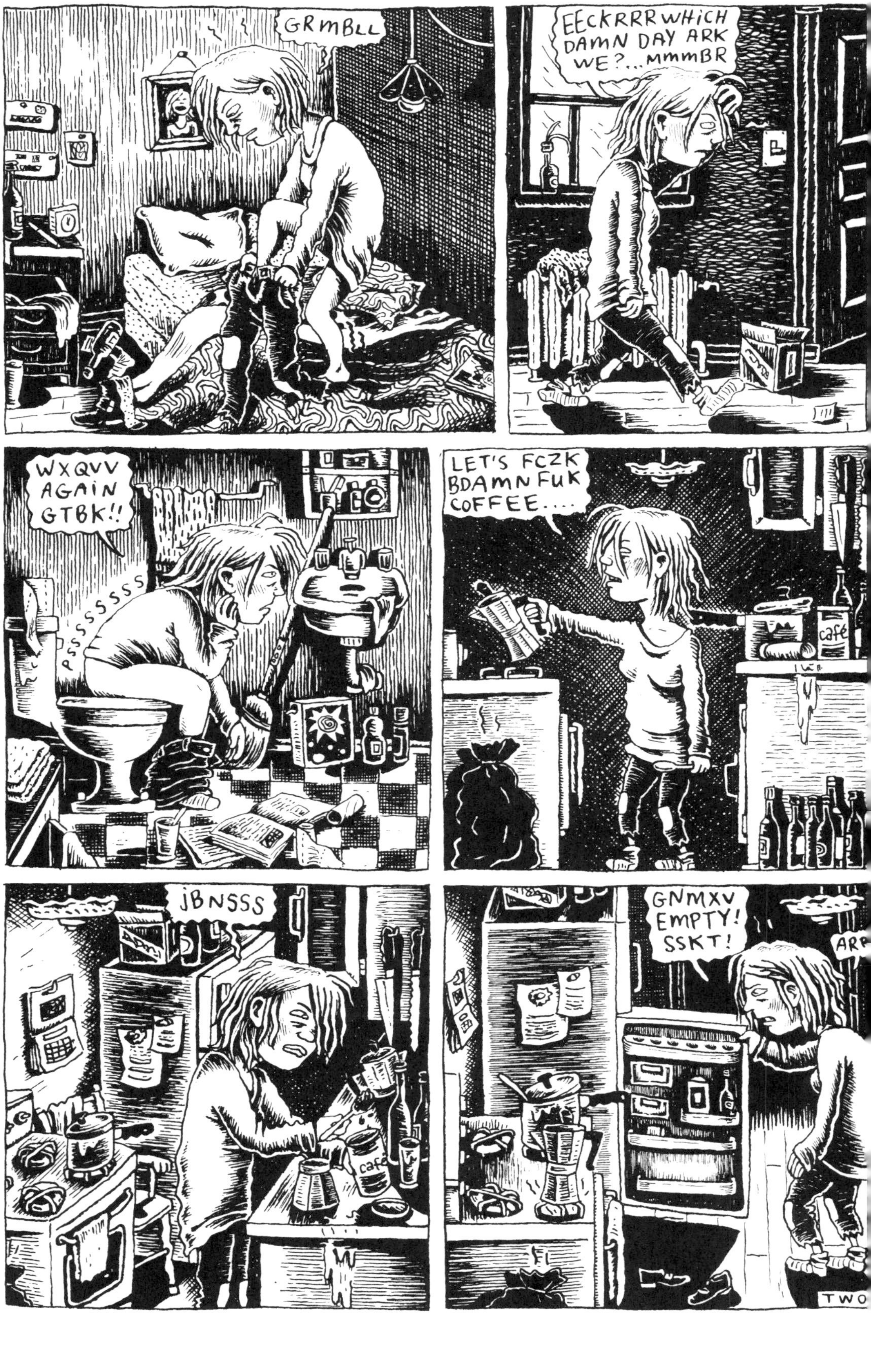
GRMBLL
EECKRRR WHICH DAMN DAY ARK WE?...MMMBR
WXQVV AGAIN GTBK!!
PSSSSSSSS
LET'S FCZK BDAMN FUK COFFEE...
café
JBNSSS
café
GNMXV EMPTY! SSKT!

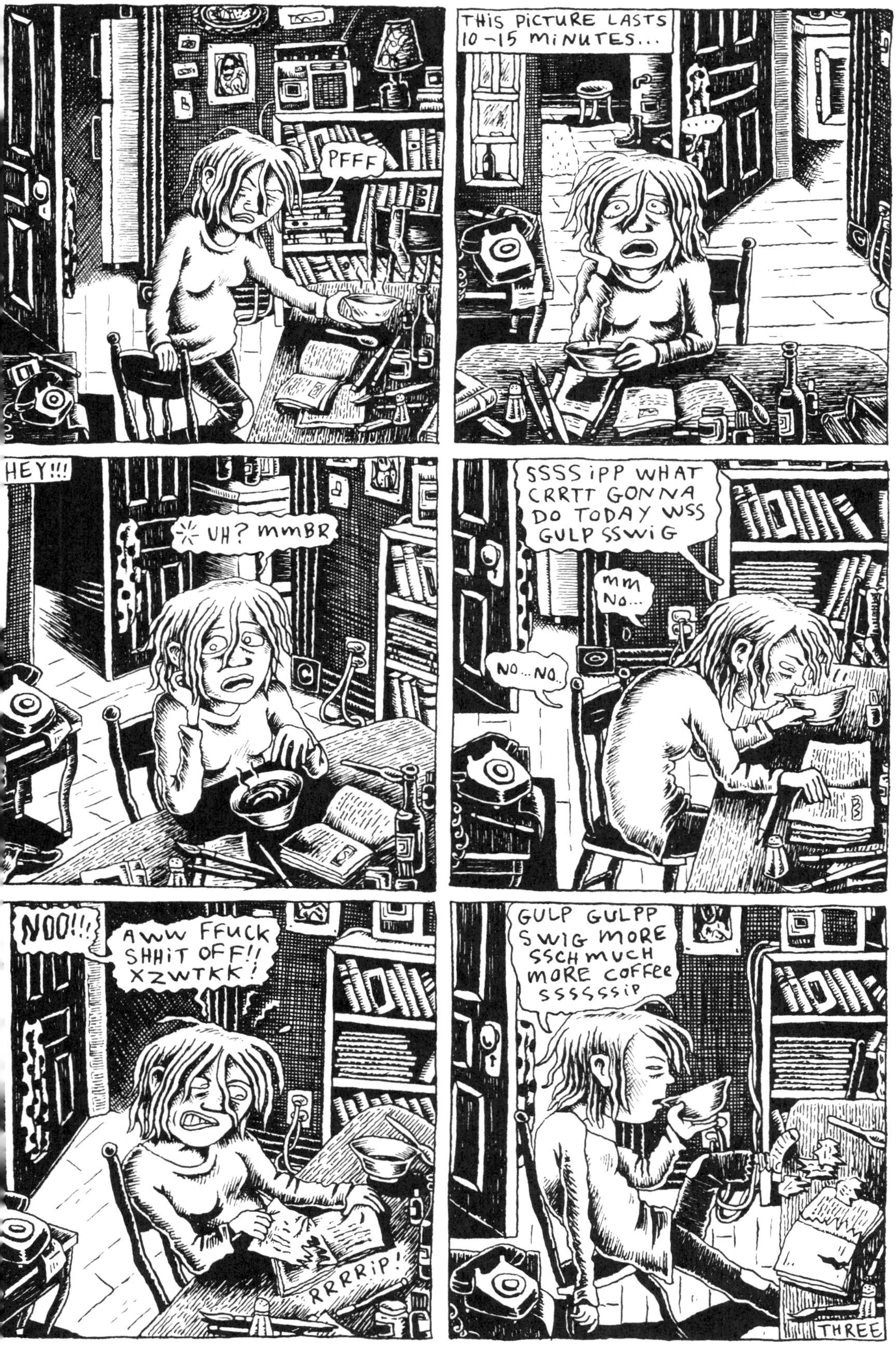
PFFF
THIS PICTURE LASTS 10 -15 MINUTES...
HEY!!!
UH? MMBR
SSSSIPP WHAT CRRTT GONNA DO TODAY WSS GULP SSWIG
MM NO...
NO...NO..
NOO!!!
AWW FFUCK SHHIT OFF!! XZWTKK!
RRRRIP!
GULP GULPP SWIG MORE SSCHMUCH MORE COFFEE SSSSSSIP
THREE

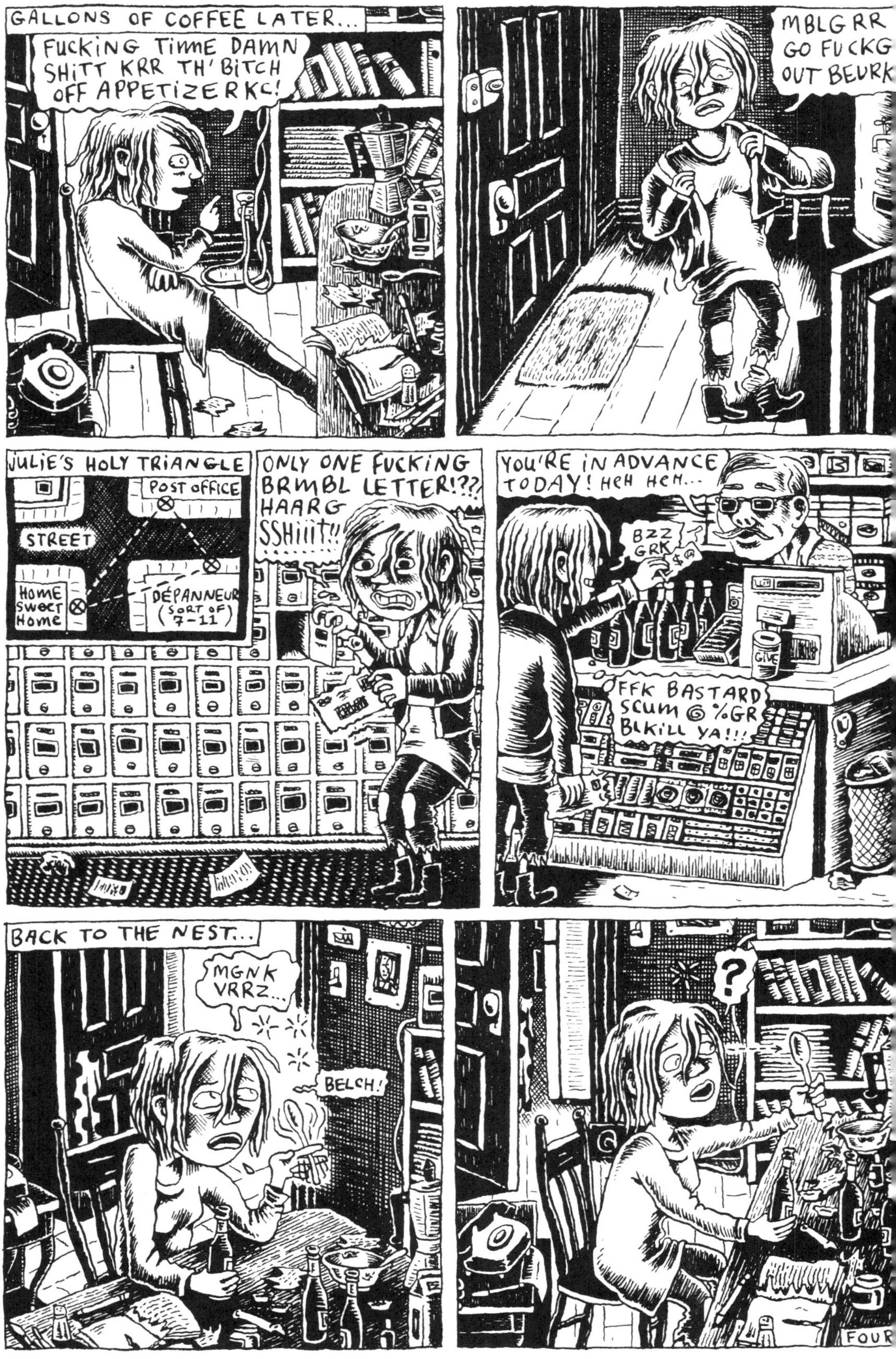
GALLONS OF COFFEE LATER...
FUCKING TIMME DAMN SHITT KRR TH' BITCH OFF APPETIZERKC!
MBLGRR GO FUCKG OUT BEURK
JULIE'S HOLY TRIANGLE
POST OFFICE
STREET
HOME SWEET HOME
DÉPANNEUR (SORT OF 7-11)
ONLY ONE FUCKING BRMBL LETTER!??
HAARG SSHIIIT!!
YOU'RE IN ADVANCE TODAY! HEH HEH...
BZZ GRK
FFK BASTARD SCUM @ %GR BLKILL YA!!!
GIVE
BACK TO THE NEST...
MGNK VRRZ...
BELCH!
?
FOUR

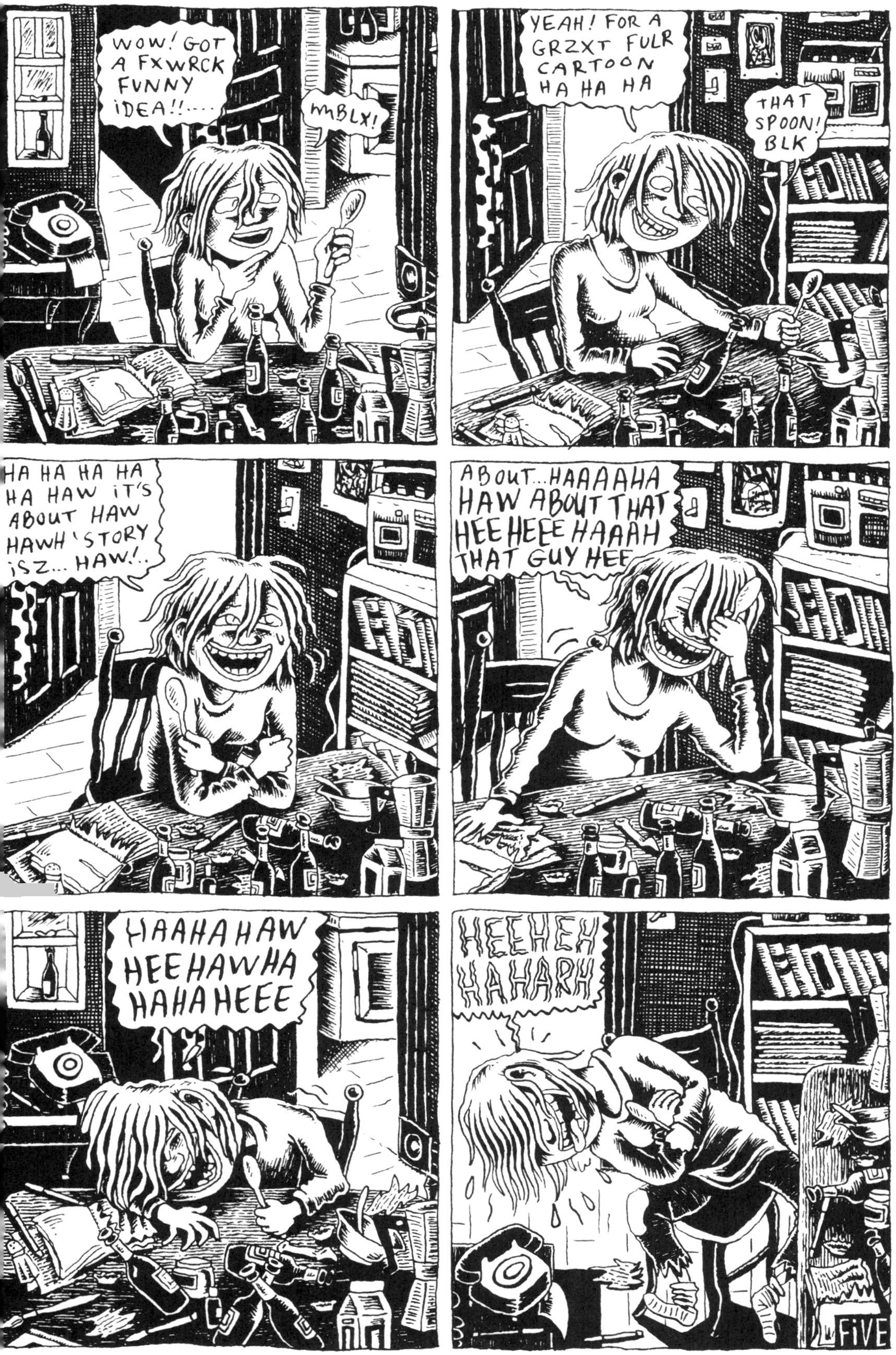
WOW! GOT A FXWRCK FUNNY IDEA!!....
MBLX!
YEAH! FOR A GRZXT FULR CARTOON HA HA HA
THAT SPOON! BLK
HA HA HA HA HA HAW IT'S ABOUT HAW HAWH 'STORY ISZ... HAW!..
ABOUT...HAAAAHA HAW ABOUT THAT HEEHEEE HAAAH THAT GUY HEE
HAAHAHAW HEEHAWHA HAHAHEEE
HEEHEH HAHARH
FIVE

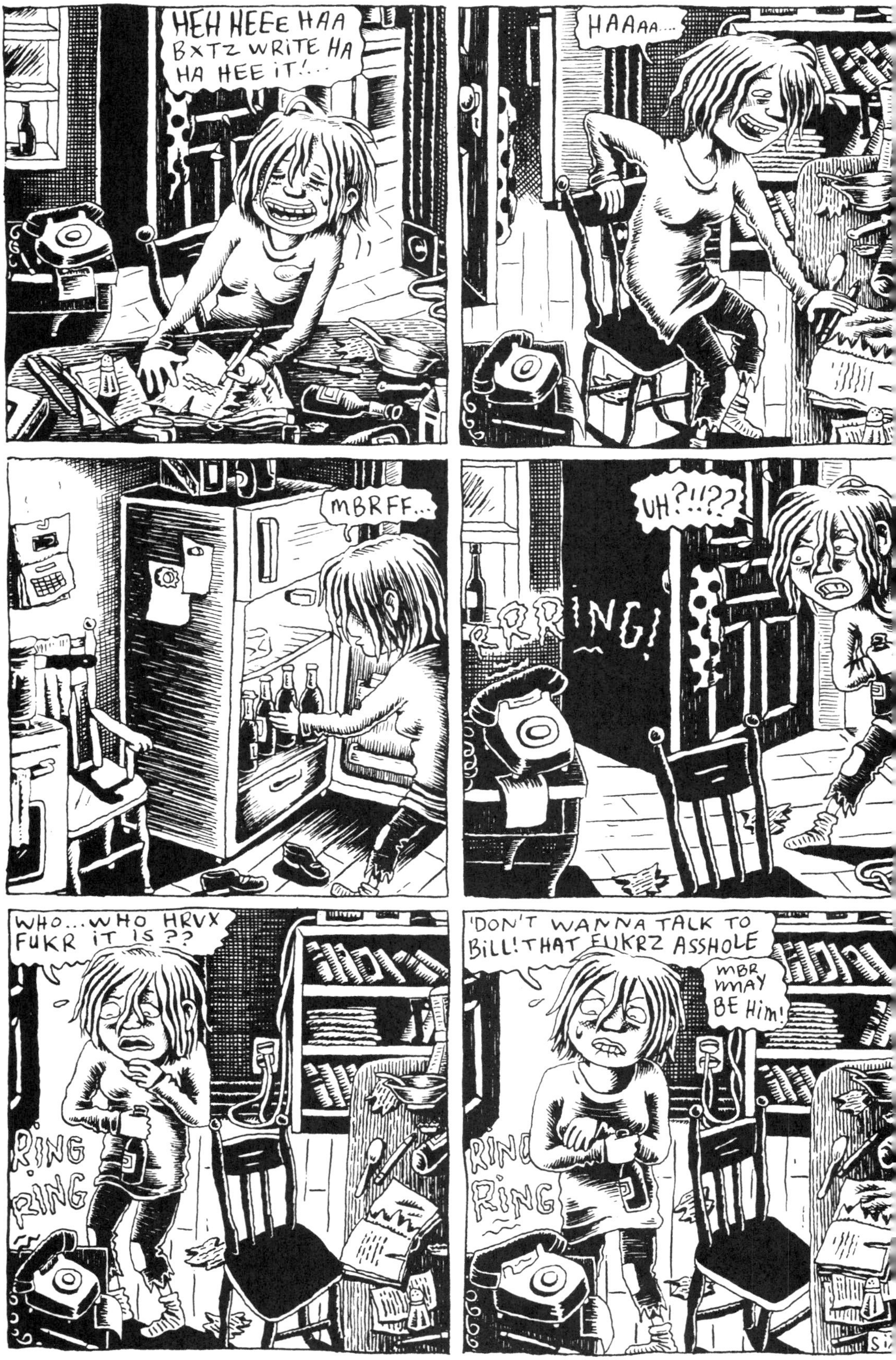
HEH HEEE HAA BXTZ WRITE HA HA HEE IT!...
HAAAA....
MBRFF...
UH?!!??
RRRING!
WHO... WHO HRVX FUKR IT IS??
RING RING
'DON'T WANNA TALK TO BILL! THAT FUKRZ ASSHOLE
MBR MAY BE HIM!
RING RING

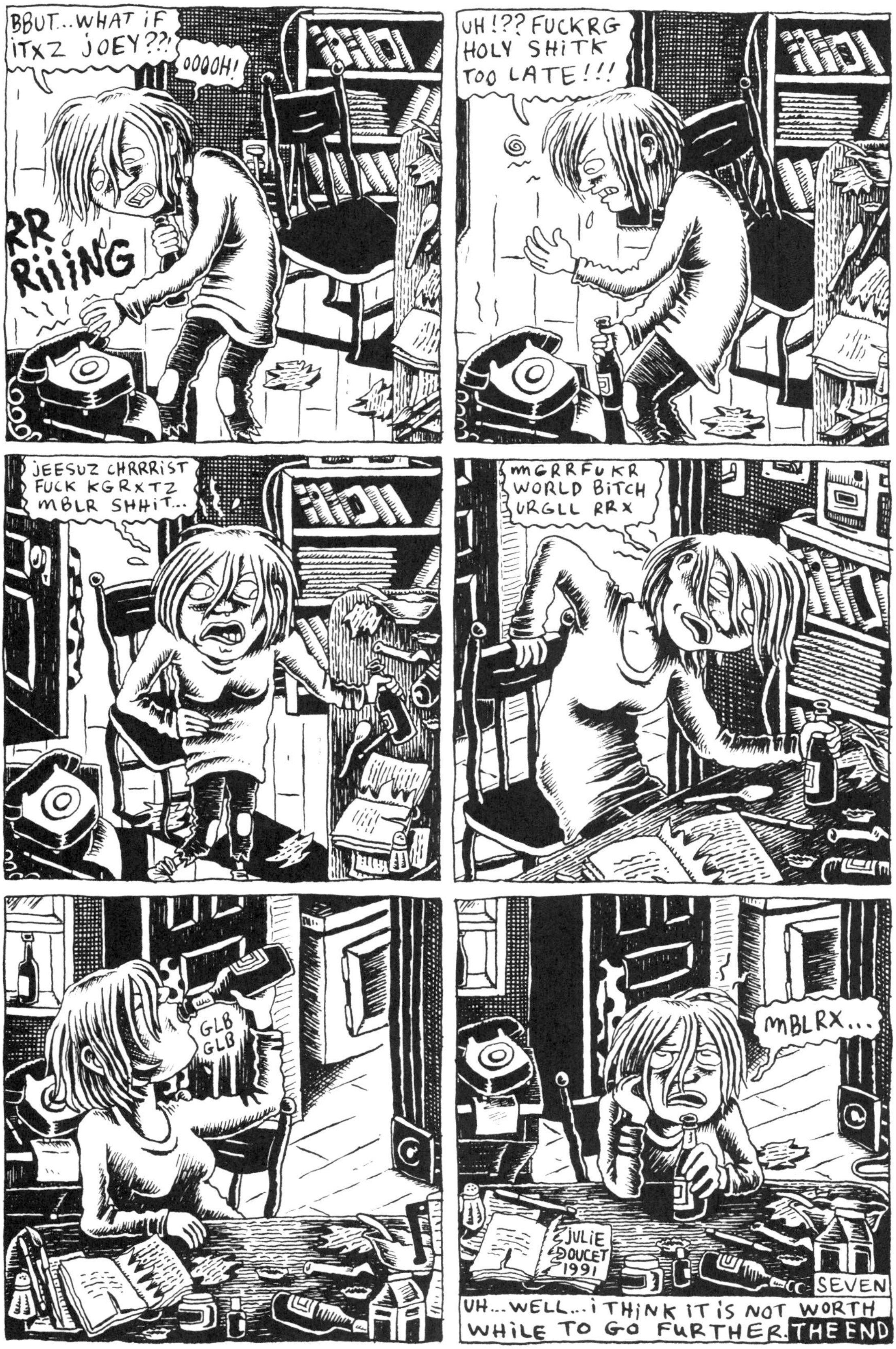
BBUT... WHAT IF ITXZ JOEY??!
OOOOH!
RR RIIING
UH!?? FUCKRG HOLY SHITK TOO LATE!!!
JEESUZ CHRRRIST FUCK KGRXTZ MBLR SHHIT...
MGRRFUKR WORLD BITCH URGLL RRX
GLB GLB
MBLRX...
JULIE DOUCET 1991
SEVEN
UH... WELL... I THINK IT IS NOT WORTH WHILE TO GO FURTHER.
THE END

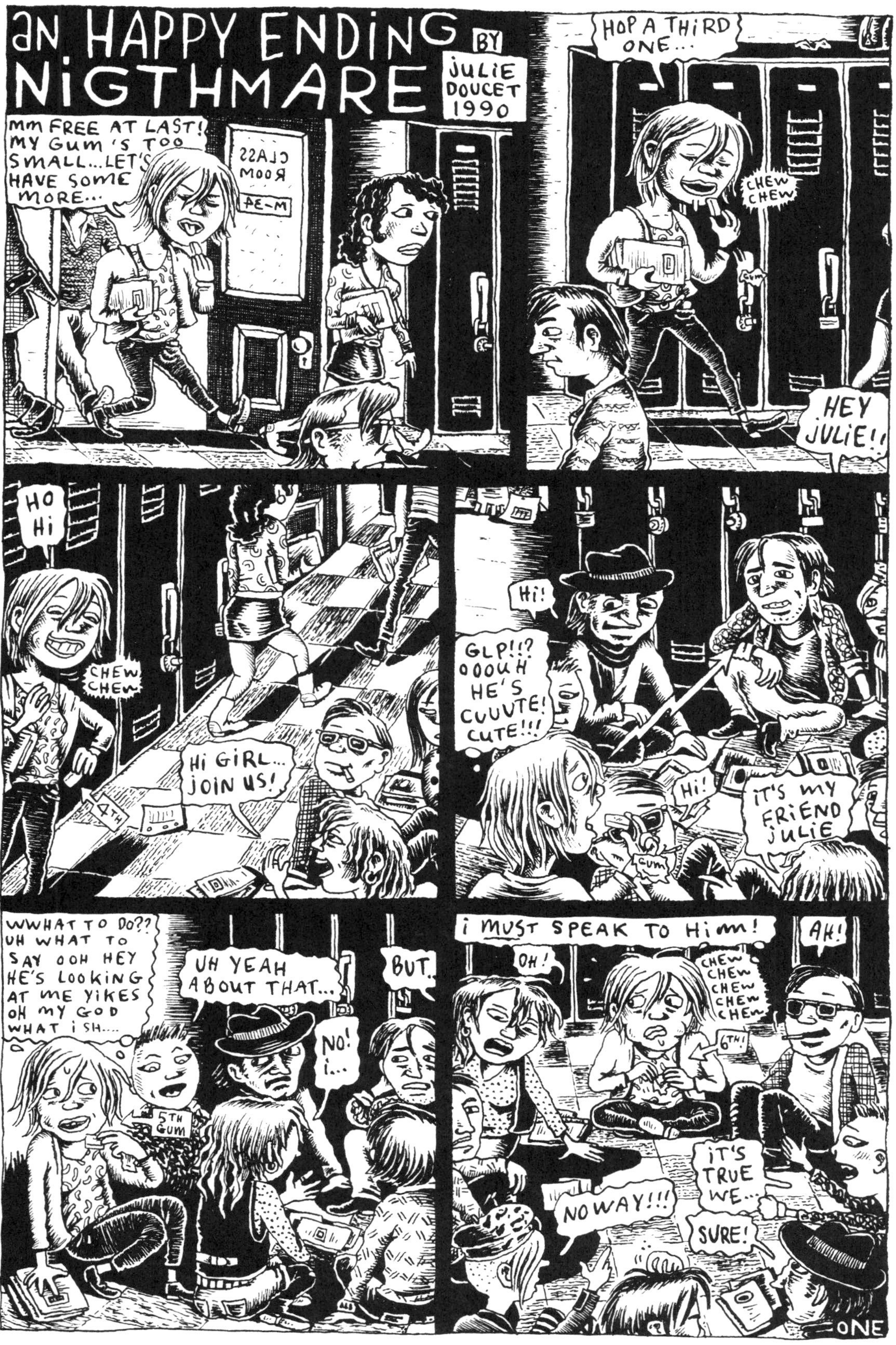
AN HAPPY ENDING NIGTHMARE
BY JULIE DOUCET 1990
MM FREE AT LAST! MY GUM'S TOO SMALL...LET'S HAVE SOME MORE...
CLASS ROOM
HOP A THIRD ONE...
CHEW CHEW
GUM
HEY JULIE!!
HO Hi
CHEW CHEW
Hi GIRL... JOIN US!
4TH
Hi!
GLP!!? OOOUH HE'S CUUUTE! CUTE!!!
Hi!
IT'S MY FRIEND JULIE
GUM
WWHAT TO DO?? UH WHAT TO SAY OOH HEY HE'S LOOKING AT ME YIKES OH MY GOD WHAT I SH....
UH YEAH ABOUT THAT...
BUT..
NO! I...
5TH GUM
I MUST SPEAK TO HIM!
AH!
OH!
CHEW CHEW CHEW CHEW CHEW
6TH!
IT'S TRUE WE...
NO WAY!!!
SURE!
ONE

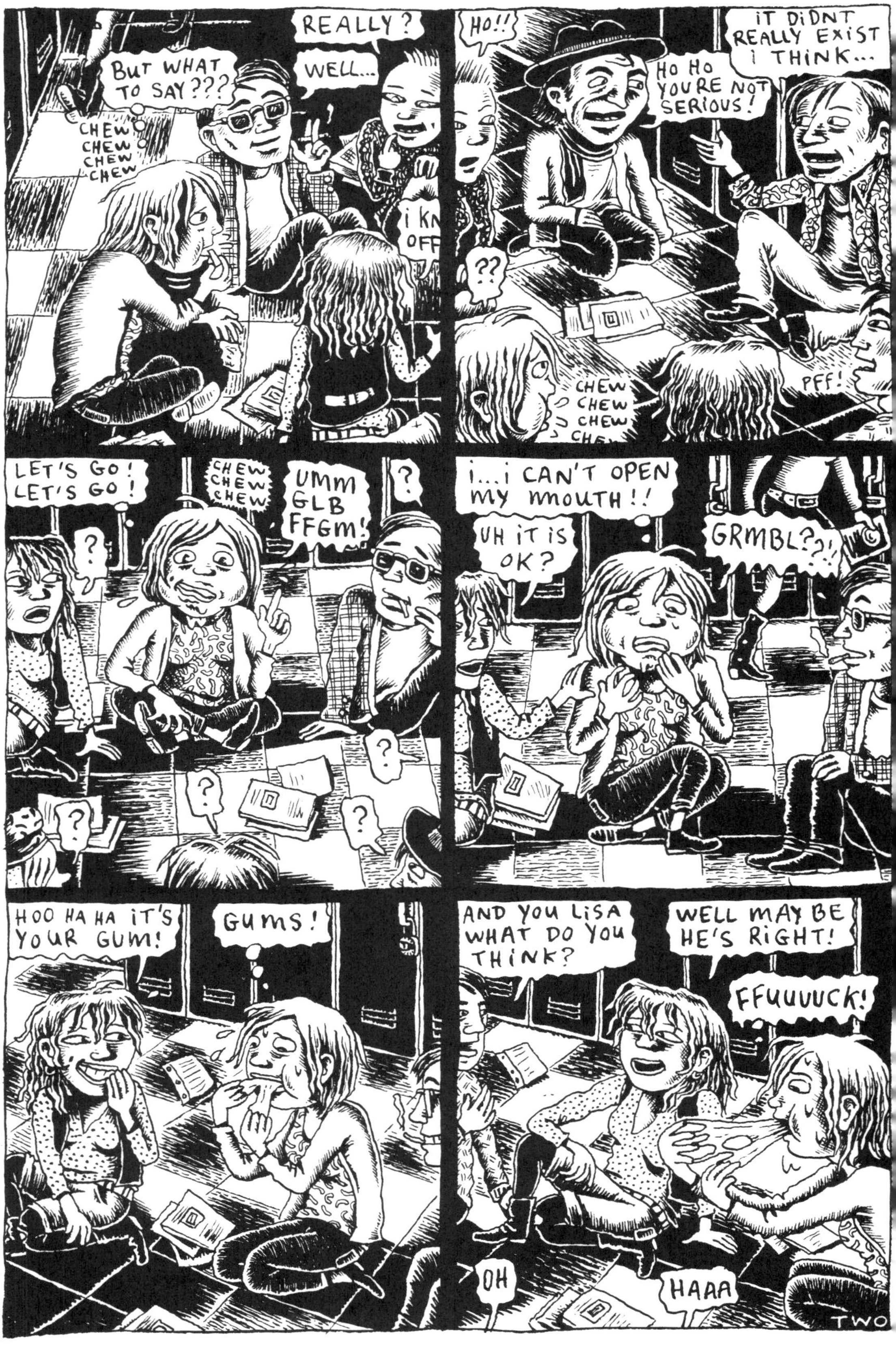
REALLY?
BUT WHAT TO SAY???
WELL...
CHEW CHEW CHEW CHEW
HO!!
IT DIDNT REALLY EXIST I THINK...
HO HO YOU'RE NOT SERIOUS!
??
PFF!
CHEW CHEW CHEW
LET'S GO! LET'S GO!
CHEW CHEW CHEW
UMM GLB FFGM!
?
?
?
?
?
?
I...I CAN'T OPEN MY MOUTH!!
UH IT IS OK?
GRMBL?!
HOO HA HA IT'S YOUR GUM!
GUMS!
AND YOU LISA WHAT DO YOU THINK?
WELL MAY BE HE'S RIGHT!
FFUUUUCK!
OH
HAAA
TWO

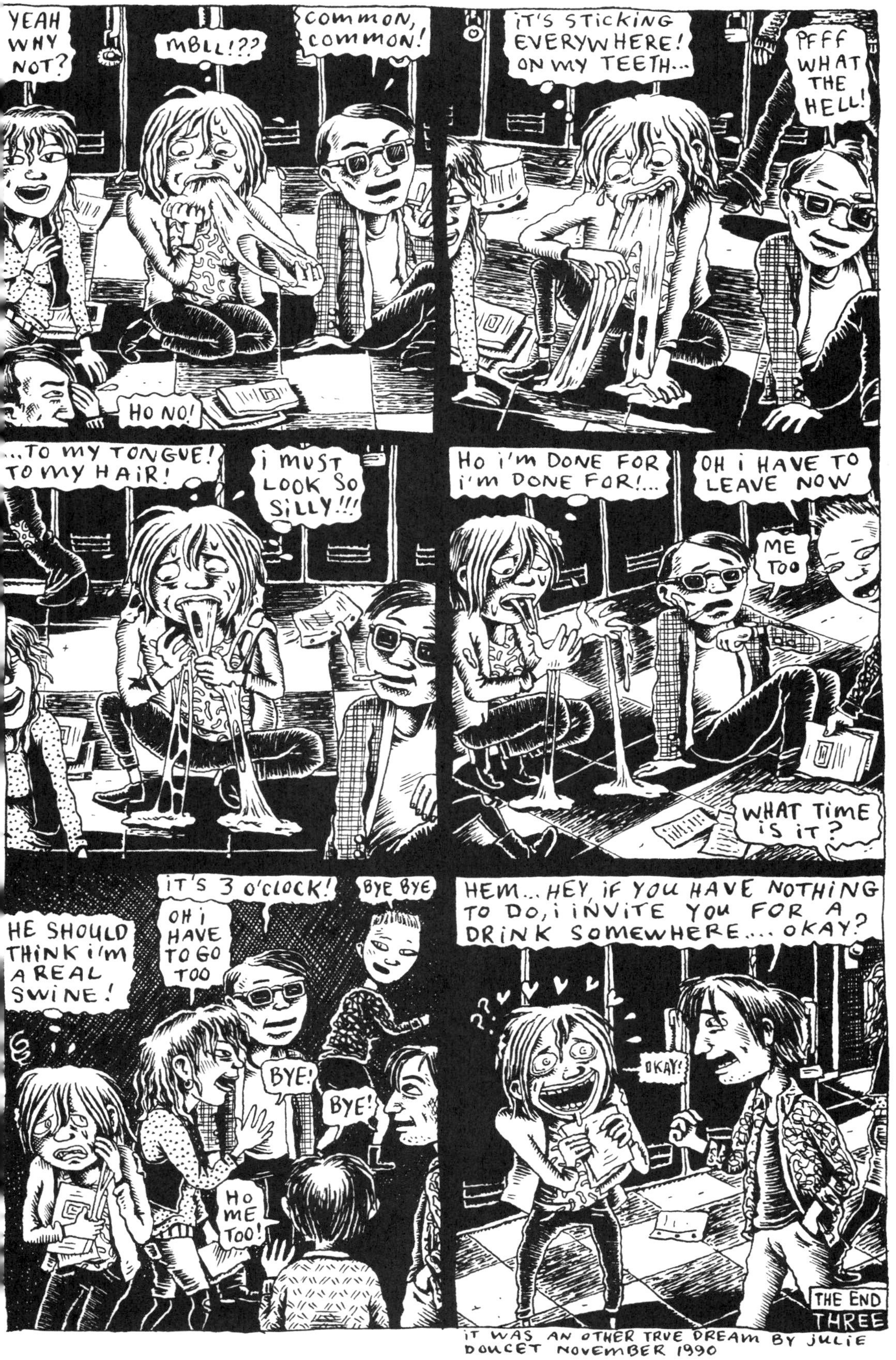
YEAH WHY NOT?
MBLL!??
COMMON, COMMON!
HO NO!
IT'S STICKING EVERYWHERE! ON MY TEETH...
PFFF WHAT THE HELL!
...TO MY TONGUE! TO MY HAIR!
I MUST LOOK SO SILLY!!!
HO I'M DONE FOR I'M DONE FOR!...
OH I HAVE TO LEAVE NOW
ME TOO
WHAT TIME IS IT?
HE SHOULD THINK I'M A REAL SWINE!
IT'S 3 O'CLOCK!
OH I HAVE TO GO TOO
BYE BYE
BYE!
BYE!
HO ME TOO!
HEM... HEY IF YOU HAVE NOTHING TO DO, I INVITE YOU FOR A DRINK SOMEWHERE... OKAY?
OKAY!
THE END THREE

IT WAS AN OTHER TRUE DREAM BY JULIE DOUCET NOVEMBER 1990

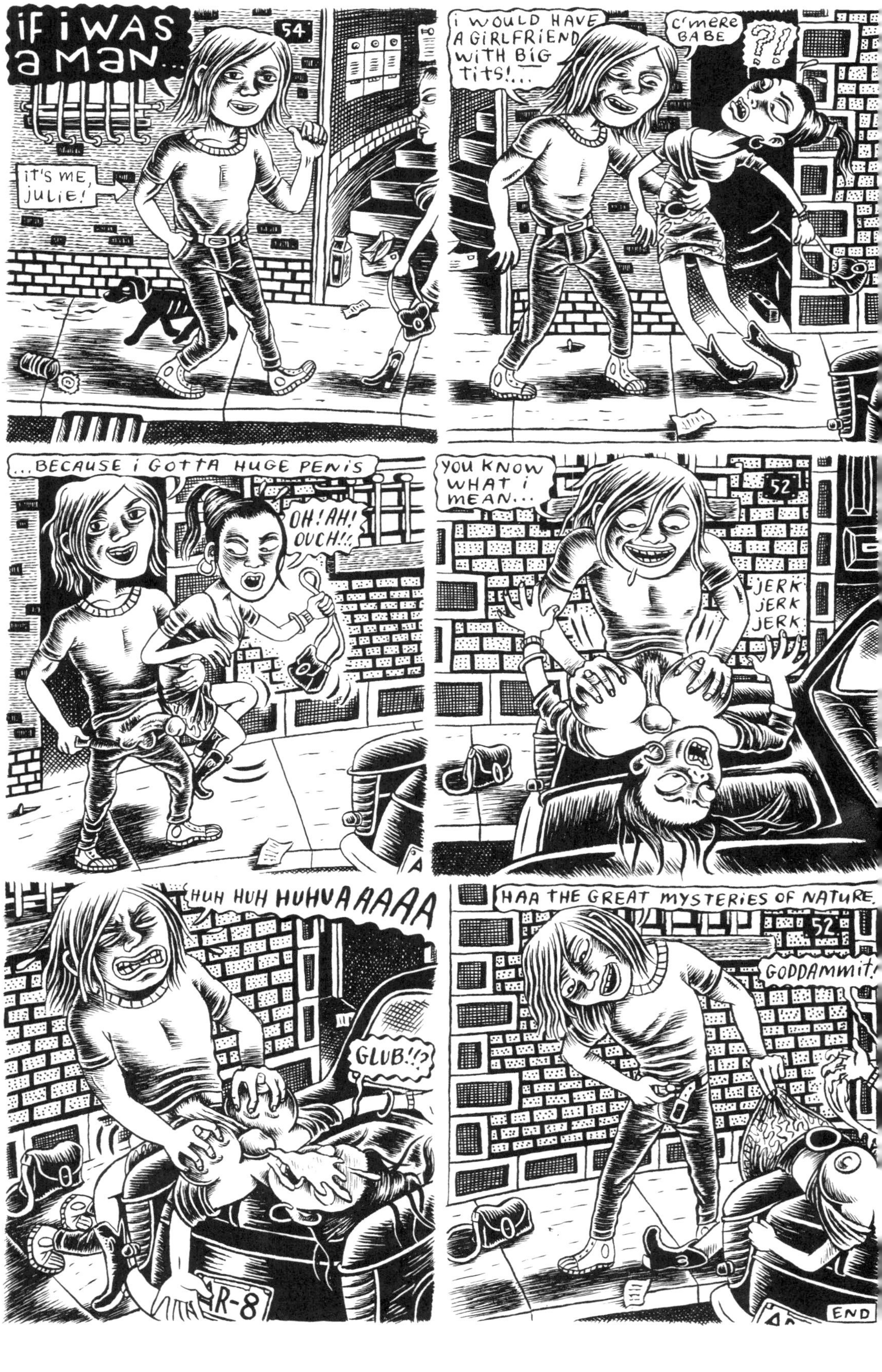
if i WAS a MAN...
54
it's ME, JULIE!
i WOULD HAVE A GIRLFRIEND WITH BIG TITS!...
C'mere BABE
?!
...BECAUSE i GOTTA HUGE PENIS
OH! AH! OUCH!!
YOU KNOW WHAT i MEAN...
52
JERK JERK JERK
HUH HUH HUHUAAAAA
GLUB!!?
R-8
HAA THE GREAT MYSTERIES OF NATURE.
52
GODDAMMIT!
END

RE GREt

A DREAM BY JULiE DOUCET

dREAMT SEPT. 5 1991

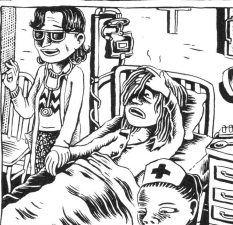

ONE

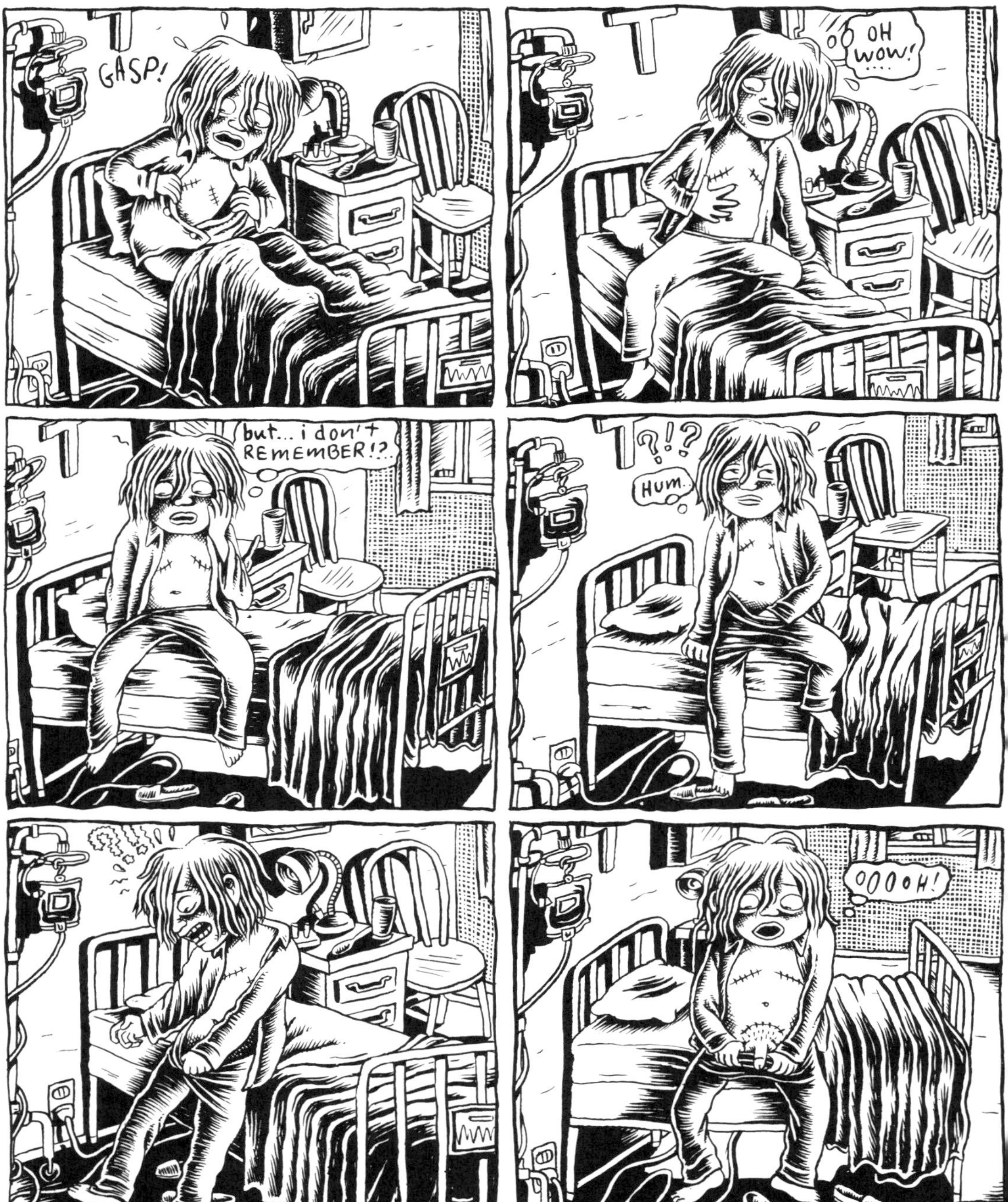
GASP!
OH WOW!
but... i don't REMEMBER!?..
?!?
Hum..
OOOOH!

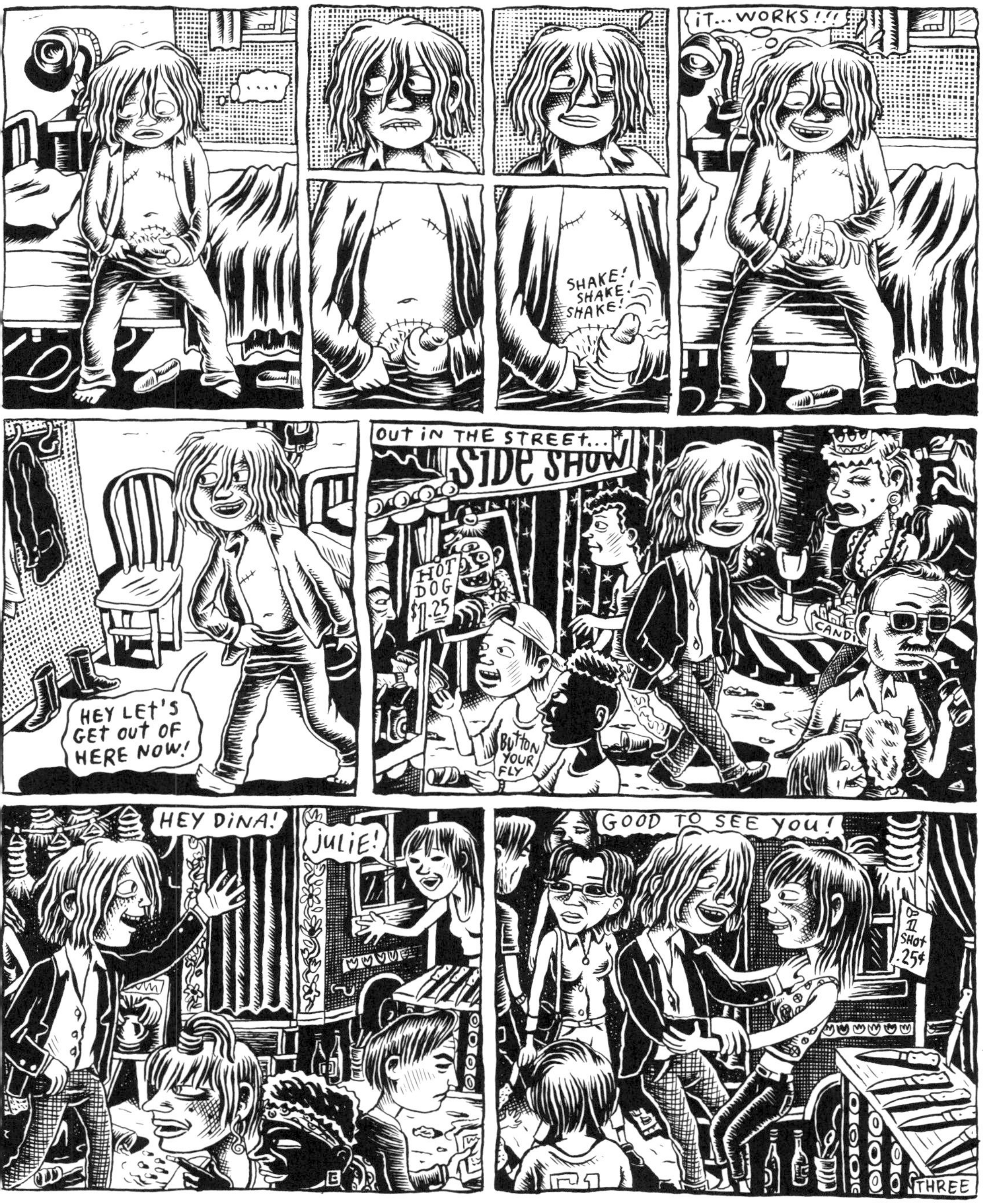
. . . .
iT... WORKS!!!
SHAKE! SHAKE! SHAKE!
HEY LET'S GET OUT OF HERE NOW!
OUT iN THE STREET...
SIDE SHOW
HOT DOG $1.25
BUTTON YOUR FLY
CANDY
HEY DiNA!
julie!
GOOD TO SEE you!
SHOT .25¢

DO YOU KNOW WHAT HAPPENED TO ME?
NO, NO TELL ME!
WELL, PSSSH PSSH! SH SSSPSH... !?!! PSSH! SSSSH....
WH...!?? WOW!!!
?
COME TO MY PLACE TONIGHT JULIE, OK?...
OH YEAH!
AFTER WORK AT MY PLACE
.25¢
OKAY, LATER!
OOH I CAN'T WAIT...
18 and PLUS
MICKY DOLENZ OF THE MONKEES!
YOU DIDN'T FORGET ME DO YOU, JULIE?
?!!
FOUR

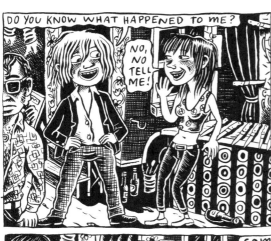

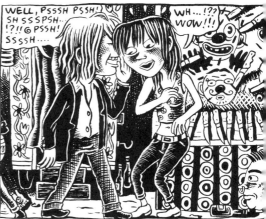

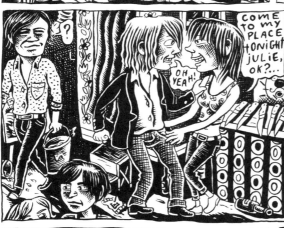

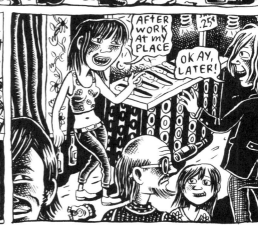

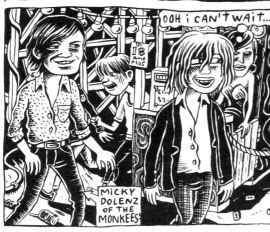

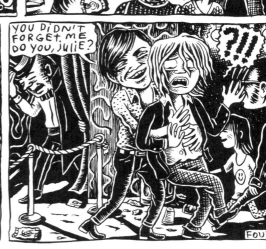

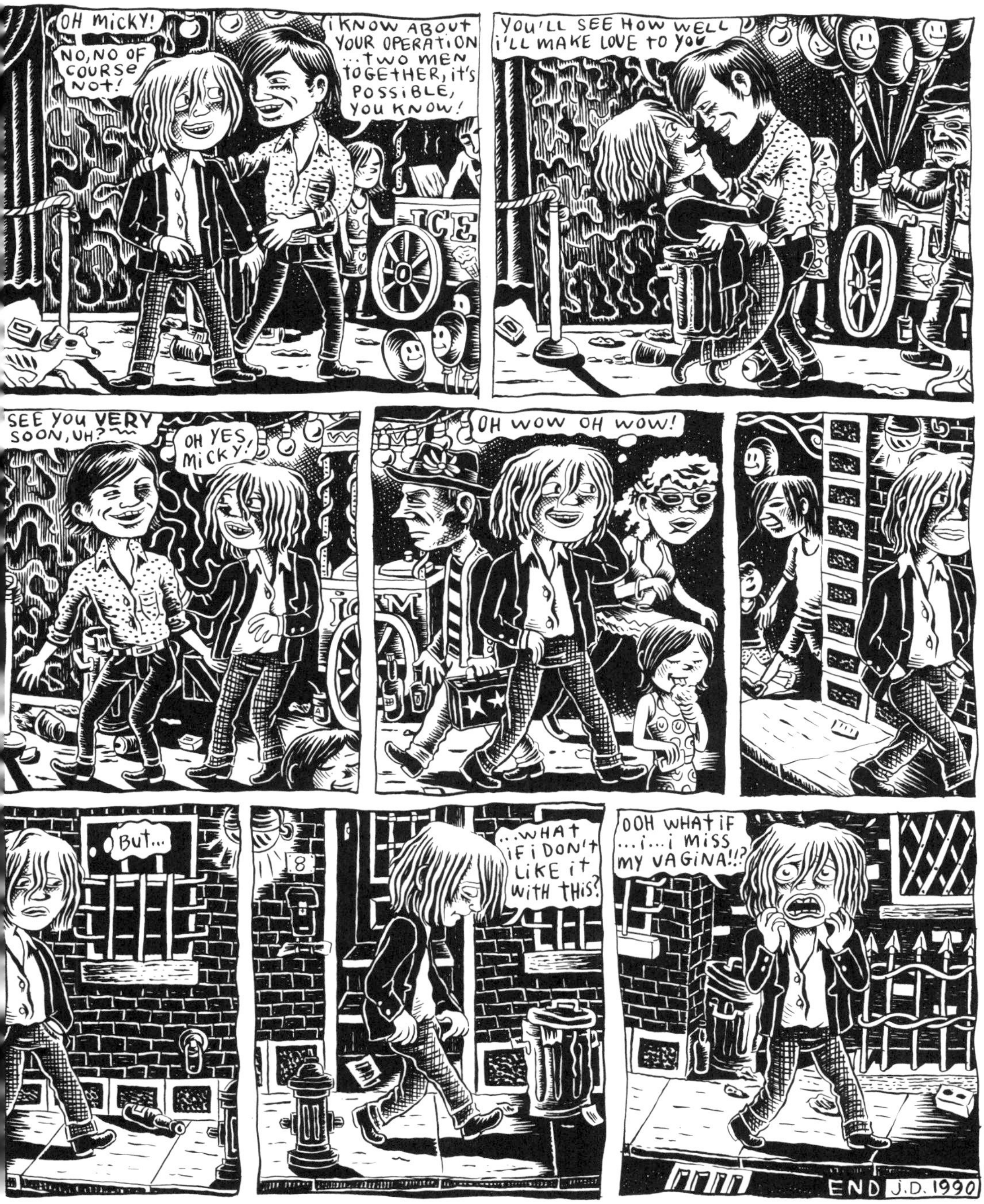
OH MICKY!
NO, NO OF COURSE NOT!
I KNOW ABOUT YOUR OPERATION ...TWO MEN TOGETHER, IT'S POSSIBLE, YOU KNOW!
YOU'LL SEE HOW WELL I'LL MAKE LOVE TO YOU
ICE
SEE YOU VERY SOON, UH?
OH YES, MICKY!
OH WOW OH WOW!
But...
8
...WHAT IF I DON'T LIKE IT WITH THIS?
OOH WHAT IF ...I...I MISS MY VAGINA!!?
END
J.D. 1990

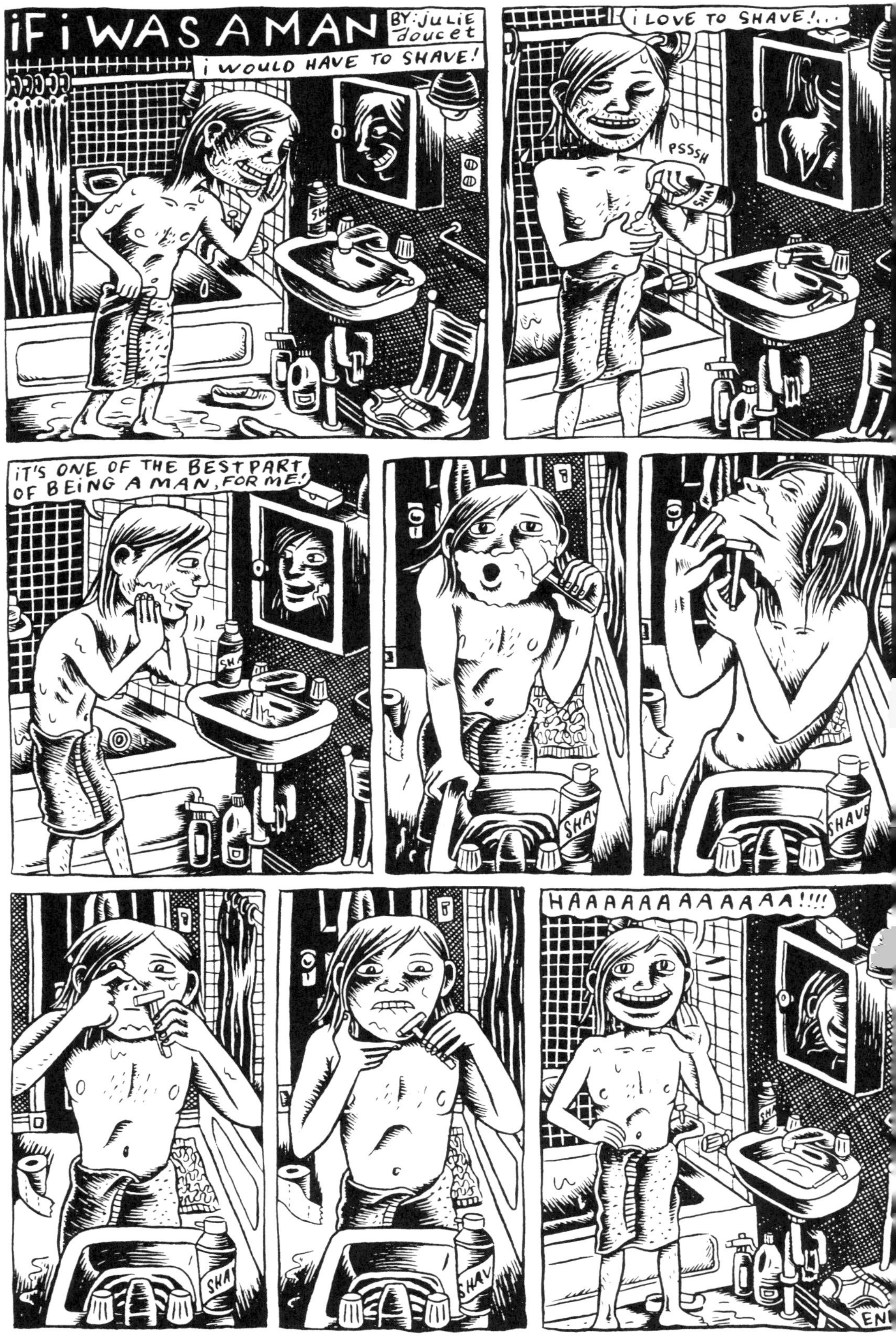
iF i WAS A MAN
BY: julie doucet
i WOULD HAVE TO SHAVE!
i LOVE TO SHAVE!...
PSSSH
IT'S ONE OF THE BEST PART OF BEING A MAN, FOR ME!
HAAAAAAAAAAAA!!!!

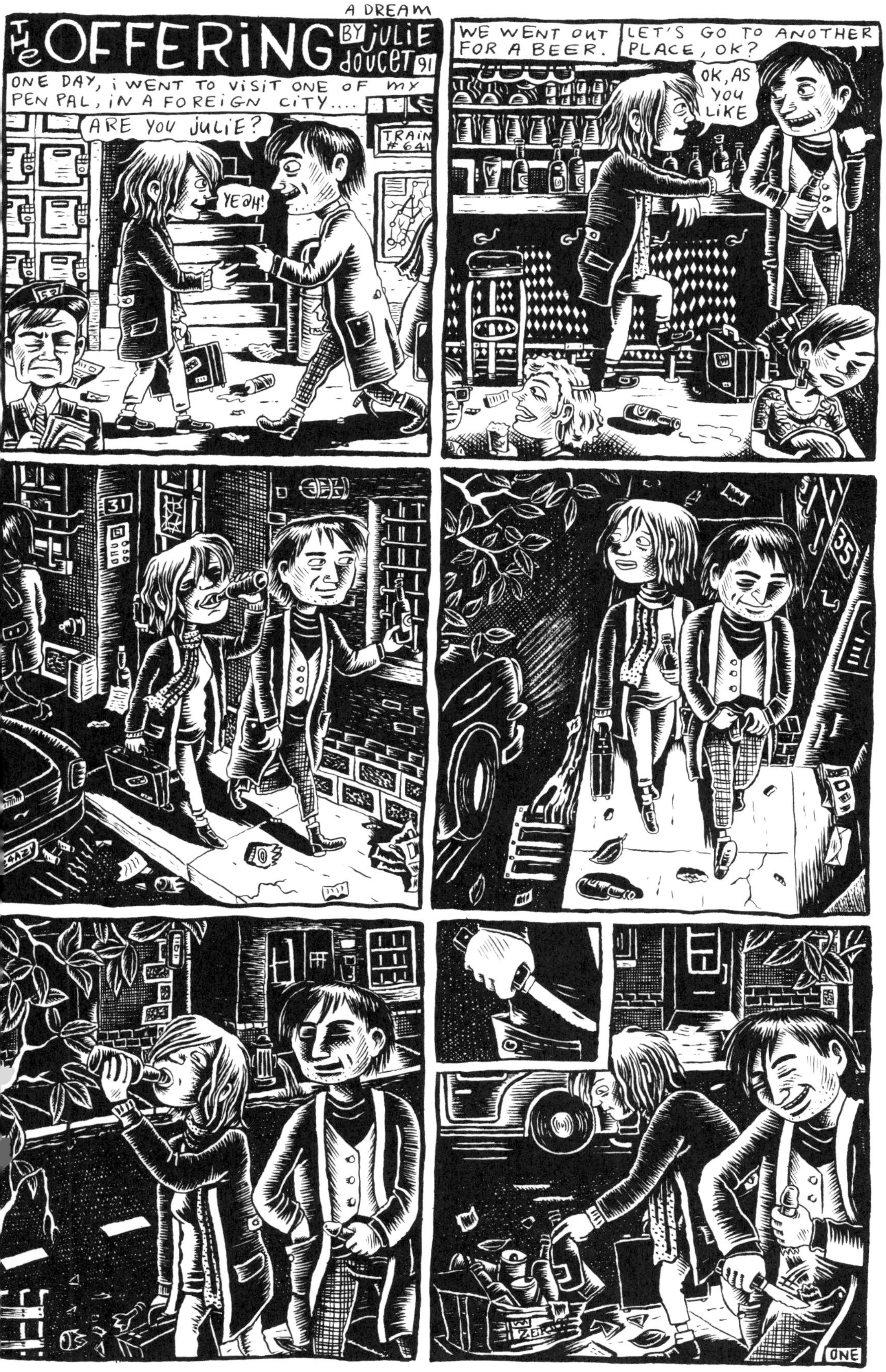
A DREAM
THE OFFERING BY JULIE DOUCET 91
ONE DAY, I WENT TO VISIT ONE OF MY PEN PAL, IN A FOREIGN CITY....
ARE YOU JULIE?
YEAH!
TRAIN #641
WE WENT OUT FOR A BEER.
LET'S GO TO ANOTHER PLACE, OK?
OK, AS YOU LIKE
31
35
ONE

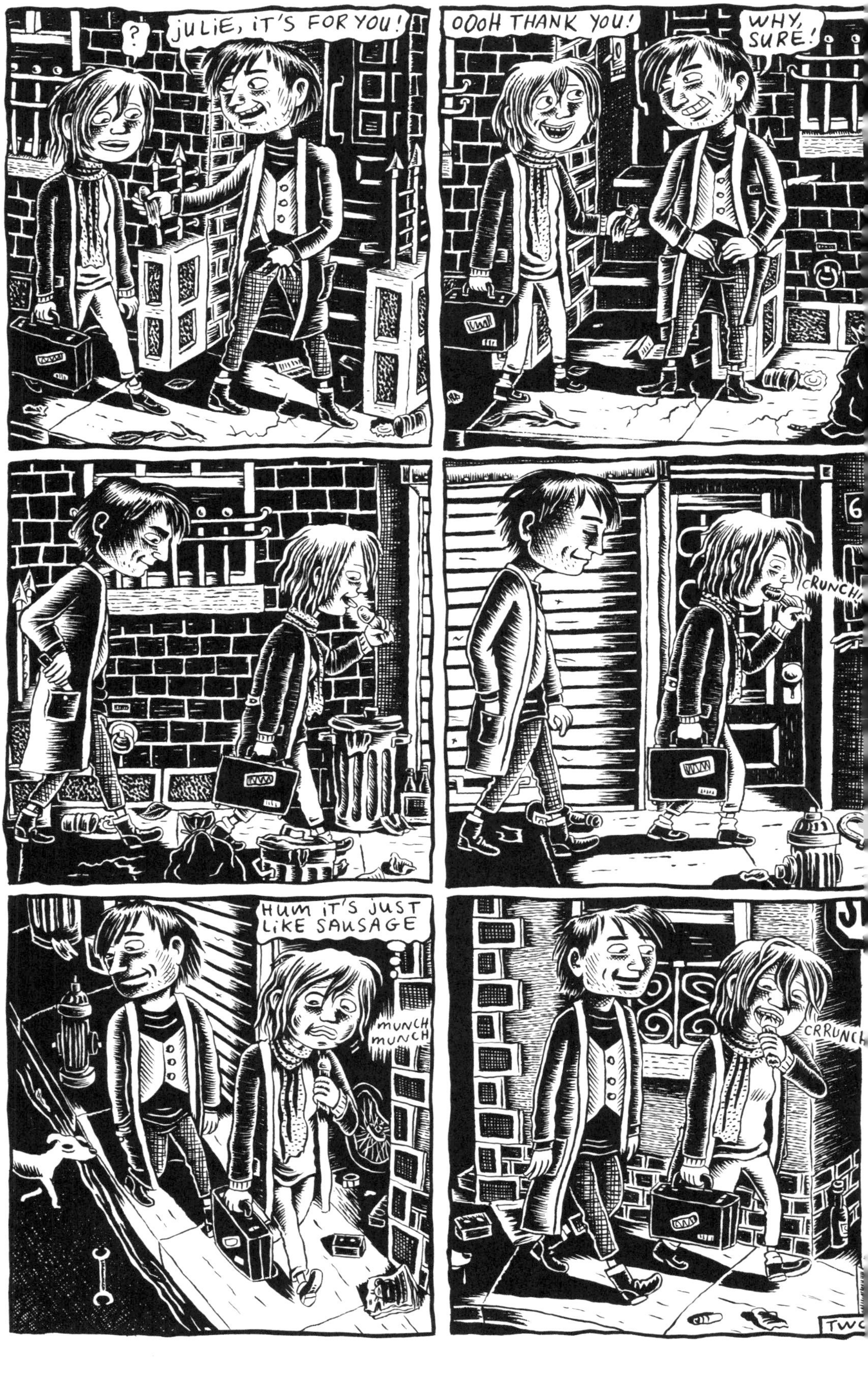
?
JULIE, IT'S FOR YOU!
OOOH THANK YOU!
WHY, SURE!
CRUNCH
HUM IT'S JUST LIKE SAUSAGE
MUNCH MUNCH
CRRUNC

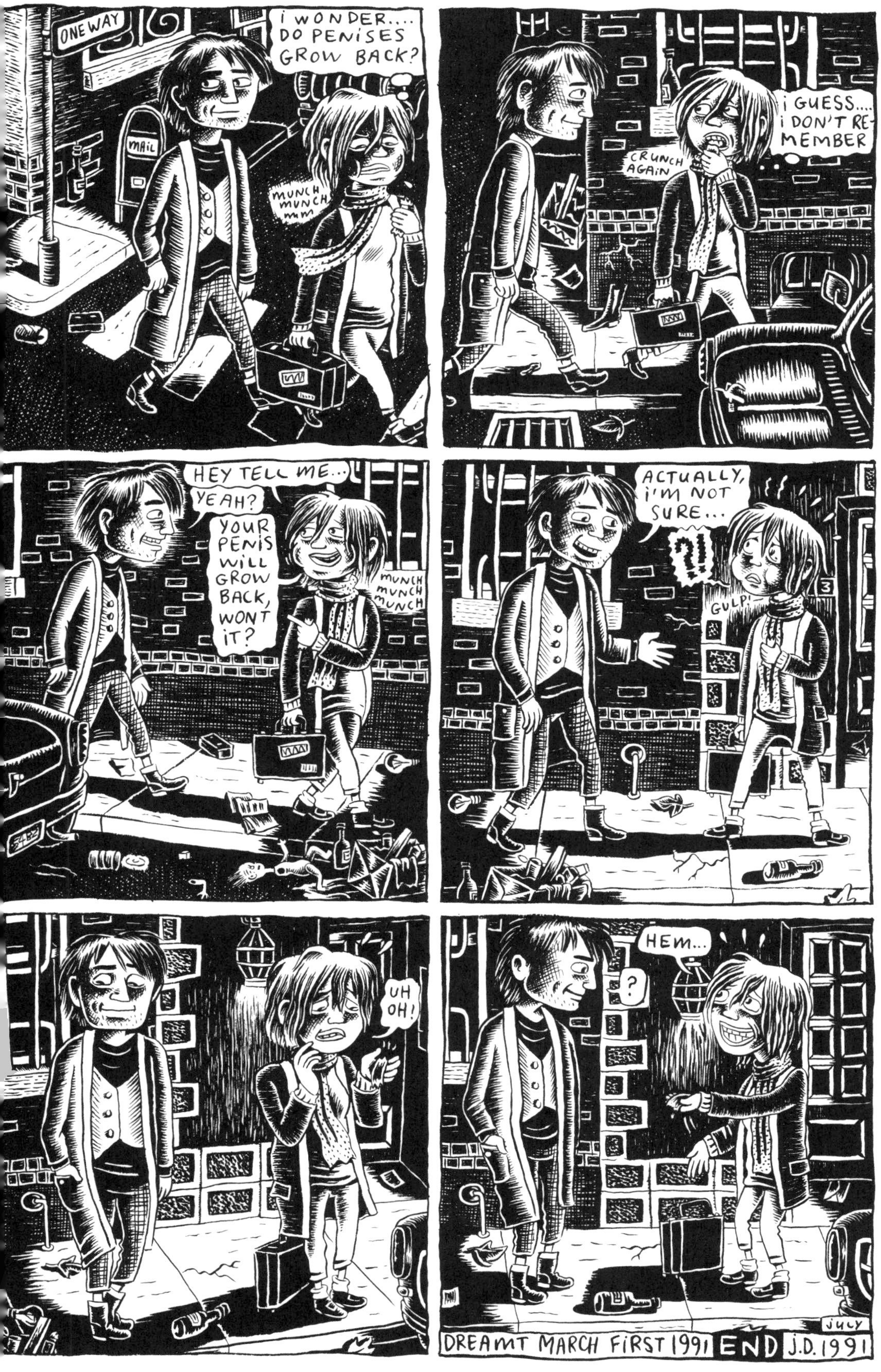
ONE WAY
MAIL
i WONDER.... DO PENISES GROW BACK?
MUNCH MUNCH MM
i GUESS.... i DON'T REMEMBER
CRUNCH AGAIN
HEY TELL ME...
YEAH?
YOUR PENIS WILL GROW BACK, WONT iT?
MUNCH MUNCH MUNCH
ACTUALLY, i'M NOT SURE...
?!
GULP!
3
UH OH!
HEM...
?
JULY
DREAMT MARCH FIRST 1991
END
J.D. 1991

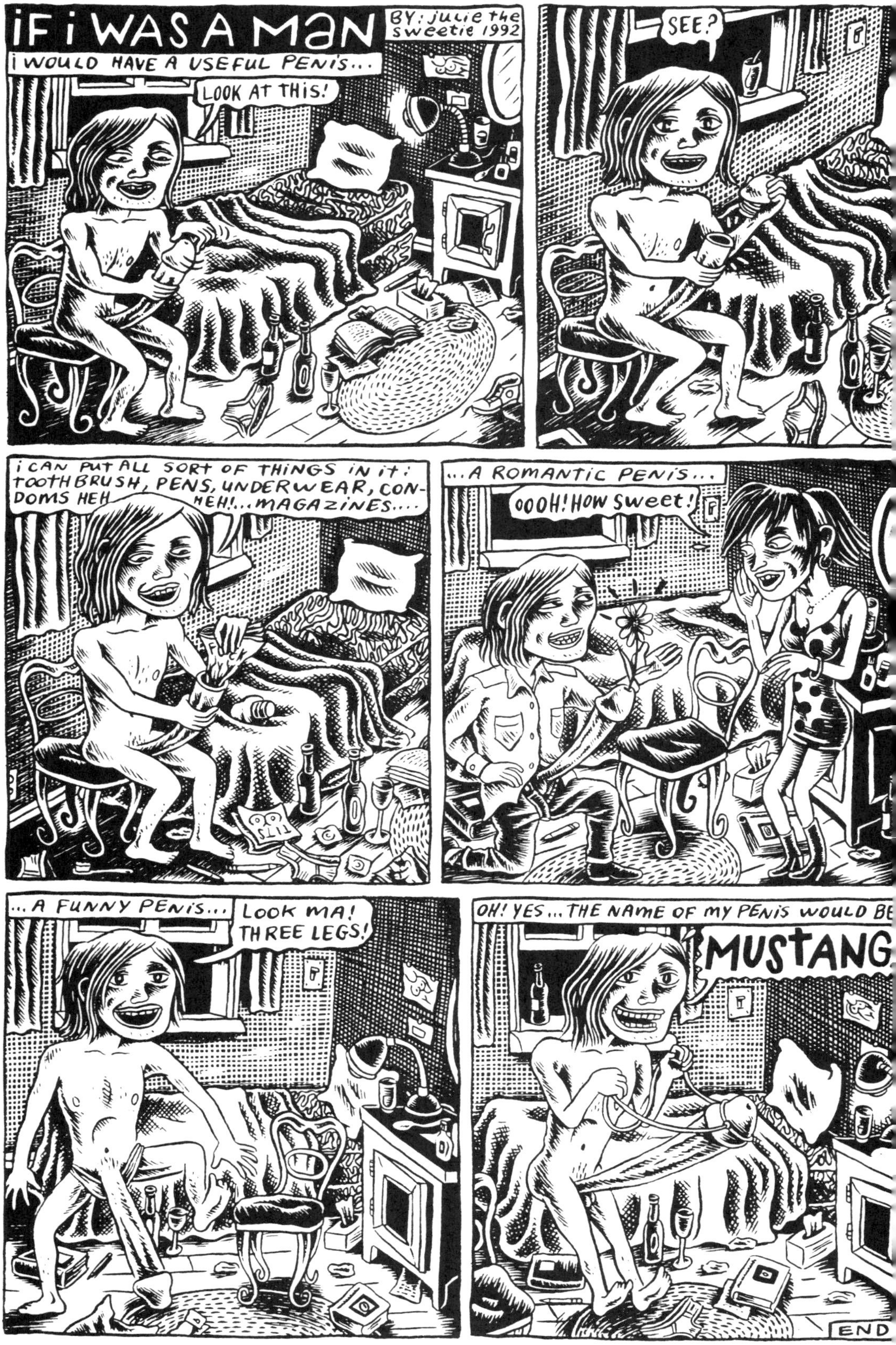
iF i WAS A MAN
BY: julie the sweetie 1992
i WOULD HAVE A USEFUL PENiS...
LOOK AT THiS!
SEE?
i CAN PUT ALL SORT OF THINGS IN iT: TOOTHBRUSH, PENS, UNDERWEAR, CONDOMS HEH HEH!... MAGAZINES...
...A ROMANTIC PENiS...
OOOH! HOW SWEET!
...A FUNNY PENiS...
LOOK MA! THREE LEGS!
OH! YES... THE NAME OF MY PENiS WOULD BE
MUSTANG
END

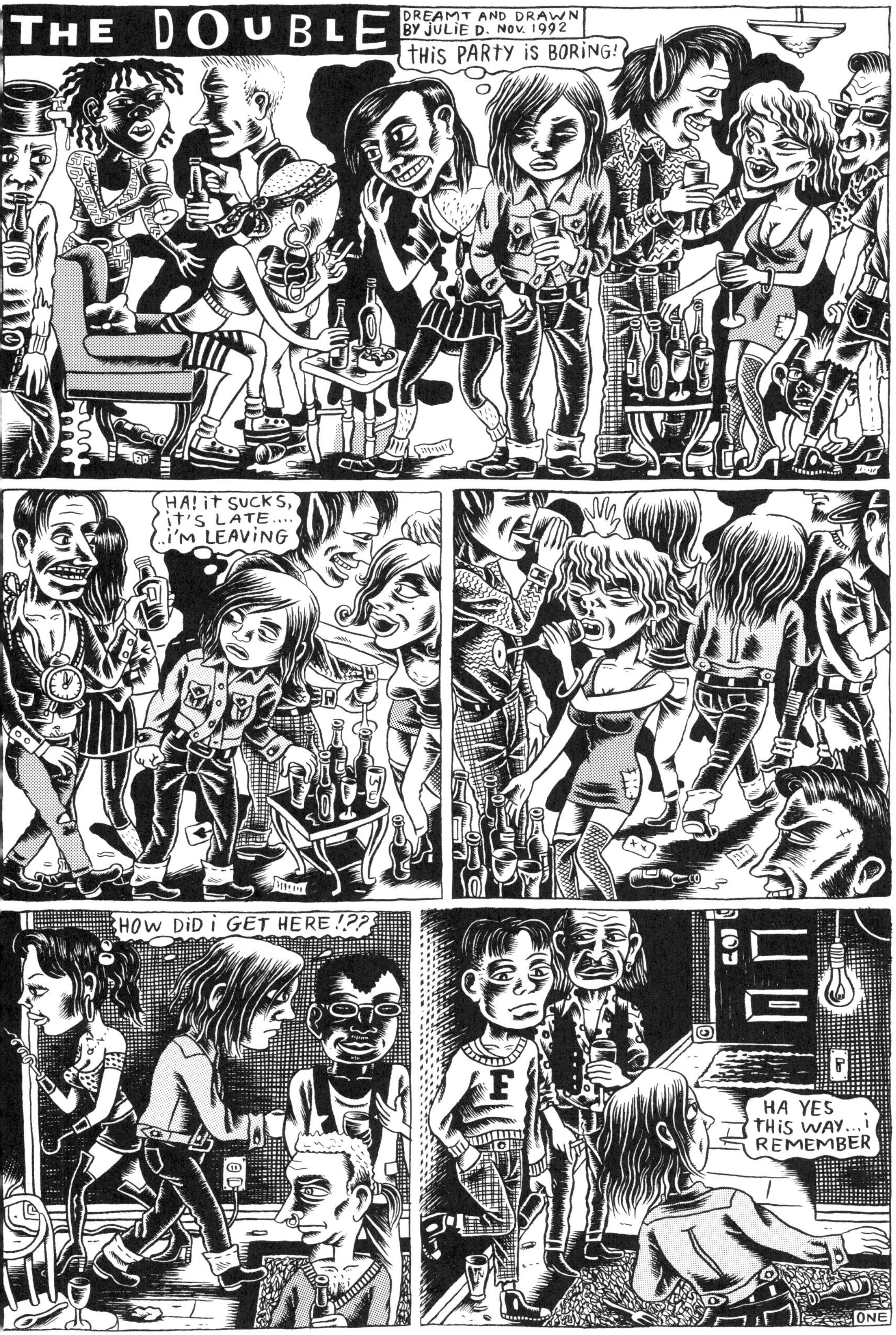
THE DOUBLE
DREAMT AND DRAWN BY JULIE D. NOV. 1992
THIS PARTY IS BORING!
HA! IT SUCKS, IT'S LATE.... ..I'M LEAVING
HOW DID I GET HERE!??
HA YES THIS WAY...I REMEMBER
ONE

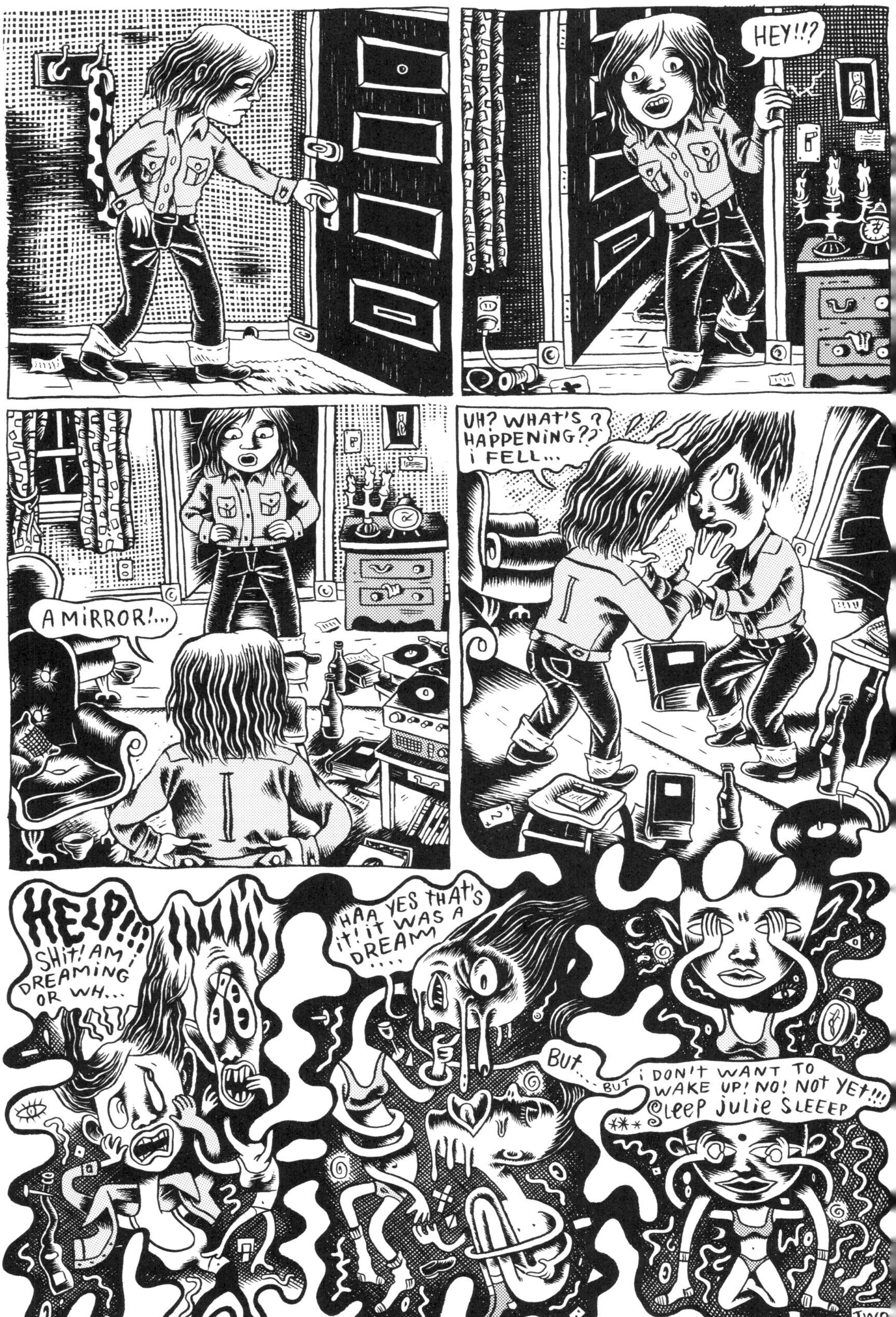
HEY!!?
UH? WHAT'S ? HAPPENING?? I FELL...
A MIRROR!...
HELP!!!
SHIT! AM I DREAMING OR WH...
HAA YES THAT'S IT! IT WAS A DREAM....
BUT...
BUT I DON'T WANT TO WAKE UP! NO! NOT YET!!!
SLEEP JULIE SLEEEP

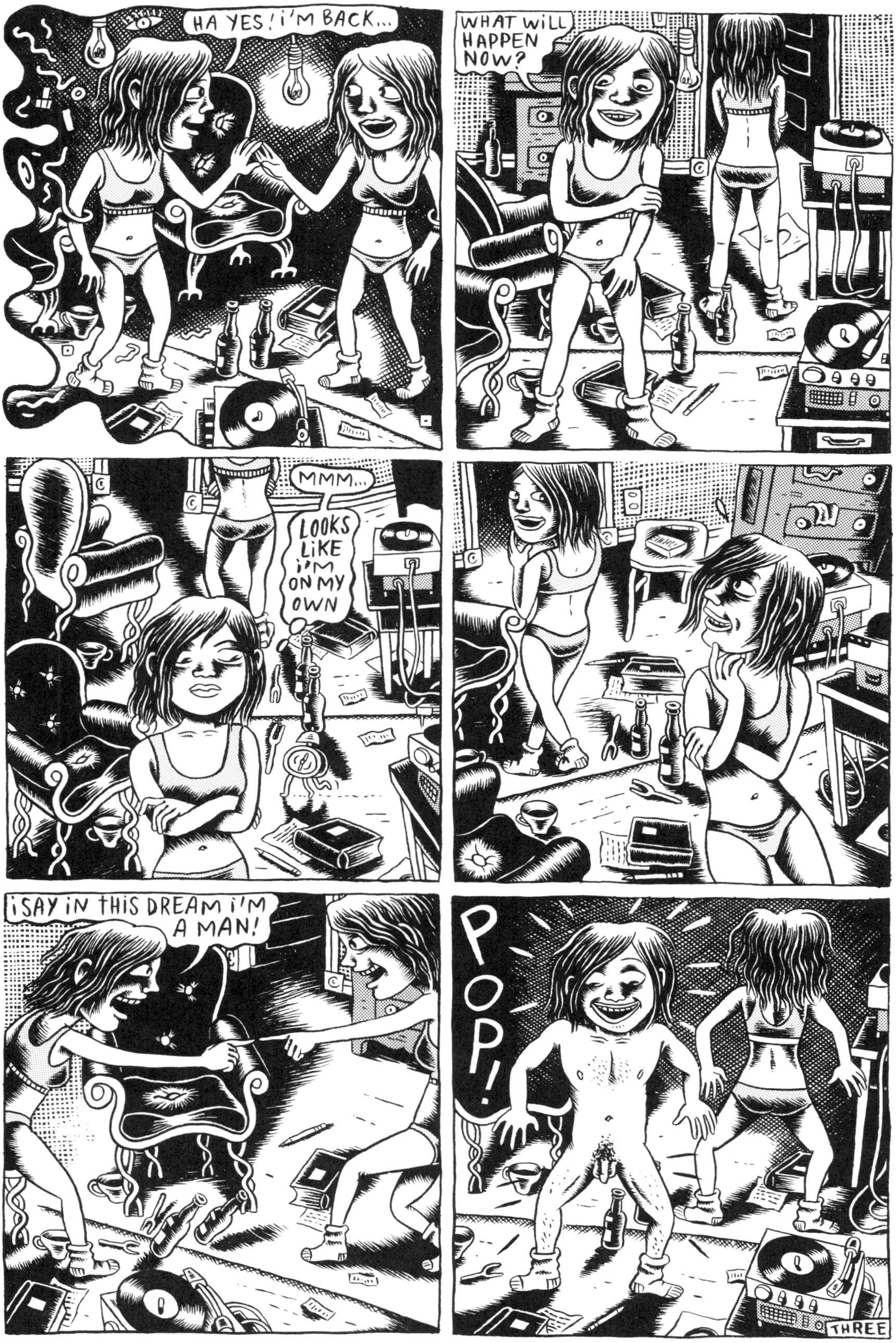
HA YES! I'M BACK...
WHAT WILL HAPPEN NOW?
MMM...
LOOKS LIKE I'M ON MY OWN
I SAY IN THIS DREAM I'M A MAN!
POP!
THREE

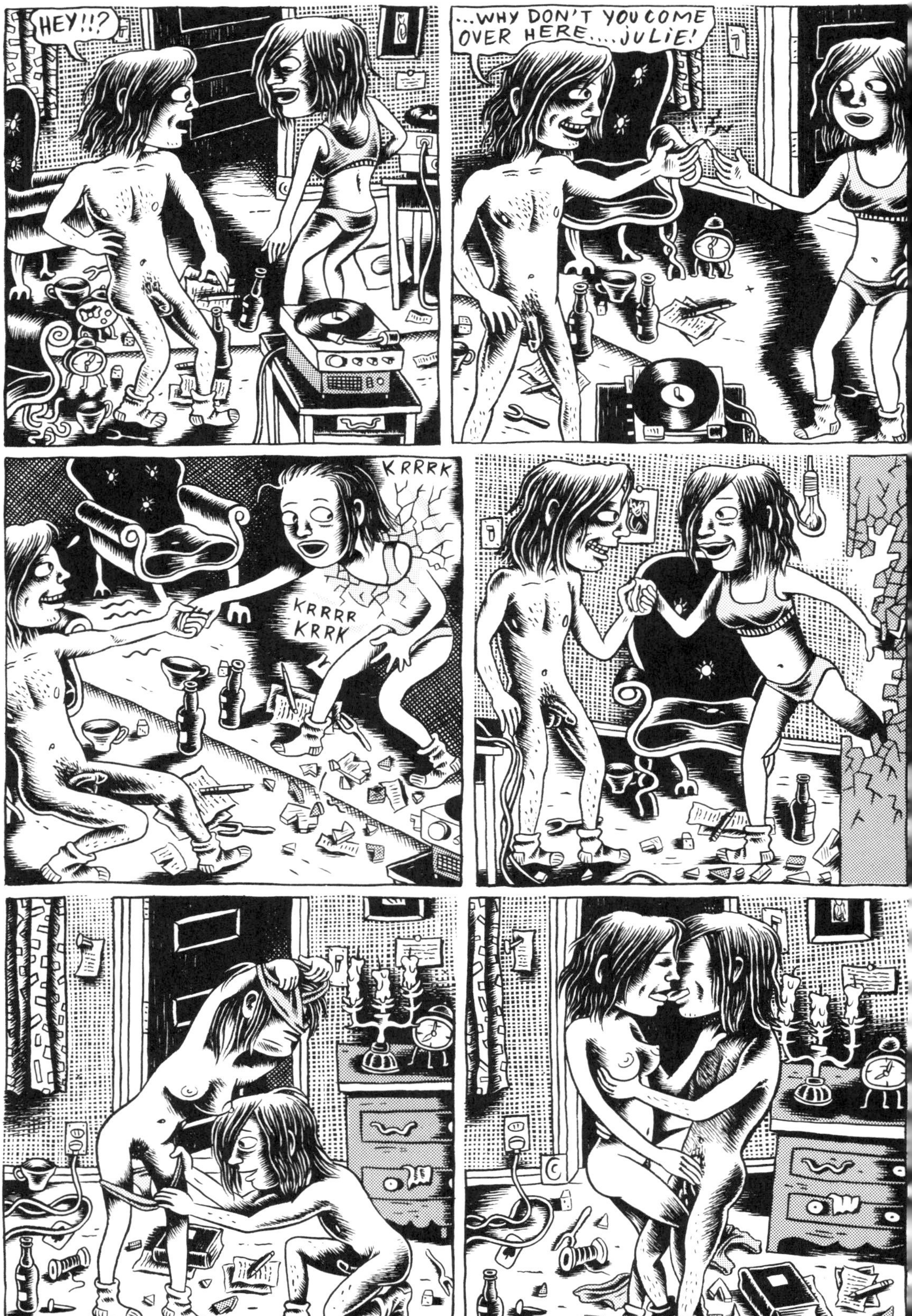
HEY!!?
...WHY DON'T YOU COME OVER HERE....JULIE!
KRRRK
KRRRR KRRK
END? J.D.92

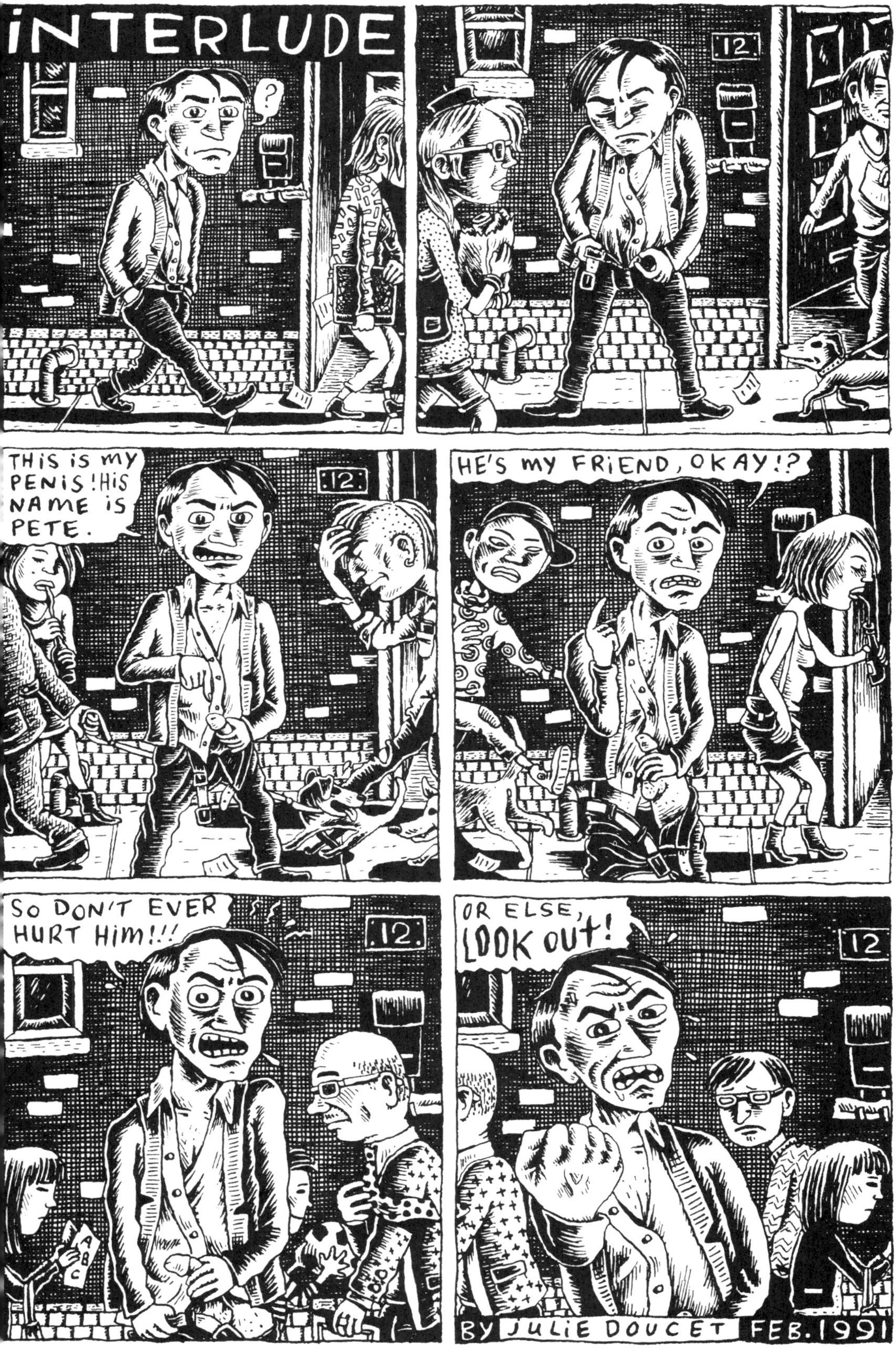
INTERLUDE
?
12
THIS IS MY PENIS! HIS NAME IS PETE.
12
HE'S MY FRIEND, OKAY!?
SO DON'T EVER HURT HIM!!!
12
OR ELSE, LOOK OUT!
12
A B C
BY JULIE DOUCET FEB. 1991

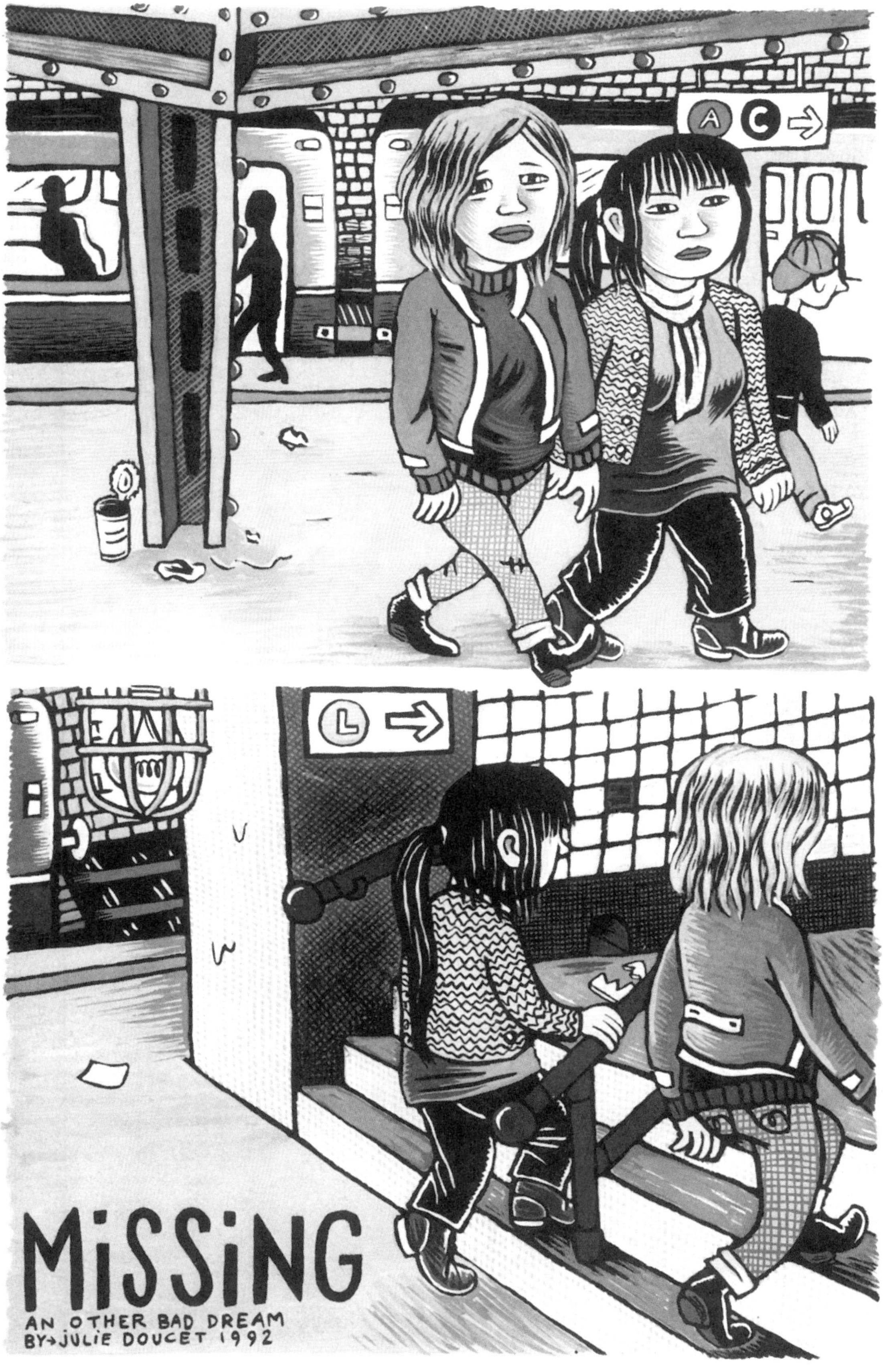
A C
L
MiSSiNG
AN OTHER BAD DREAM
BY→JULIE DOUCET 1992

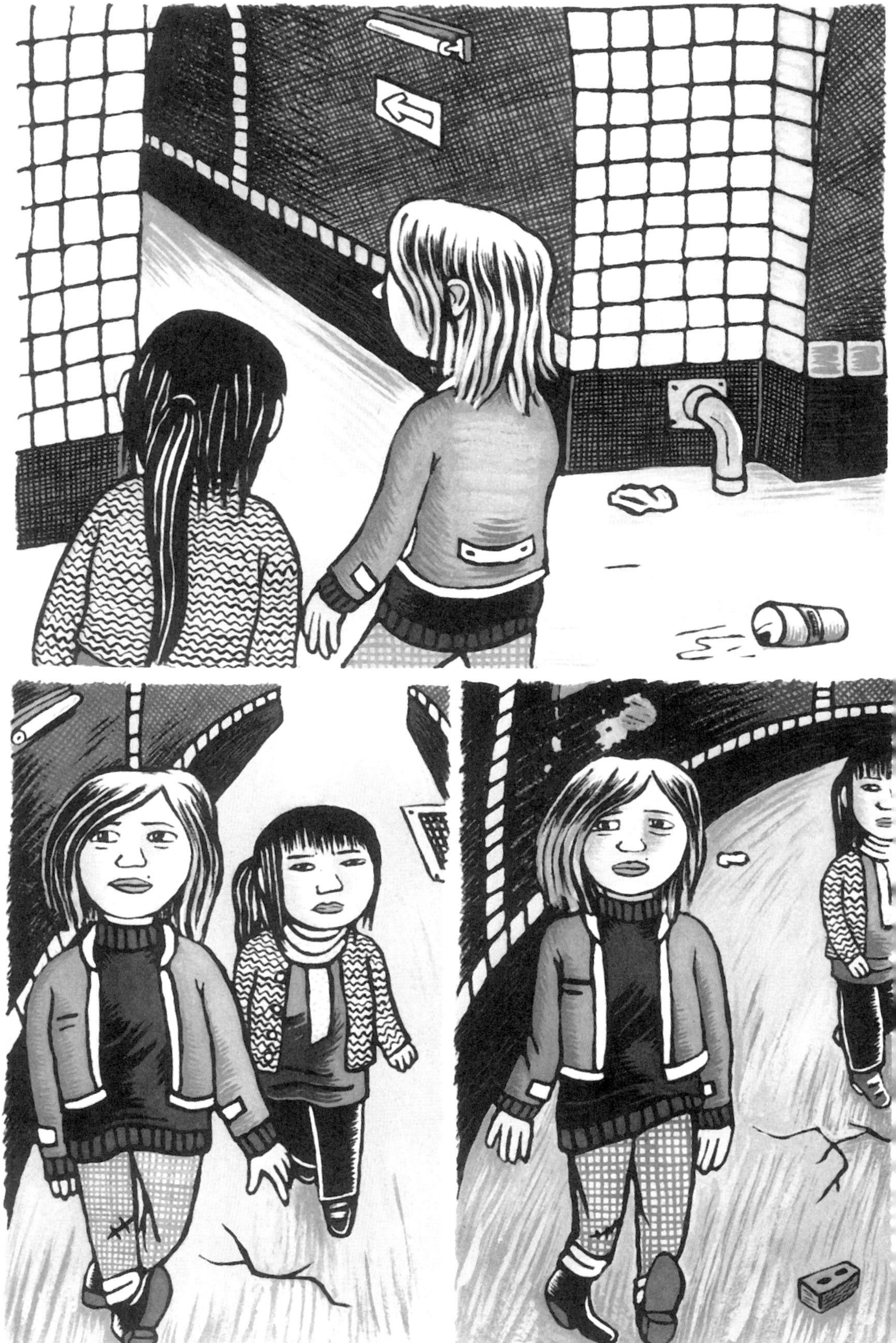

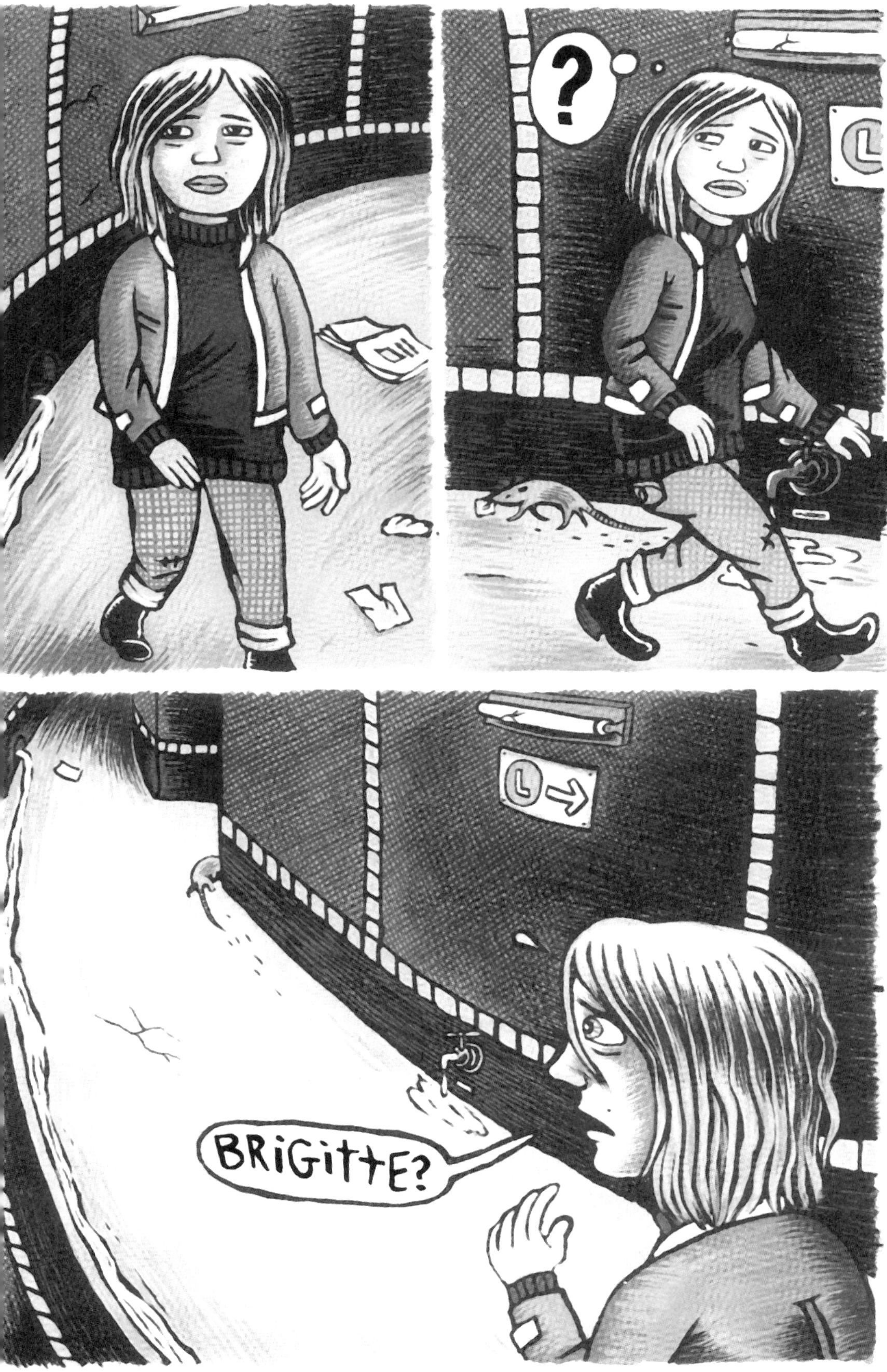
?
BRIGITTE?

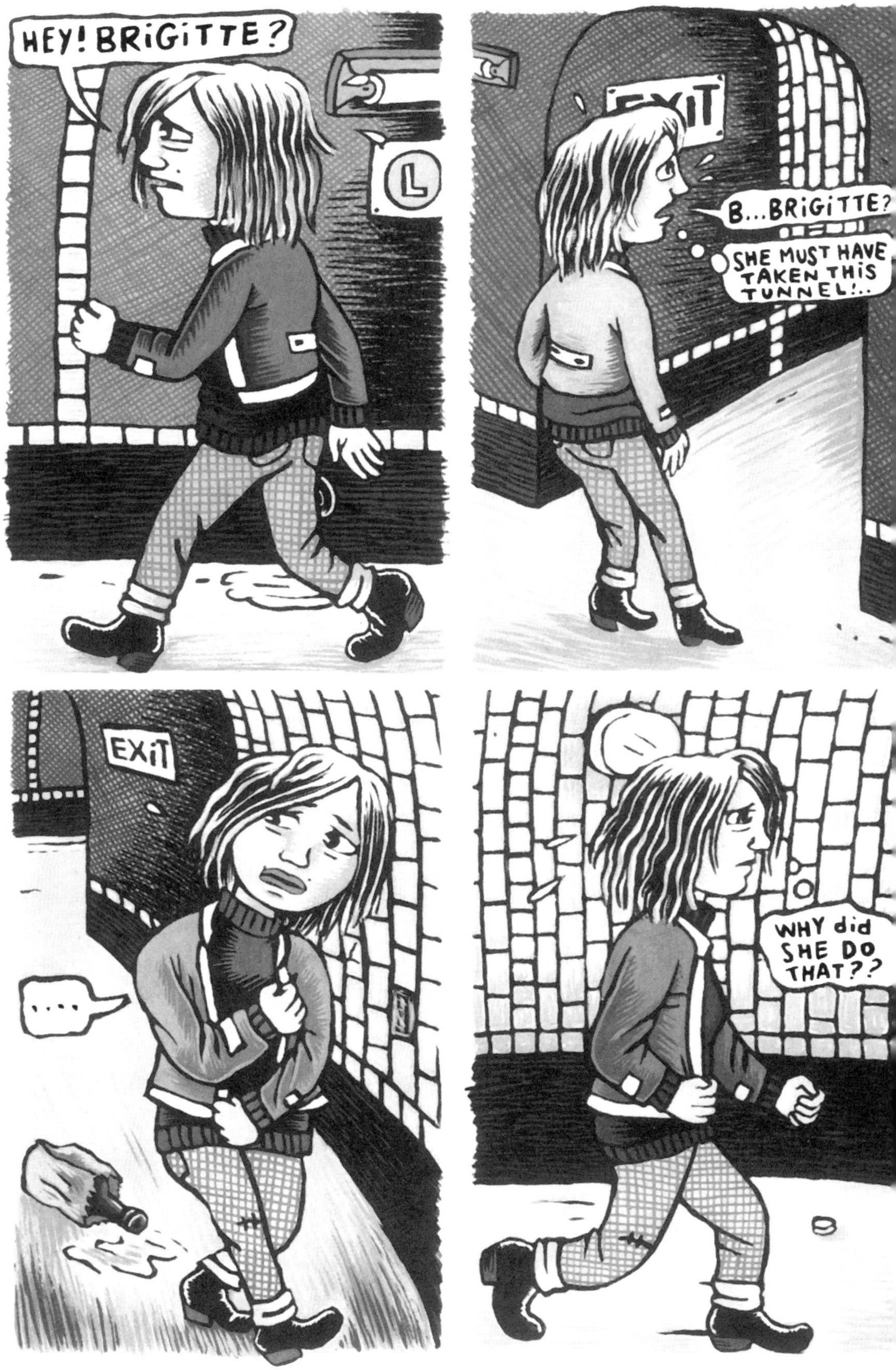
HEY! BRIGITTE?
B...BRIGITTE?
SHE MUST HAVE TAKEN THIS TUNNEL!..
EXIT
....
WHY did SHE DO THAT??

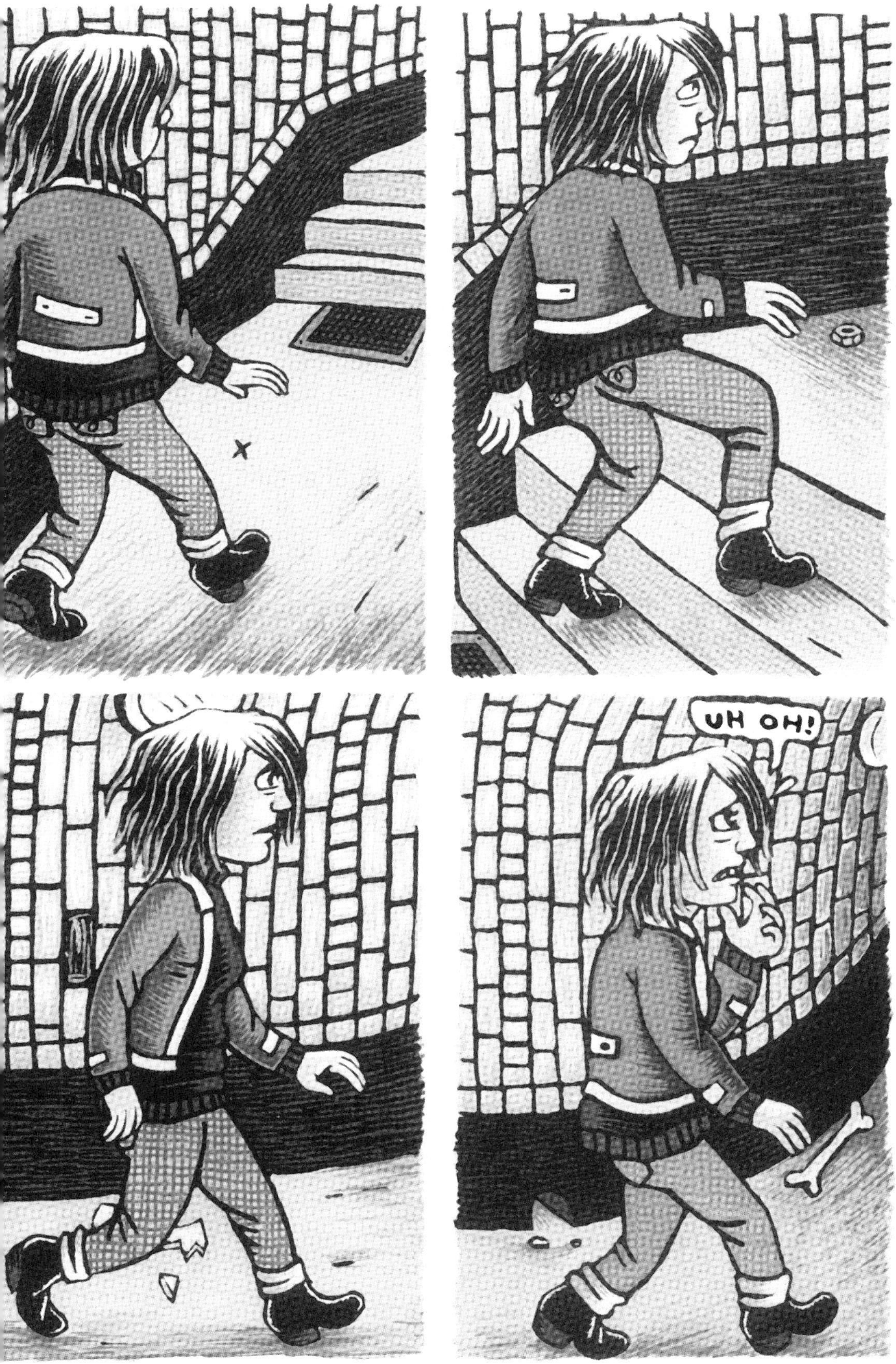
UH OH!

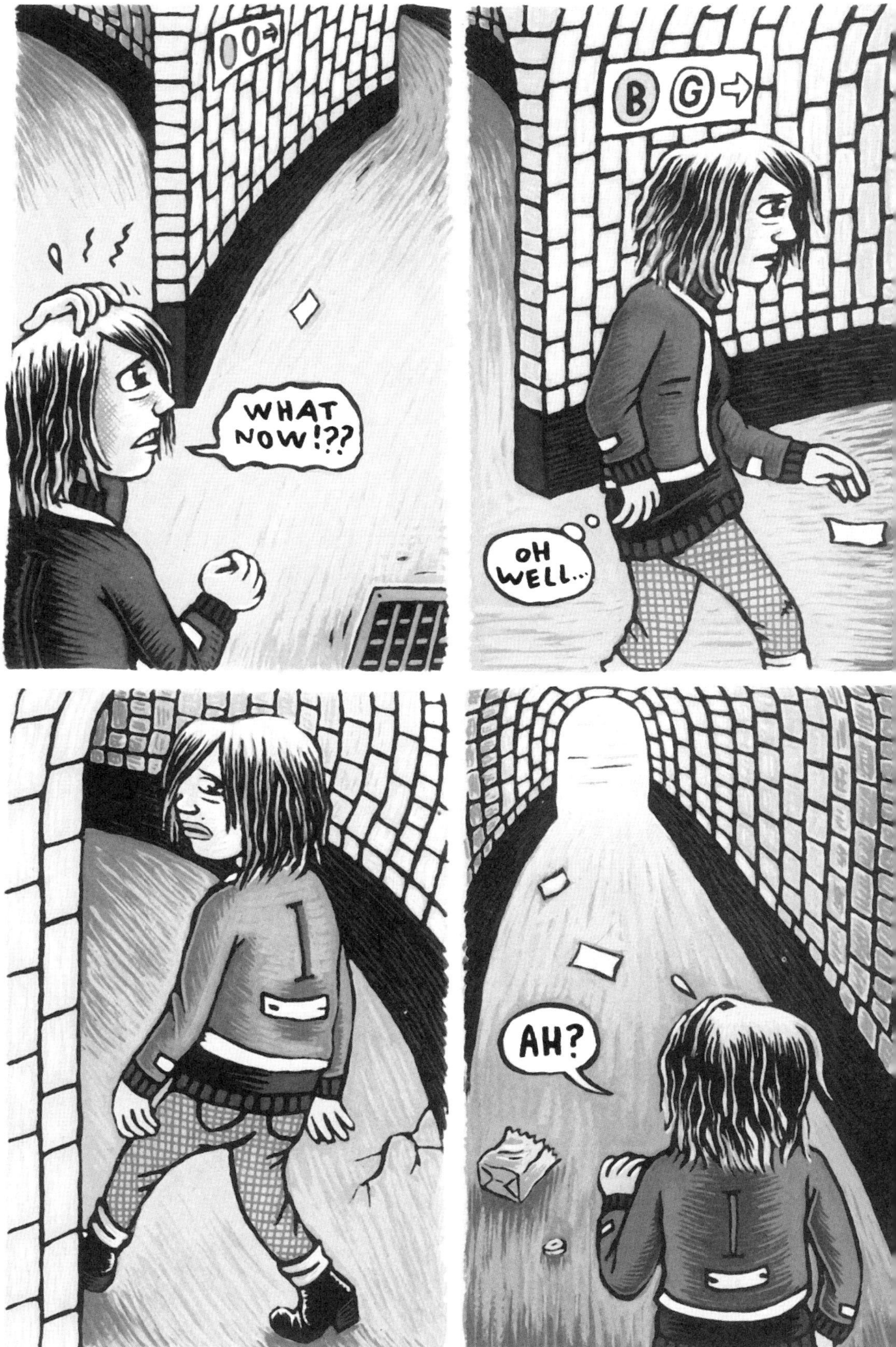
WHAT NOW!??
B G
OH WELL...
AH?

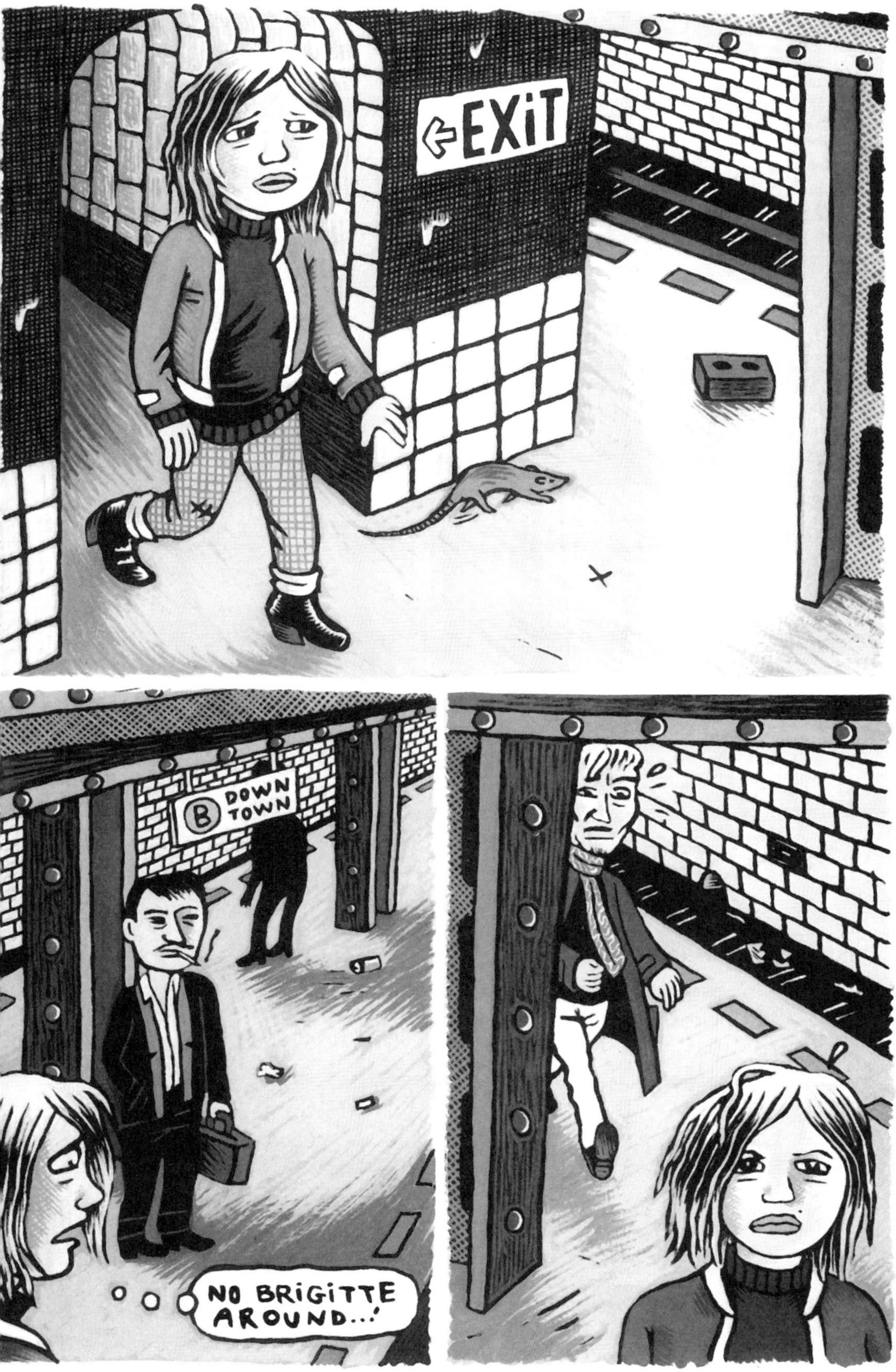
EXIT
DOWN TOWN
NO BRIGITTE AROUND...!

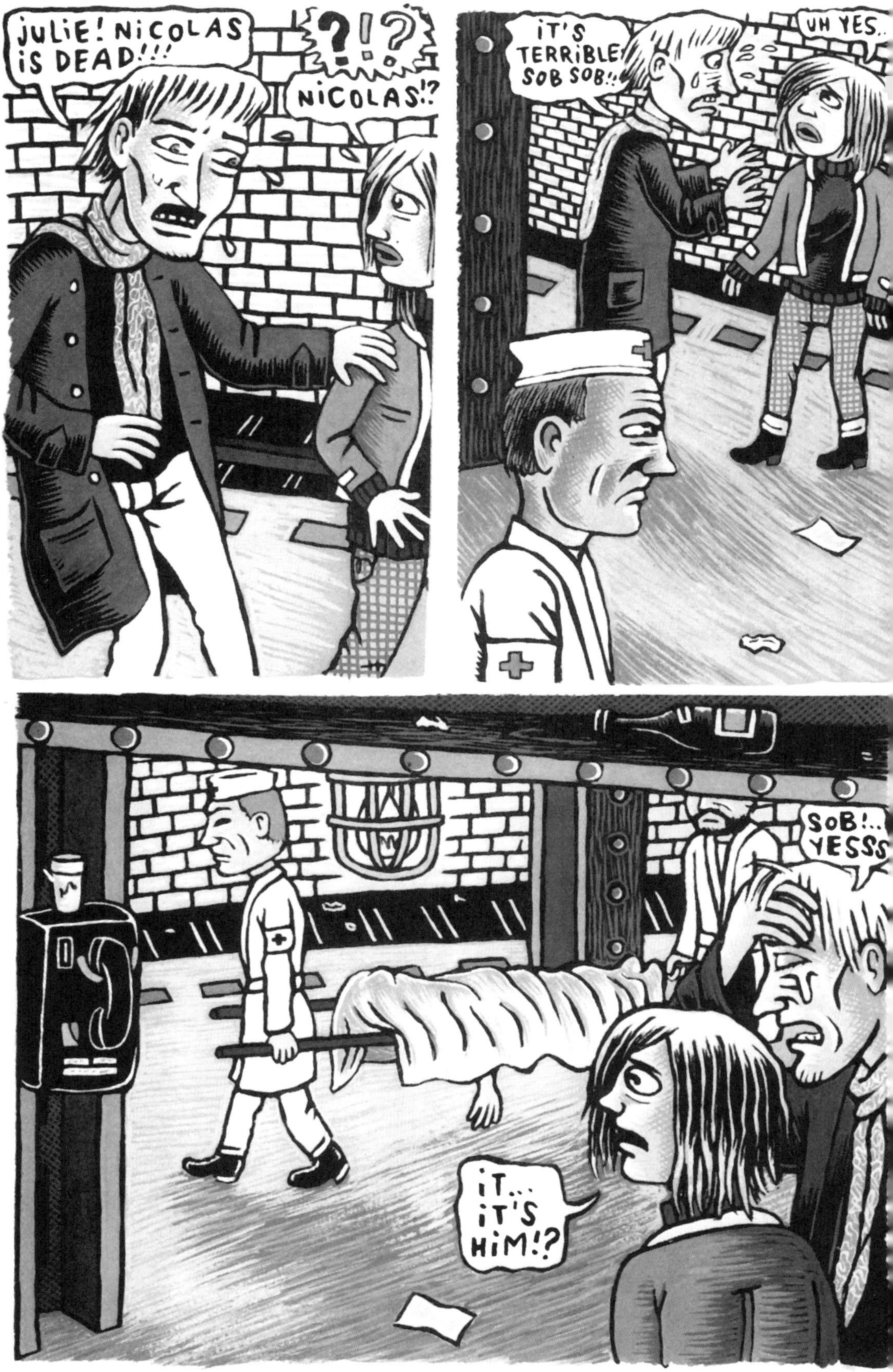
JULIE! NICOLAS IS DEAD!!!
?!?
NICOLAS!?
IT'S TERRIBLE SOB SOB!!
UH YES..
SOB!.. YESSS
IT... IT'S HIM!?

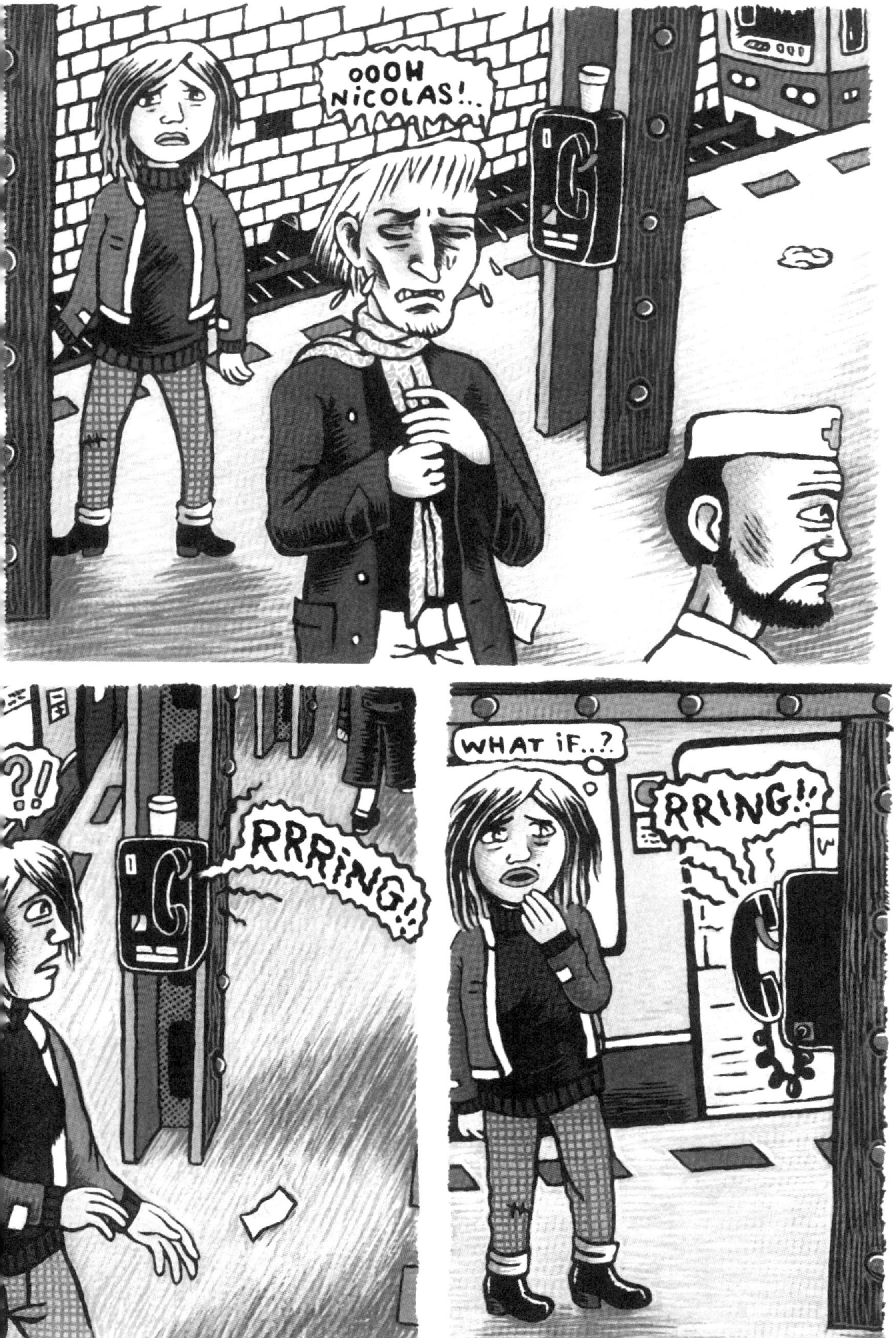
OOOH NICOLAS!..
?!
RRRING!!
WHAT IF..?
RRING!!

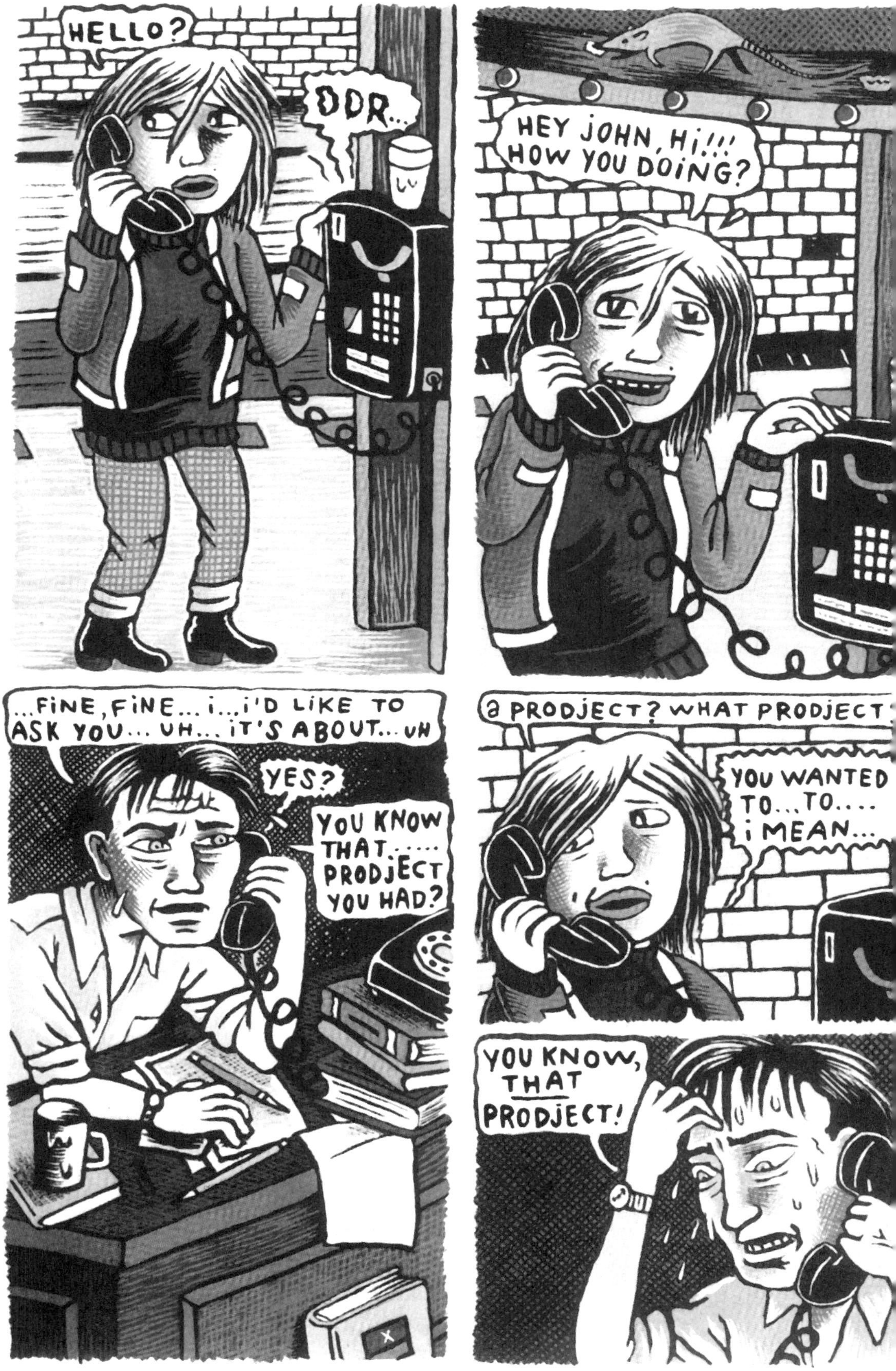
HELLO?
DDR...
HEY JOHN, Hi!!!
HOW YOU DOING?
...FINE, FINE... i... i'D LIKE TO ASK YOU... UH... IT'S ABOUT... UH
YES?
YOU KNOW THAT..... PRODJECT YOU HAD?
a PRODJECT? WHAT PRODJECT
YOU WANTED TO... TO.... i MEAN...
YOU KNOW, THAT PRODJECT!

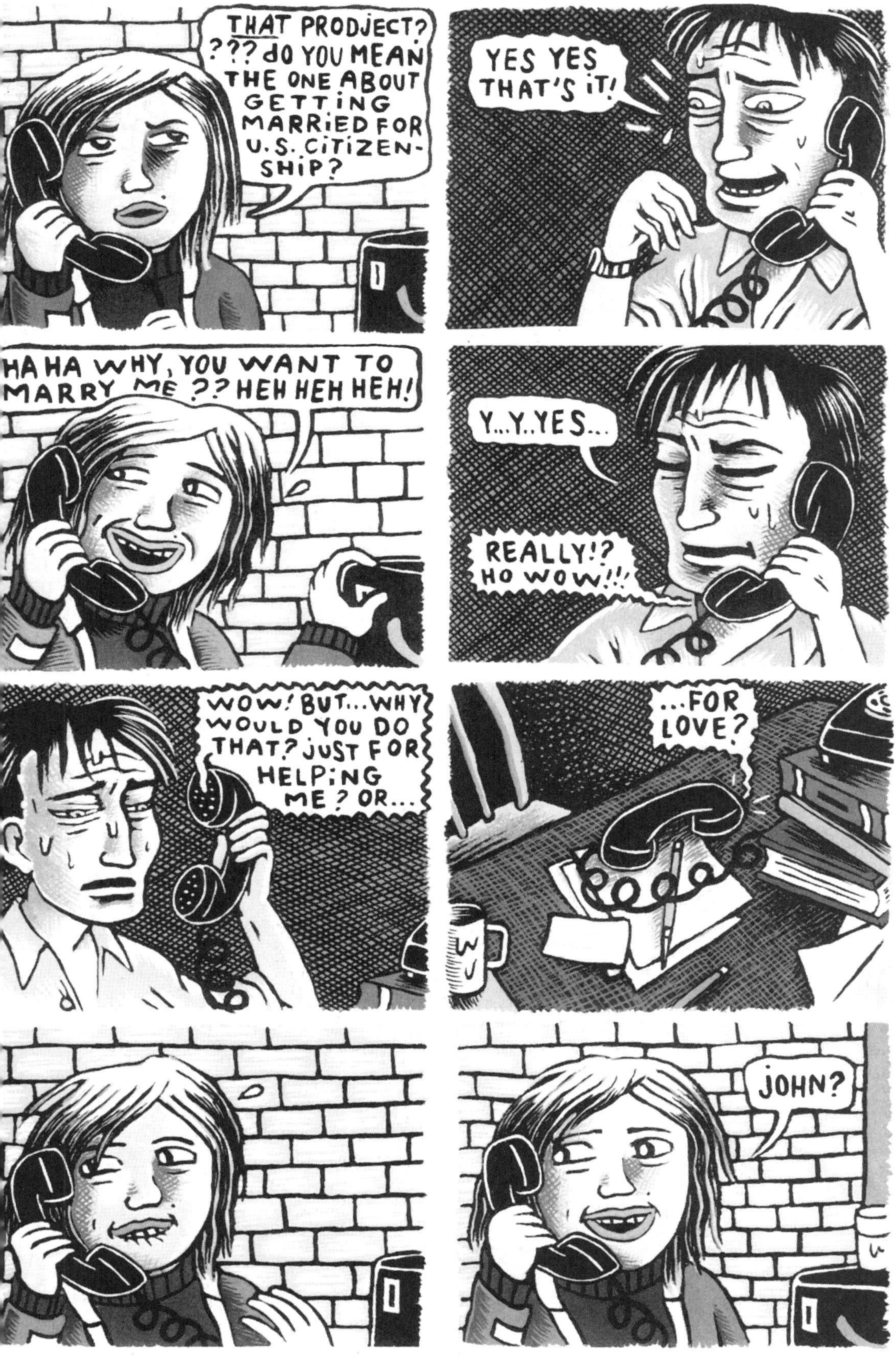
THAT PRODJECT? ??? do YOU MEAN THE ONE ABOUT GETTING MARRIED FOR U.S. CITIZENSHIP?
YES YES THAT'S IT!
HA HA WHY, YOU WANT TO MARRY ME ?? HEH HEH HEH!
Y...Y..YES...
REALLY!? HO WOW!!!
WOW! BUT...WHY WOULD YOU DO THAT? JUST FOR HELPING ME? OR...
...FOR LOVE?
JOHN?

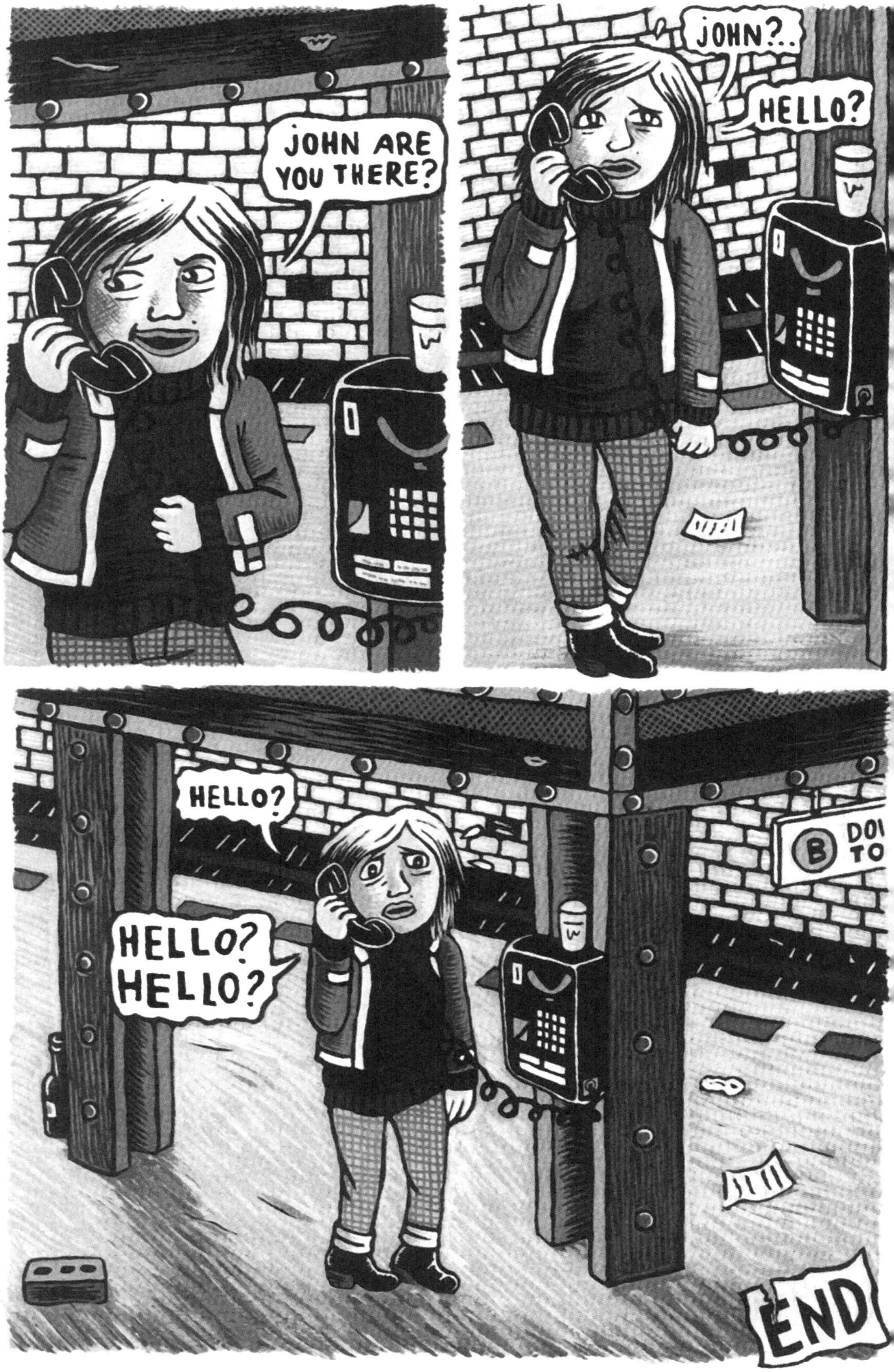
JOHN ARE YOU THERE?
JOHN?..
HELLO?
HELLO?
HELLO? HELLO?
END

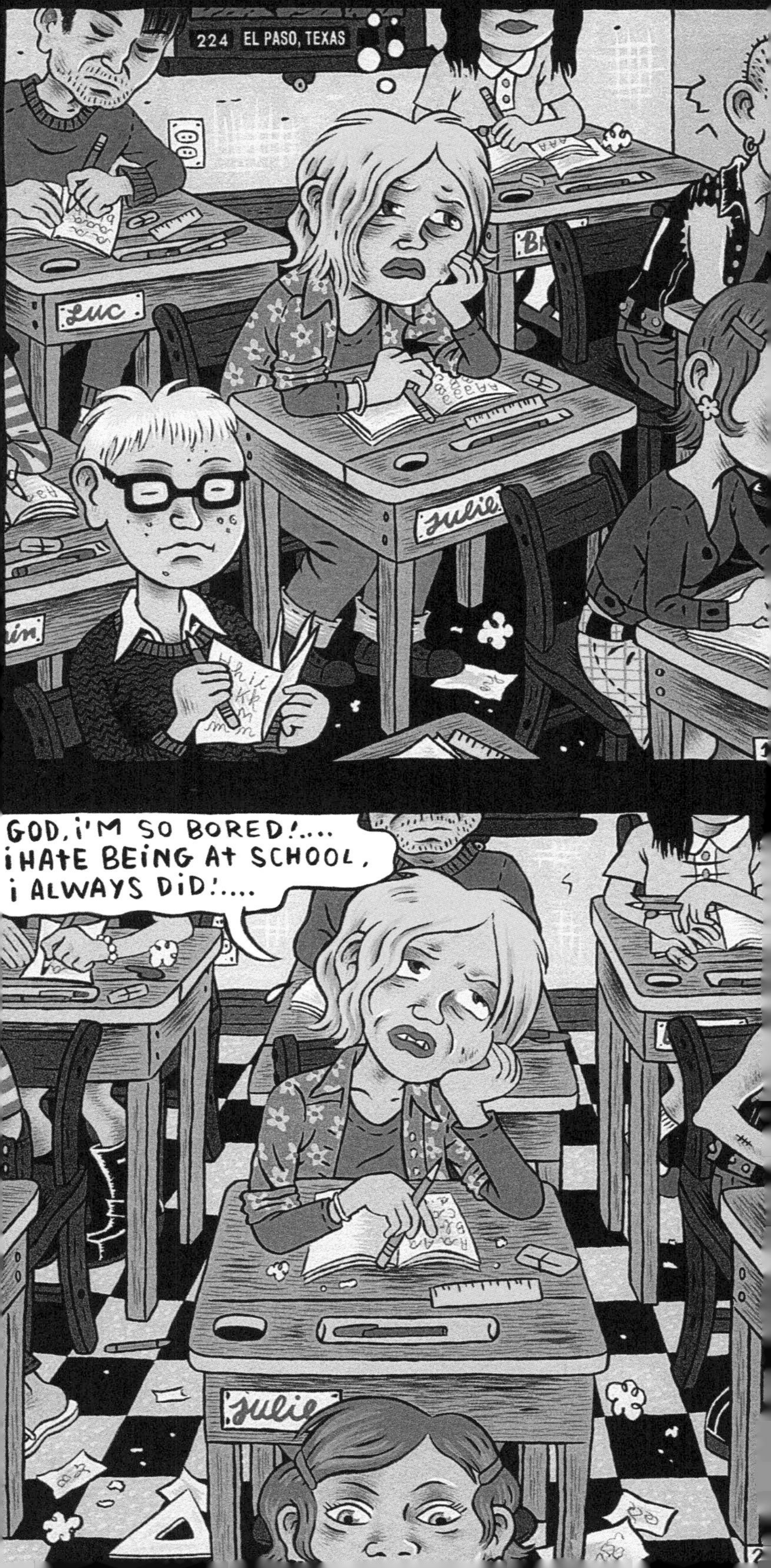
224 EL PASO, TEXAS
Luc
Julie
GOD, i'M SO BORED!....
iHATE BEING At SCHOOL,
i ALWAYS DID!....

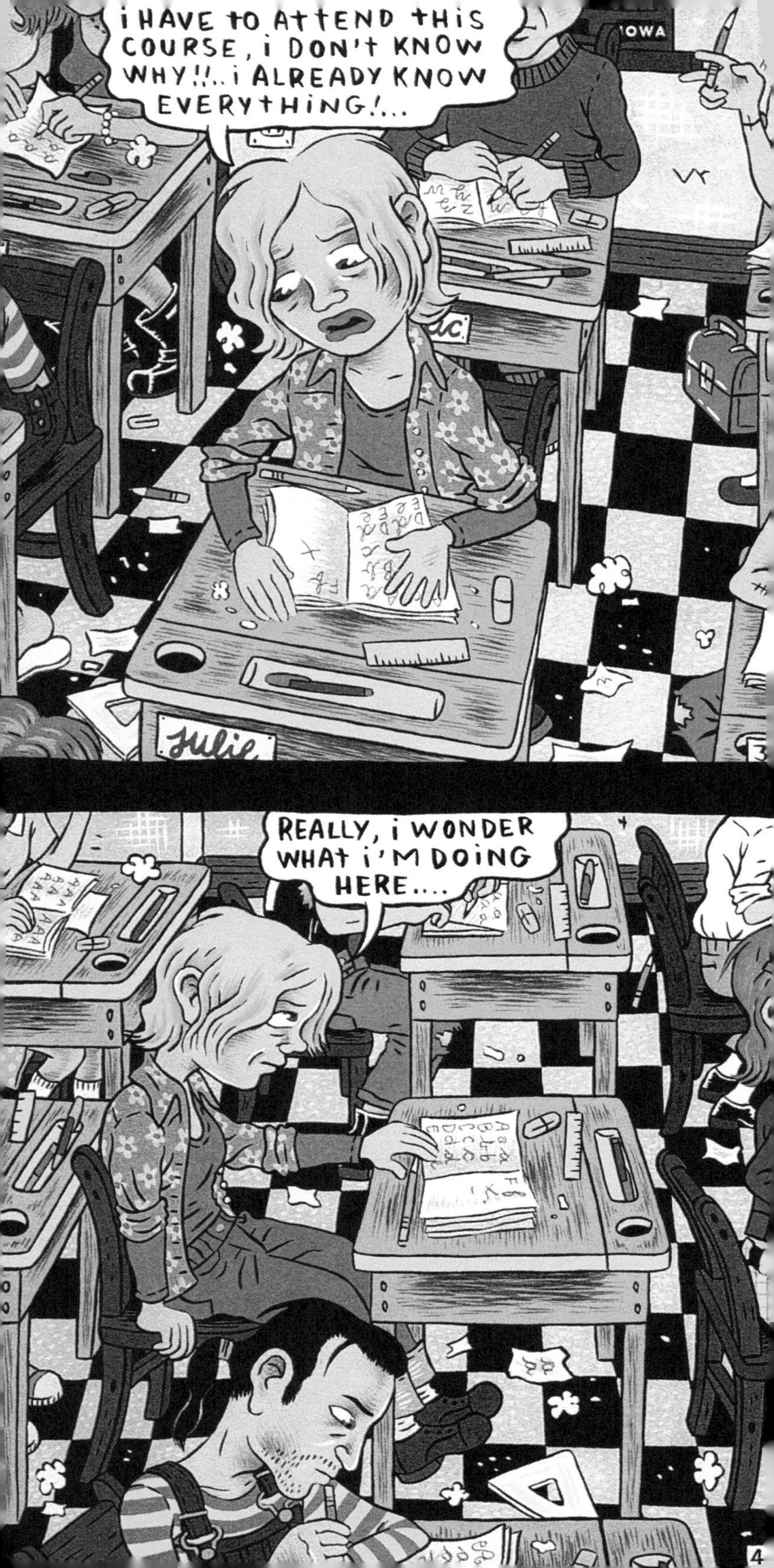
IOWA
i HAVE TO ATTEND THIS COURSE, i DON'T KNOW WHY!!.. i ALREADY KNOW EVERYTHING!...
Julie
REALLY, i WONDER WHAT i'M DOING HERE....

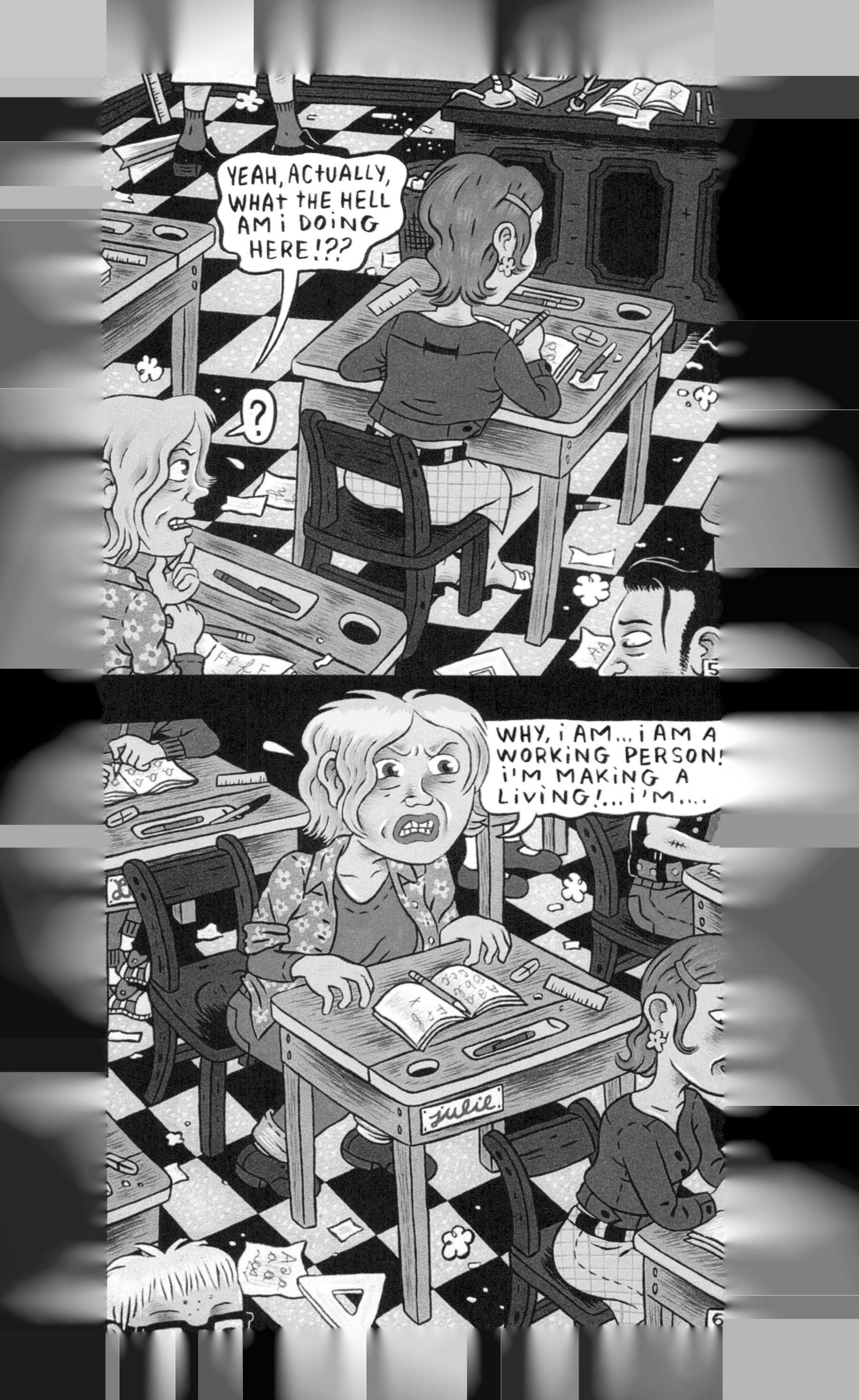
YEAH, ACTUALLY, WHAT THE HELL AM i DOING HERE!??
?
WHY, i AM... i AM A WORKING PERSON! i'M MAKING A LIVING!... i'M....
julie

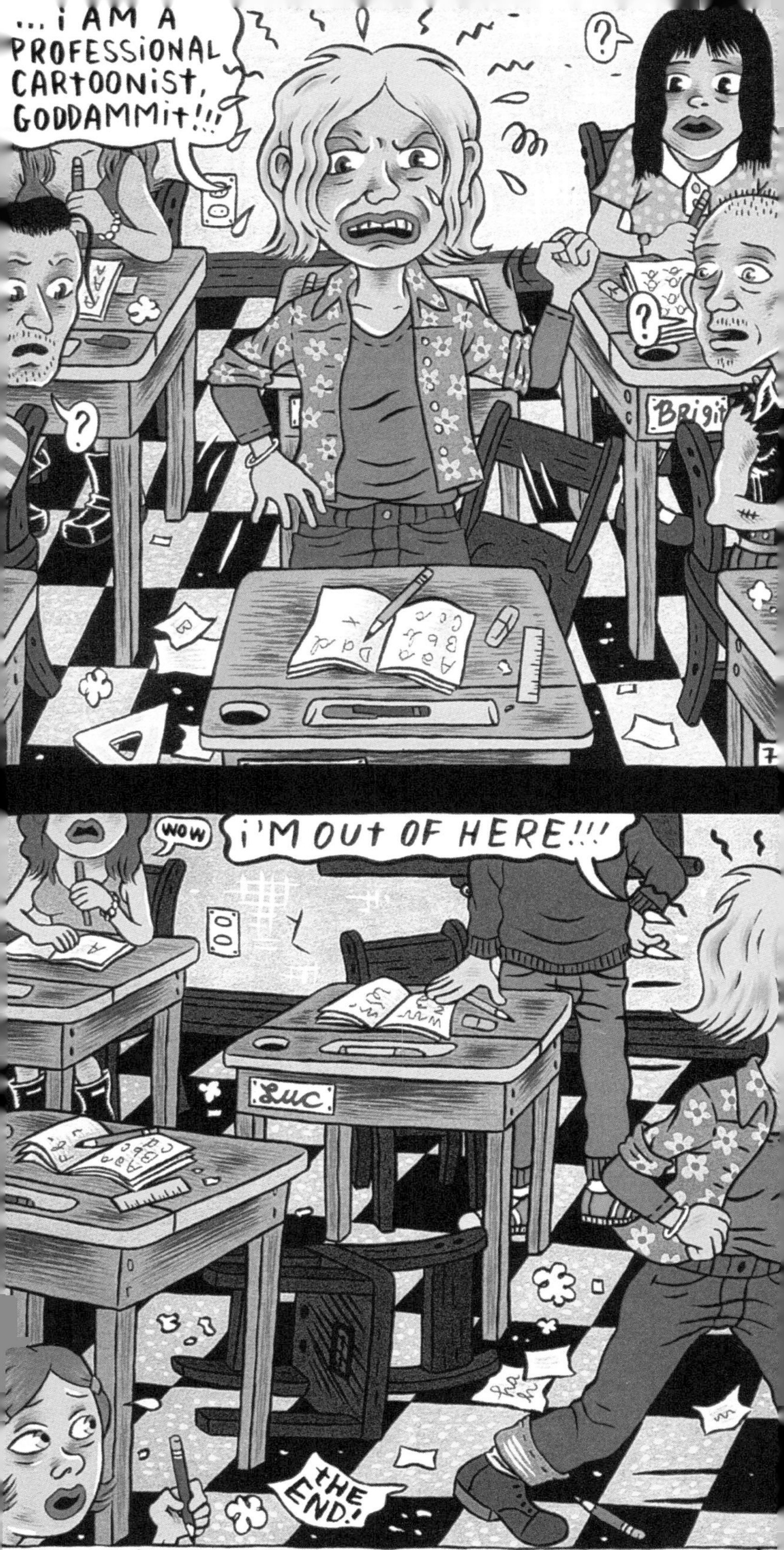
...i AM A PROFESSIONAL CARTOONIST, GODDAMMIT!!!
?
?
?
Brigit
7
WOW
i'M OUT OF HERE!!!
Luc
tHE END!

a RECURRING SCHOOL NIGHTMARE – JULIE DOUCET, JULY 1995 | 8

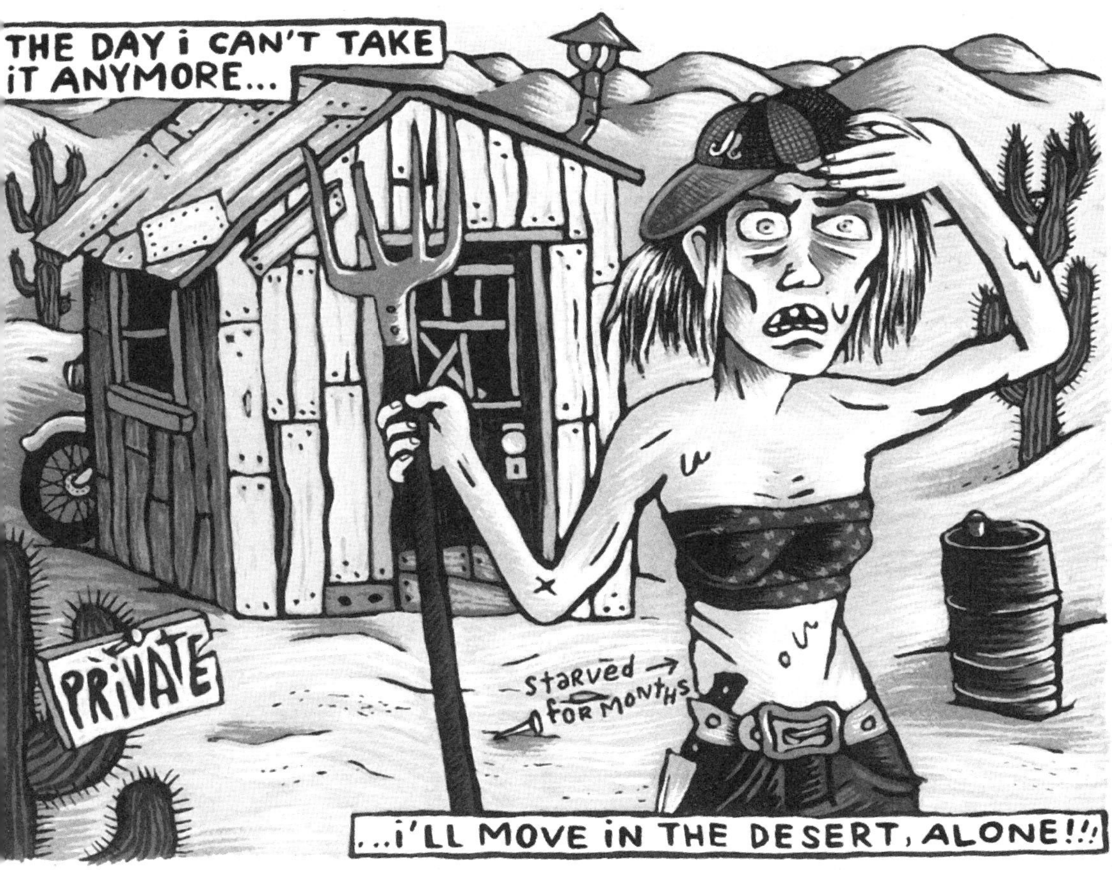
THE DAY i CAN'T TAKE iT ANYMORE...
PRiVATE
starved for MONTHS
...i'LL MOVE iN THE DESERT, ALONE!!!

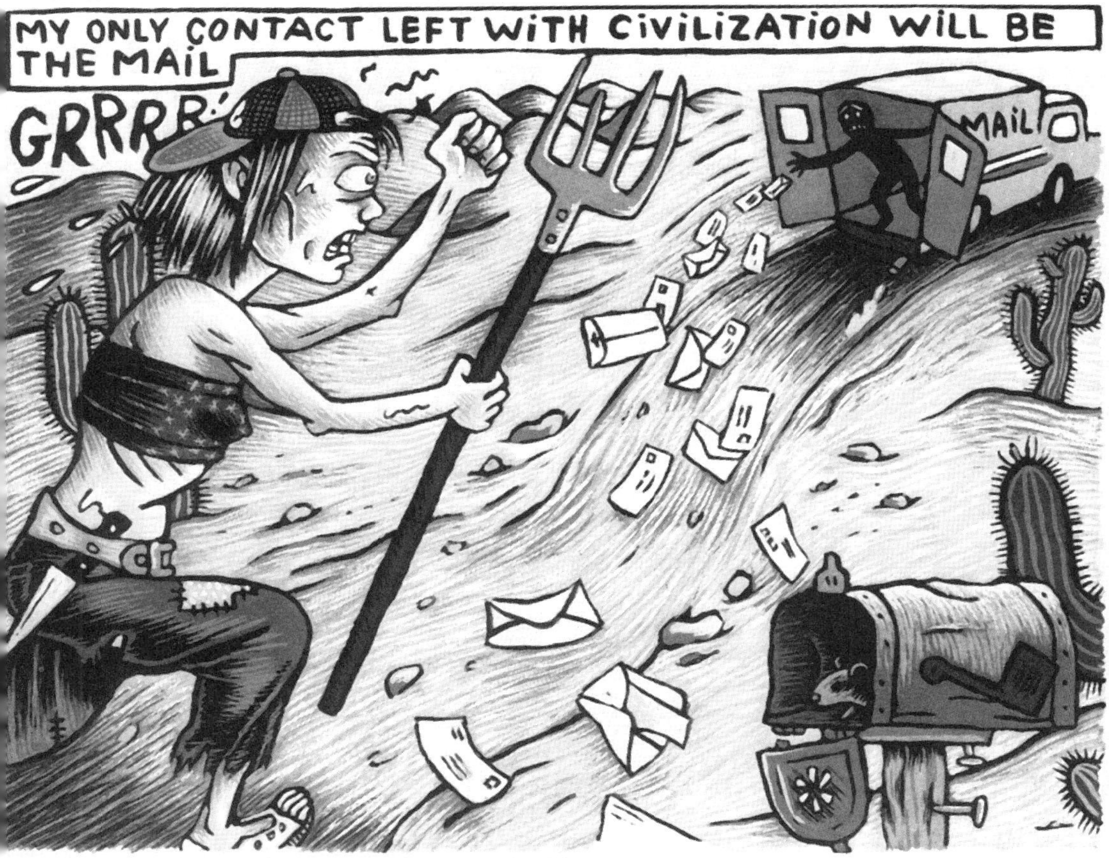
MY ONLY CONTACT LEFT WiTH CiViLIZATiON WiLL BE THE MAiL
GRRRR
MAiL

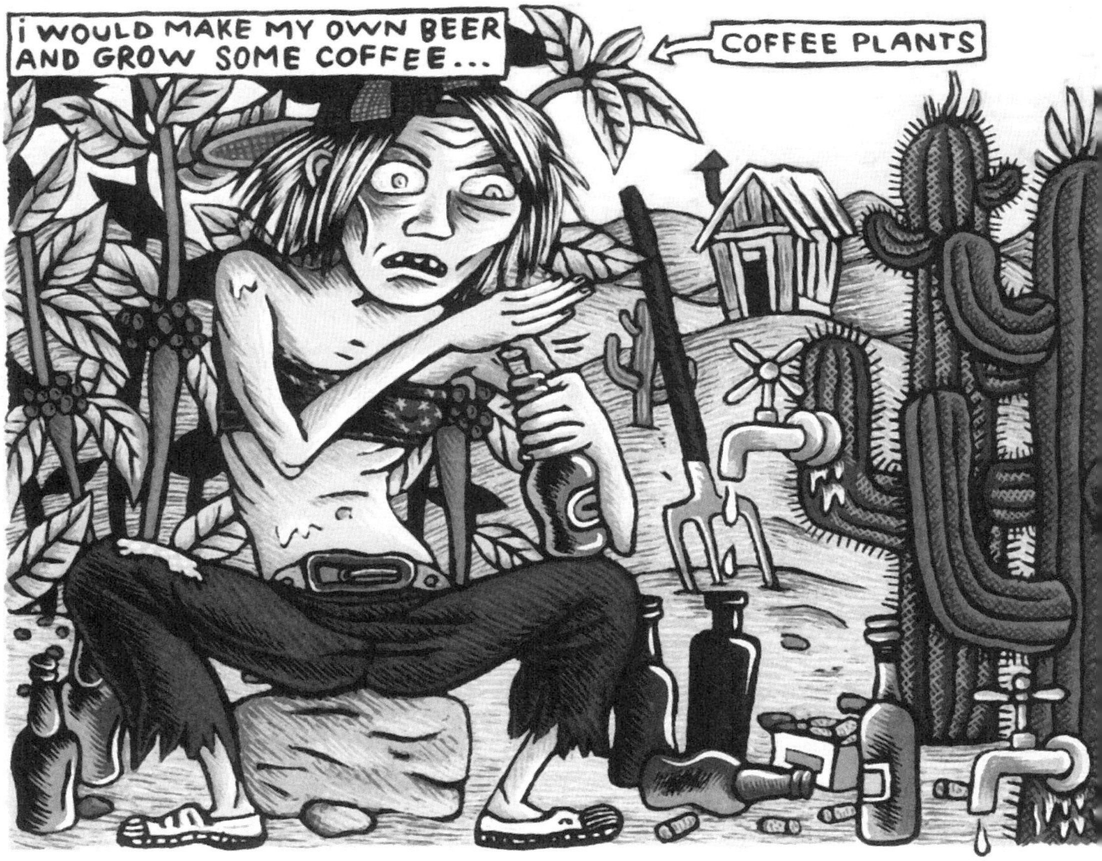
i WOULD MAKE MY OWN BEER AND GROW SOME COFFEE...
COFFEE PLANTS

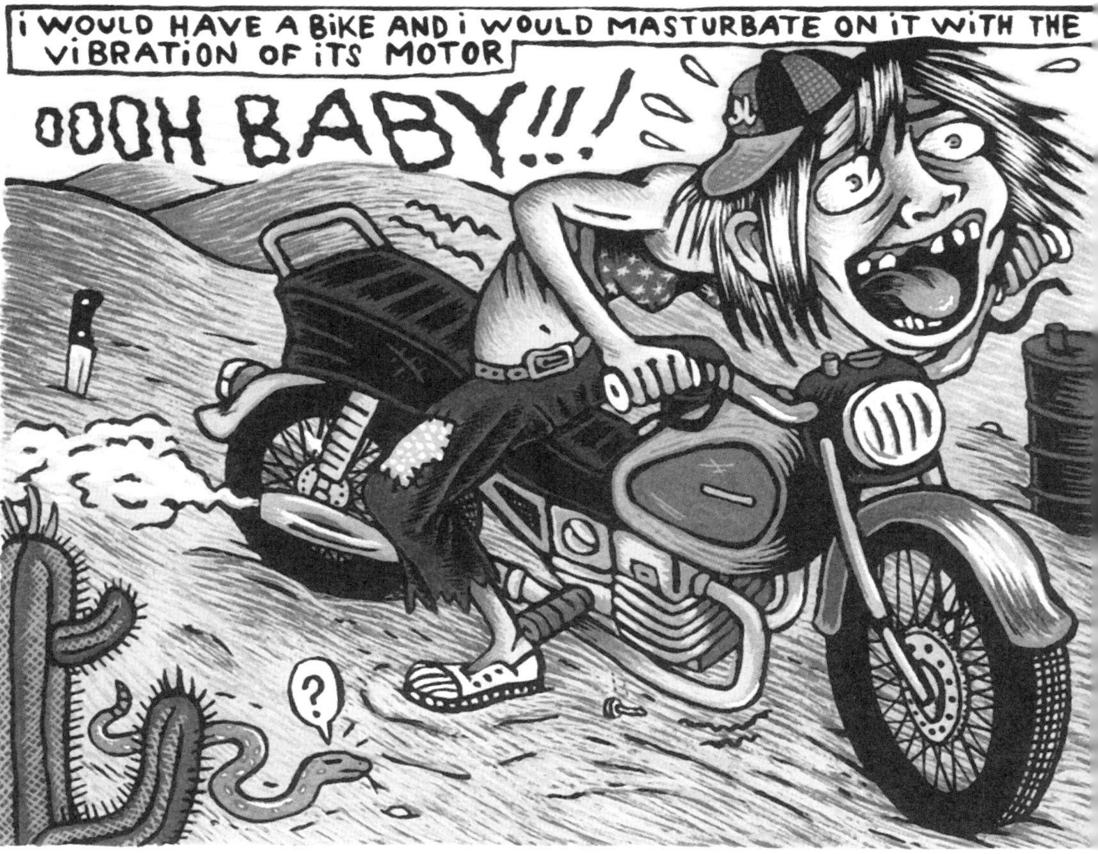
i WOULD HAVE A BiKE AND i WOULD MASTURBATE ON iT WiTH THE ViBRATiON OF iTS MOTOR
OOOH BABY!!!
?

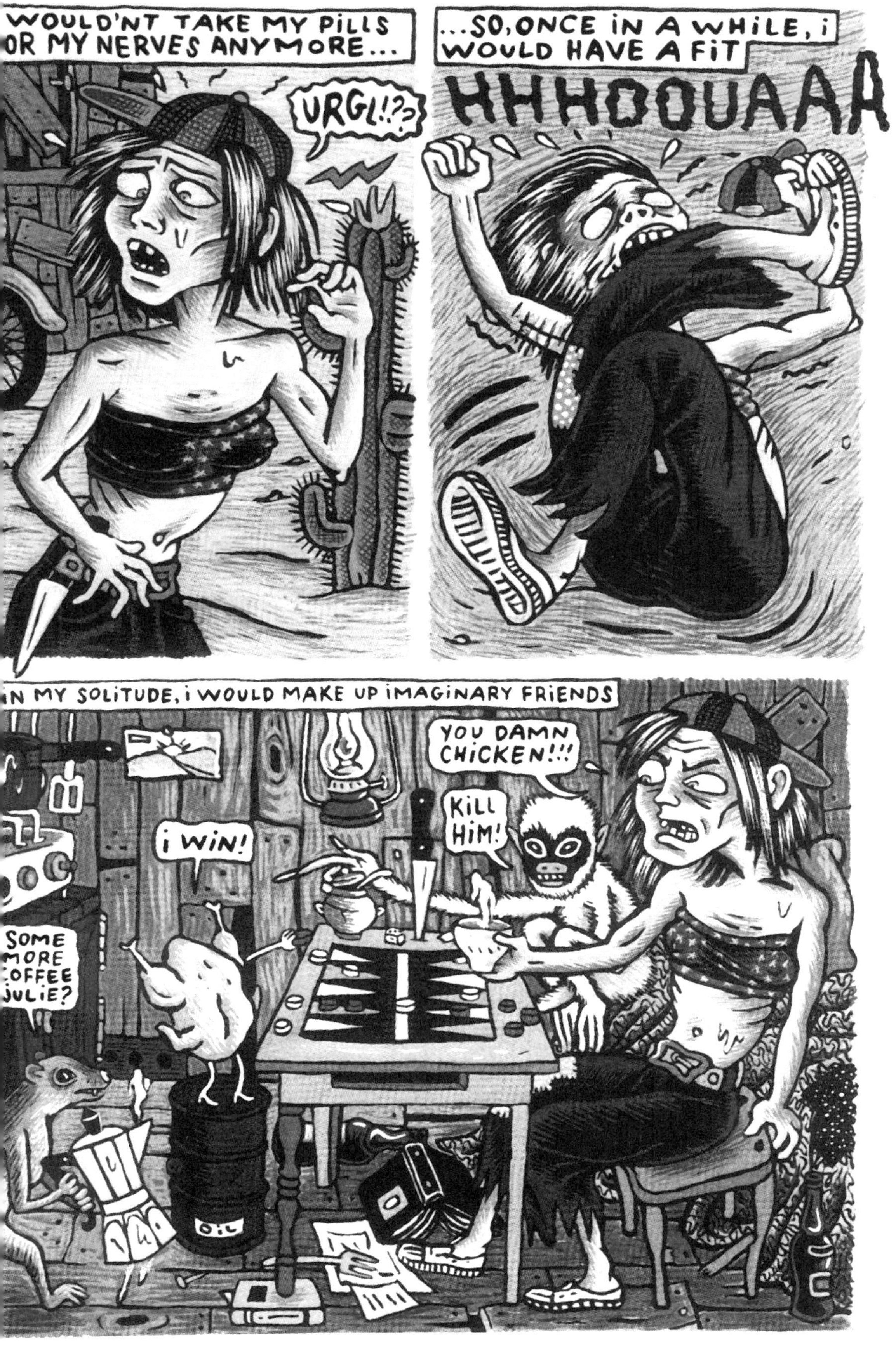
WOULD'NT TAKE MY PILLS
OR MY NERVES ANYMORE...
URGL!?
...SO, ONCE IN A WHILE, I
WOULD HAVE A FIT
HHHOOUAAA
IN MY SOLITUDE, I WOULD MAKE UP IMAGINARY FRIENDS
YOU DAMN
CHICKEN!!!
KILL
HIM!
I WIN!
SOME
MORE
COFFEE
JULIE?
OIL

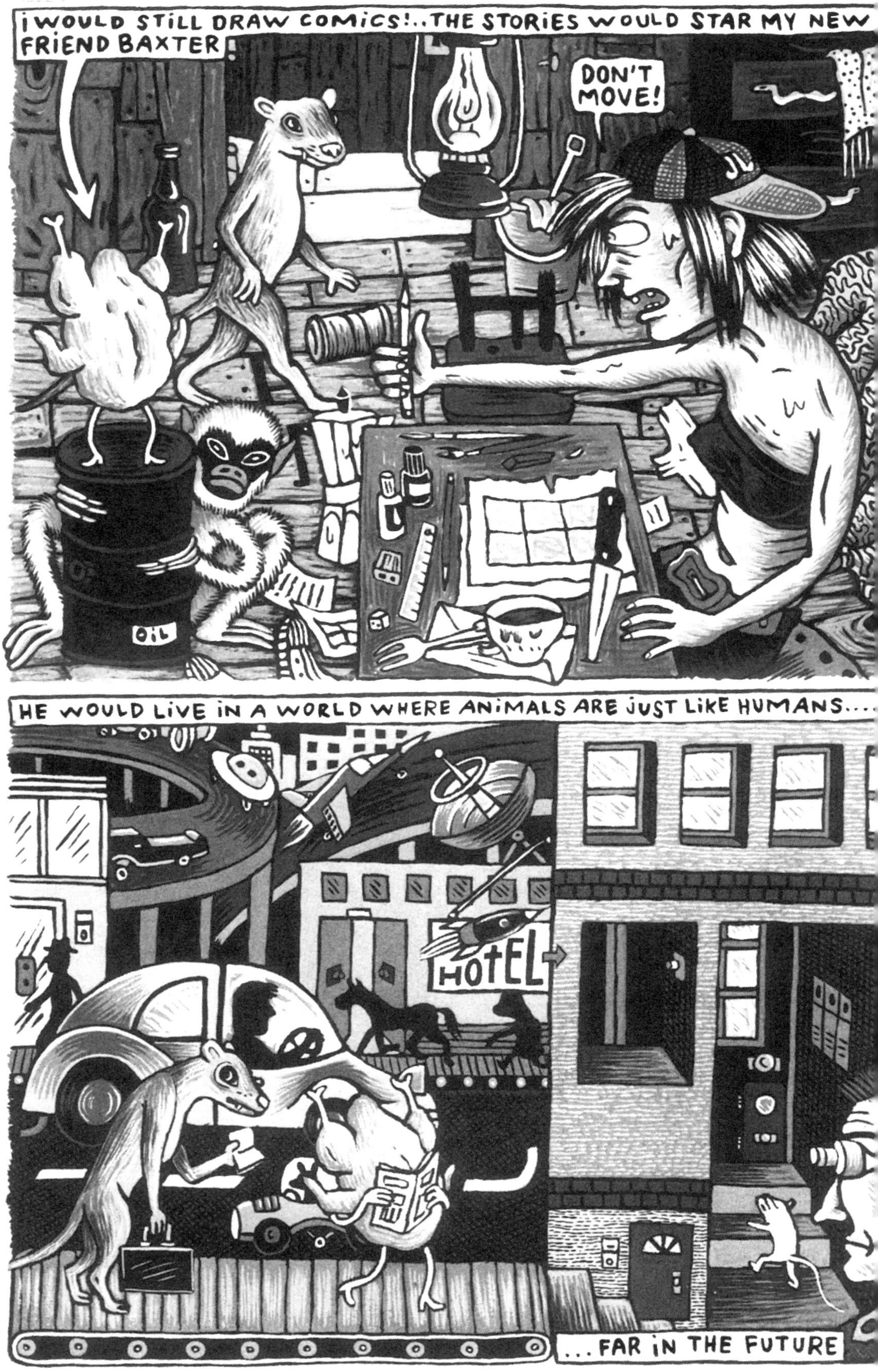
I WOULD STILL DRAW COMICS!..THE STORIES WOULD STAR MY NEW FRIEND BAXTER
DON'T MOVE!
OIL
HE WOULD LIVE IN A WORLD WHERE ANIMALS ARE JUST LIKE HUMANS....
HOTEL
...FAR IN THE FUTURE

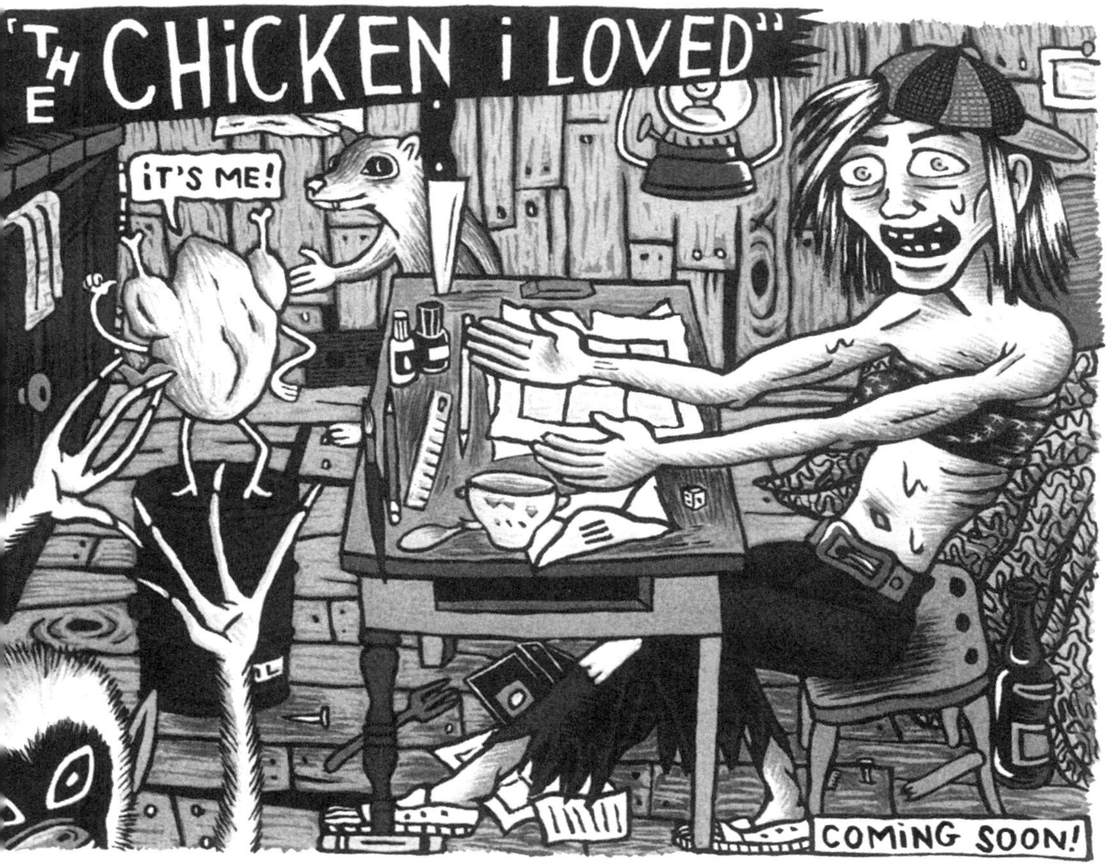
"THE CHICKEN I LOVED"
IT'S ME!
COMING SOON!

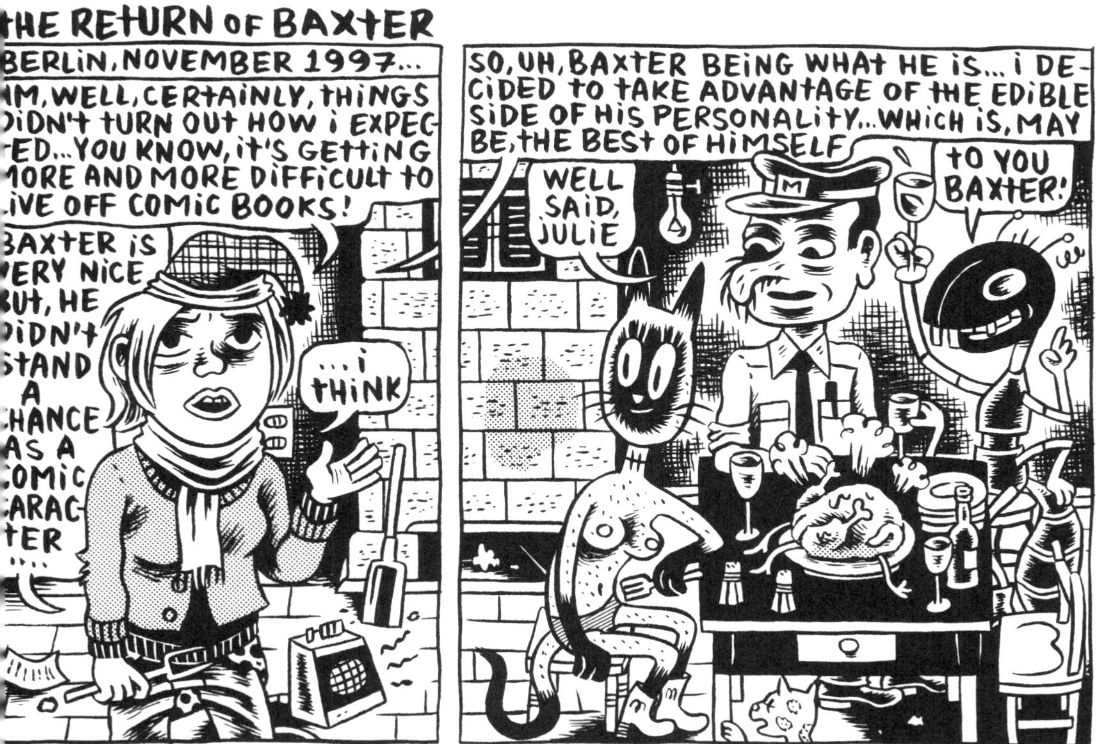
THE RETURN OF BAXTER
BERLIN, NOVEMBER 1997...
IM, WELL, CERTAINLY, THINGS
DIDN'T TURN OUT HOW I EXPEC
TED... YOU KNOW, IT'S GETTING
MORE AND MORE DIFFICULT TO
LIVE OFF COMIC BOOKS!
BAXTER IS VERY NICE BUT, HE DIDN'T STAND A CHANCE AS A COMIC CARACTER...
...I THINK
SO, UH, BAXTER BEING WHAT HE IS... I DECIDED TO TAKE ADVANTAGE OF THE EDIBLE SIDE OF HIS PERSONALITY... WHICH IS, MAY BE, THE BEST OF HIMSELF
WELL SAID, JULIE
TO YOU BAXTER!
j.d.

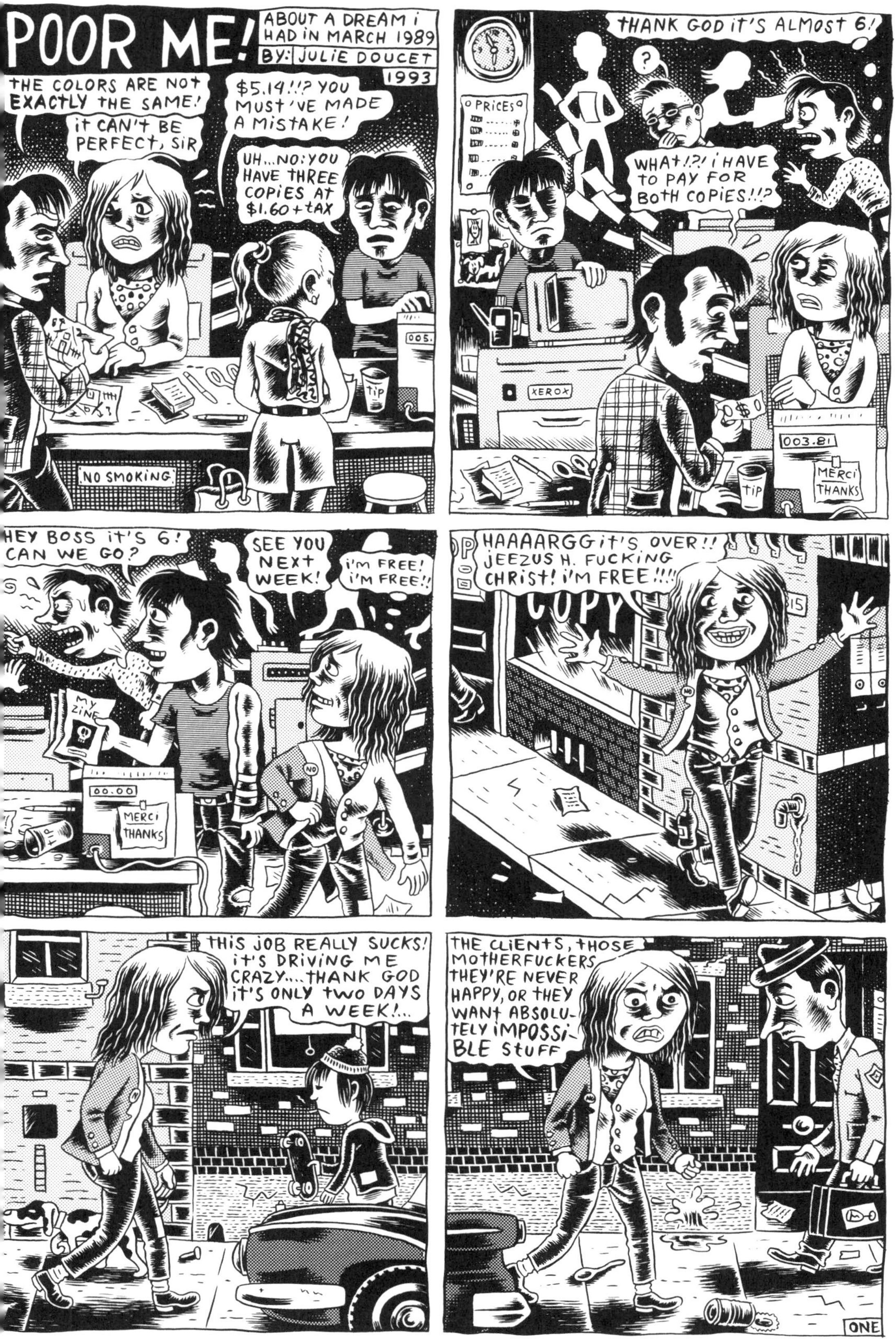
POOR ME!
ABOUT A DREAM i HAD iN MARCH 1989
BY: JULiE DOUCET 1993
THE COLORS ARE NOT EXACTLY THE SAME!
it CAN'T BE PERFECT, SiR
$5.14!!? YOU MUST'VE MADE A MiSTAKE!
UH...NO: YOU HAVE THREE COPiES AT $1.60 + tAX
NO SMOKiNG
TiP
PRiCES
THANK GOD it'S ALMOSt 6!
WHAt!?! i HAVE TO PAY FOR BOtH COPiES!!?
XEROX
003.81
MERCi THANKS
HEY BOSS it'S 6! CAN WE GO?
SEE YOU NEXt WEEK!
i'M FREE! i'M FREE!!
MY ZiNE
00.00
MERCi THANKS
HAAAARGG it'S OVER!! JEEZUS H. FUCKiNG CHRiSt! i'M FREE!!!!
COPY
THiS JOB REALLY SUCKS! it'S DRiViNG ME CRAZY....THANK GOD it'S ONLY tWO DAYS A WEEK!...
THE CLiENtS, tHOSE MOTHERFUCKERS THEY'RE NEVER HAPPY, OR tHEY WANt ABSOLUtELY iMPOSSiBLE StUFF
ONE

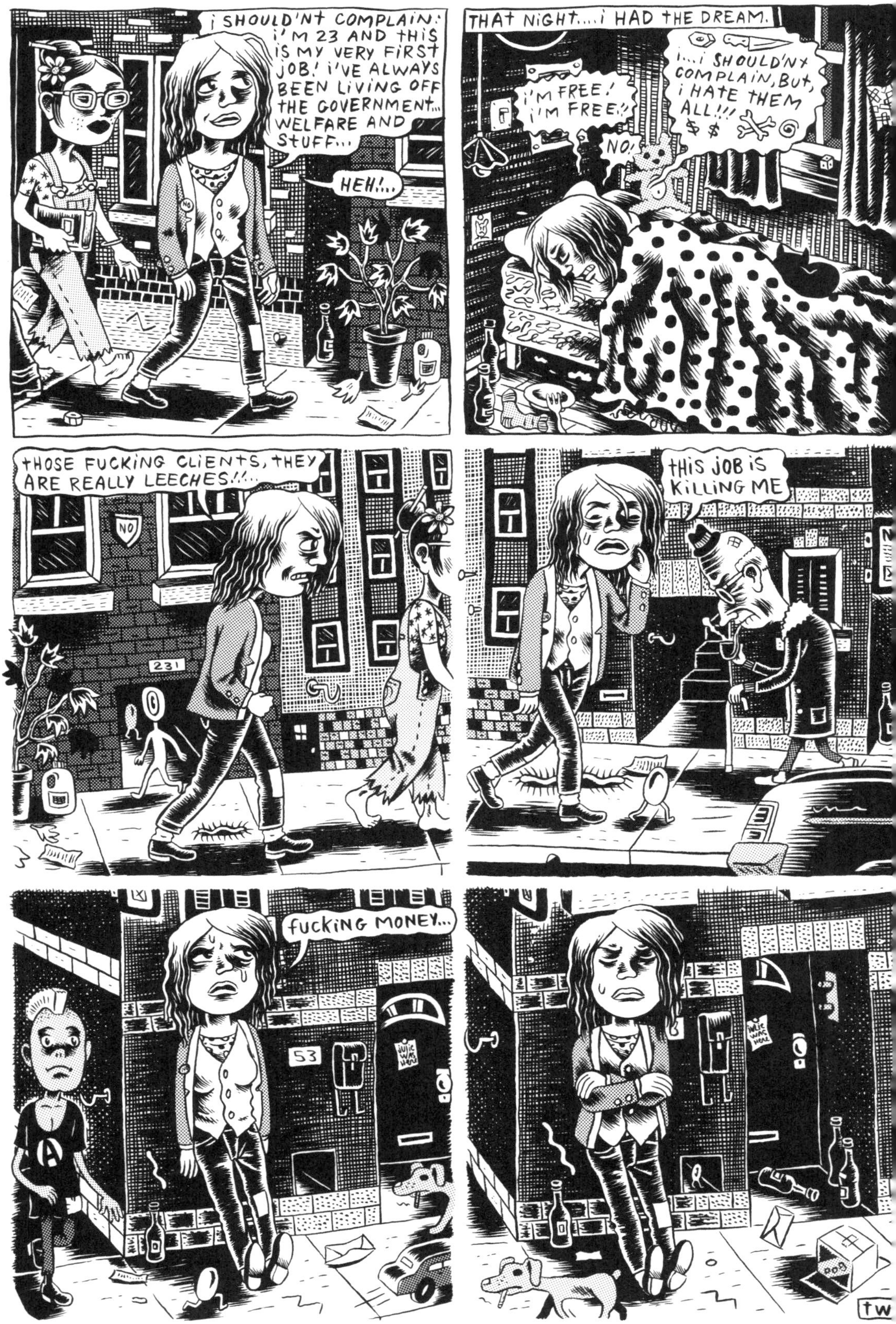
i SHOULD'N+ COMPLAIN: i'M 23 AND +HiS iS MY VERY FiRS+ JOB! i'VE ALWAYS BEEN LiViNG OFF THE GOVERNMEN+... WELFARE AND STUFF...
HEH!...
THA+ NiGH+... i HAD THE DREAM.
i'M FREE! i'M FREE!!
NO!
i... i SHOULD'N+ COMPLAiN, BU+, i HATE THEM ALL!!!
+HOSE FUCKiNG CLiEN+S, THEY ARE REALLY LEECHES!!...
NO
231
+HiS JOB iS KiLLiNG ME
fuckiNG MONEY...
53
tw

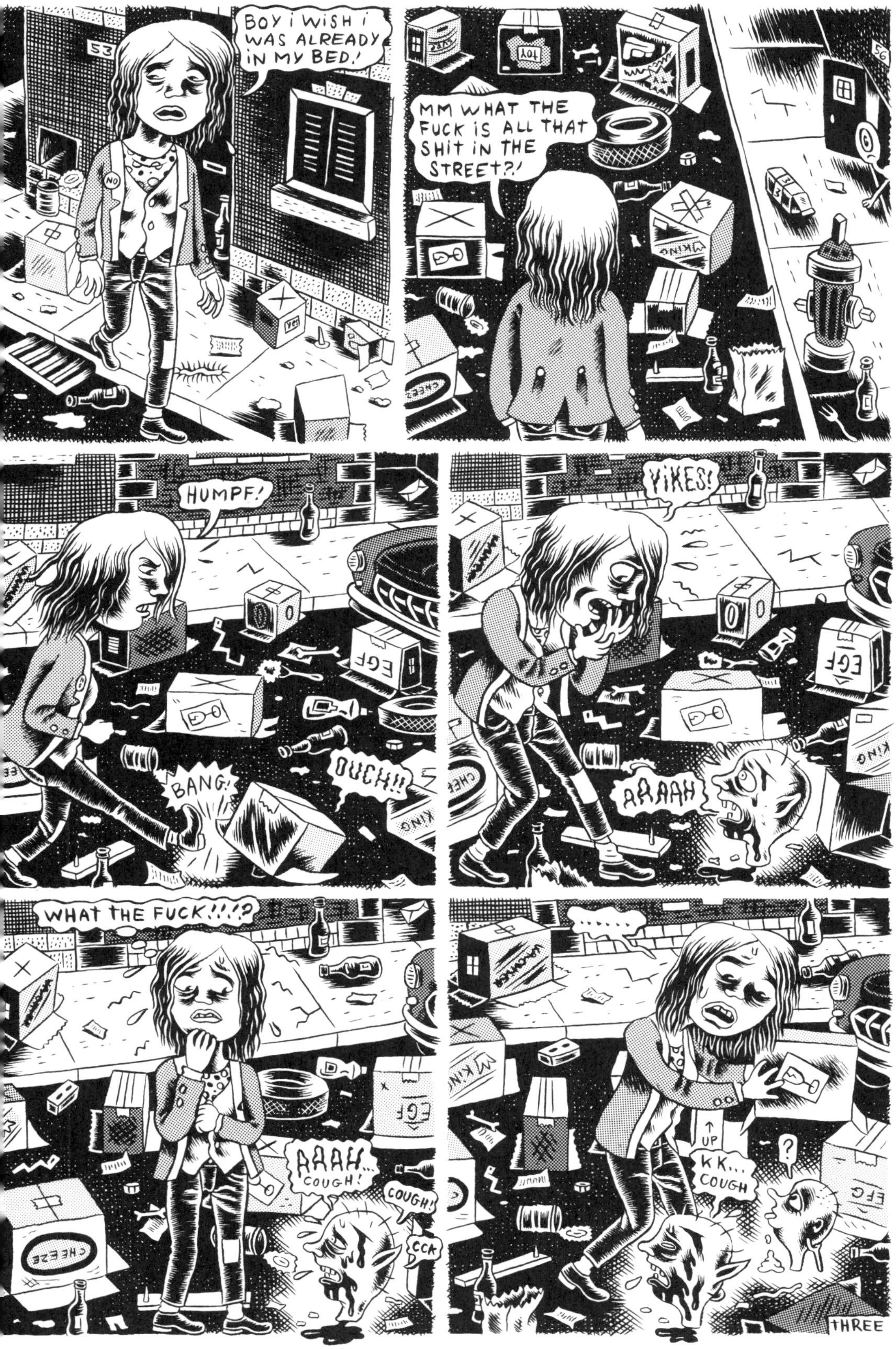
BOY i WiSH i WAS ALREADY iN MY BED!
MM WHAT THE FUCK iS ALL THAT SHiT iN THE STREET?!
HUMPF!
BANG!
OUCH!!
YiKES!
AAAAH
WHAT THE FUCK!!!?
AAAH... COUGH!
COUGH!
CCK
KK... COUGH
?

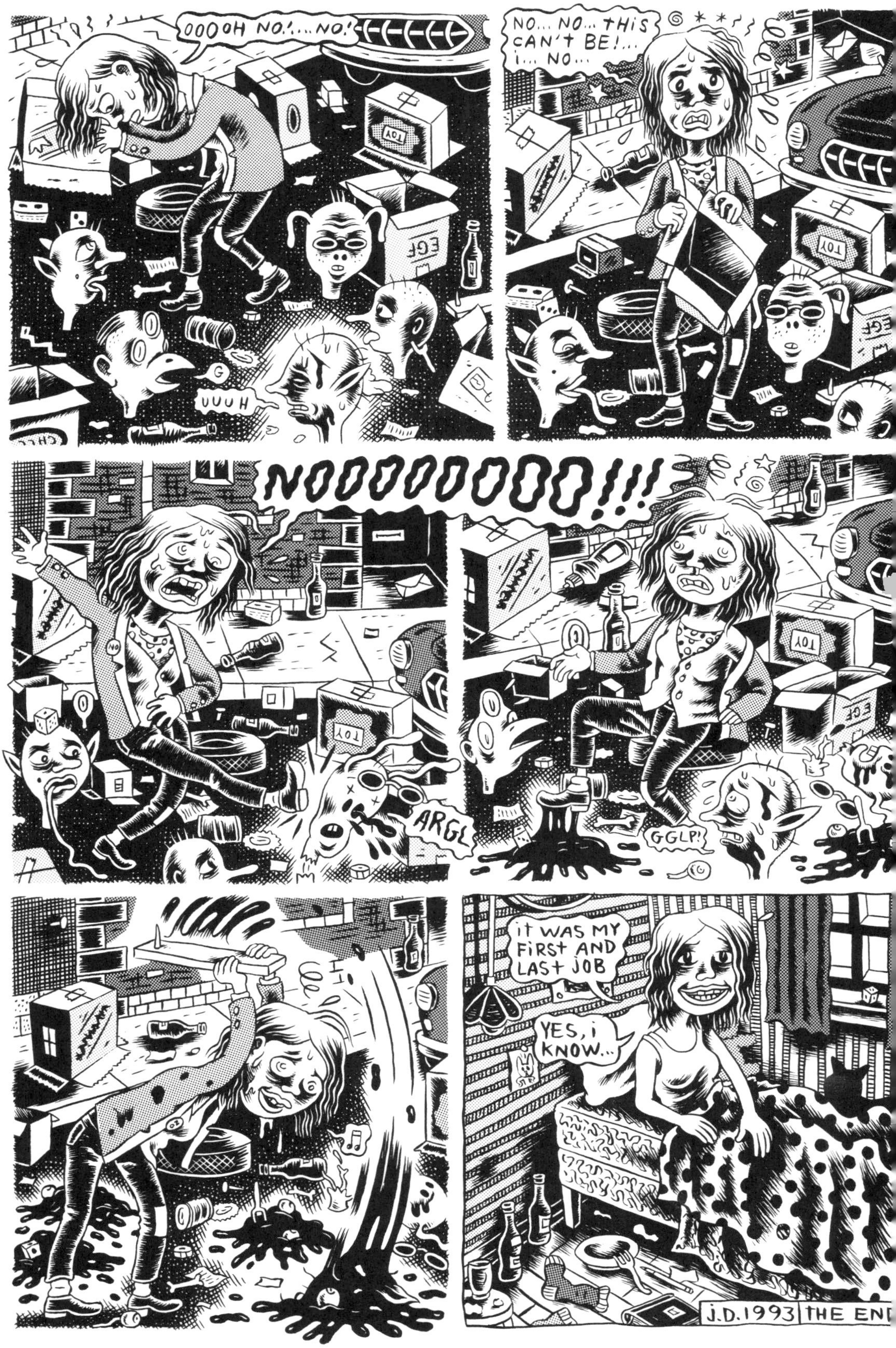
OOOOH NO!...NO!
UUUH
NO... NO... THIS CAN'T BE!... I... NO...
NOOOOOOOOO!!!
ARGL
GGLP!
IT WAS MY FIRST AND LAST JOB
YES, I KNOW...
J.D. 1993
THE END

THE RECURRING DREAM

A YEAR AGO, THAT DREAM STARTED TO COME VISIT ME, EVERY ONCE IN A WHILE... THAT DAMN DREAM! ALWAYS THE SAME STORY: I AM PREGNANT. I GIVE BIRTH, EVERY ABSURD POSSIBLE WAY. AND MY BABY ALWAYS TURNS OUT TO BE SOME SORT OF CAT!!!... WHAT DOES IT ALL MEAN? HERE'S SOME SAMPLE FOR YOU... → J.D. 1995

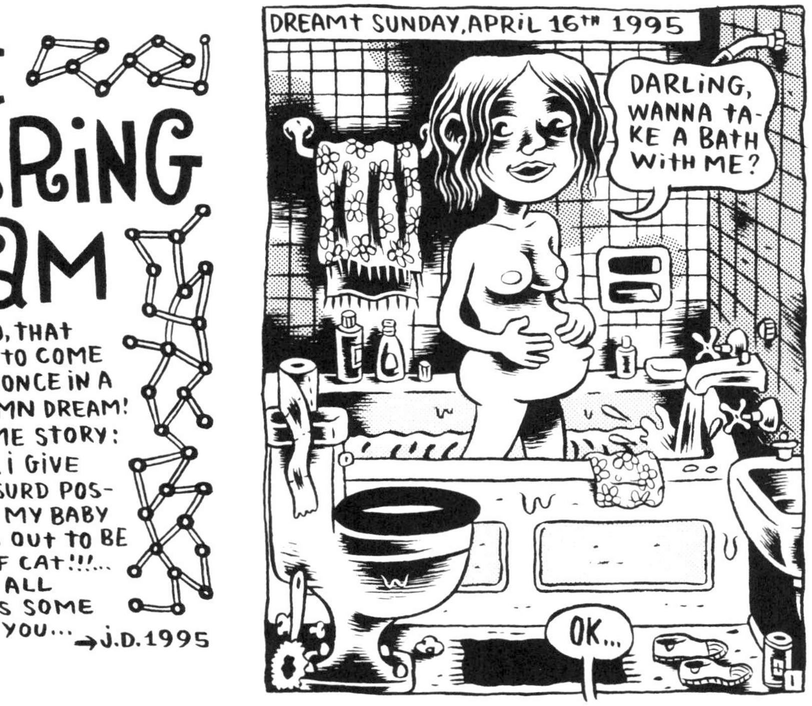
DREAMT SUNDAY, APRIL 16TH 1995
DARLING, WANNA TAKE A BATH WITH ME?
OK...
1

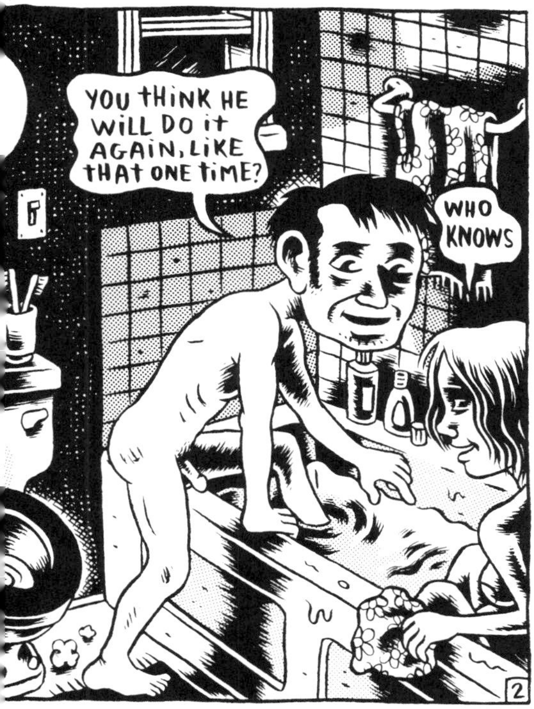
YOU THINK HE WILL DO IT AGAIN, LIKE THAT ONE TIME?
WHO KNOWS
2

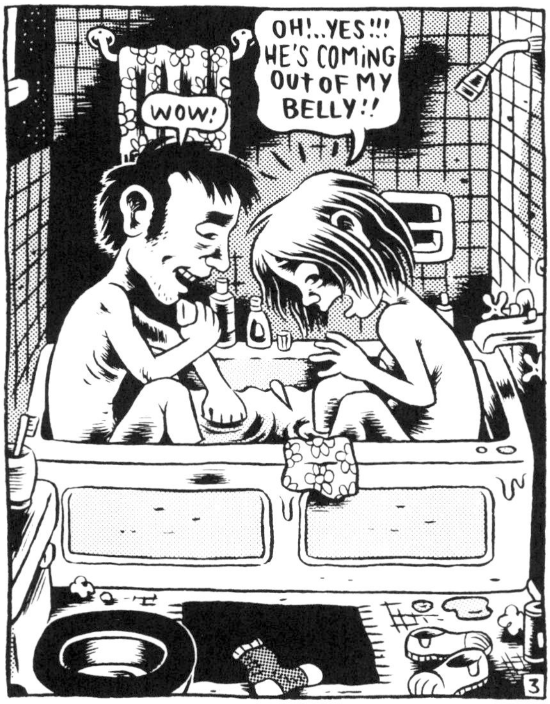
WOW!
OH!..YES!!! HE'S COMING OUT OF MY BELLY!!
3

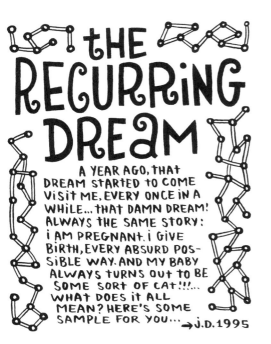

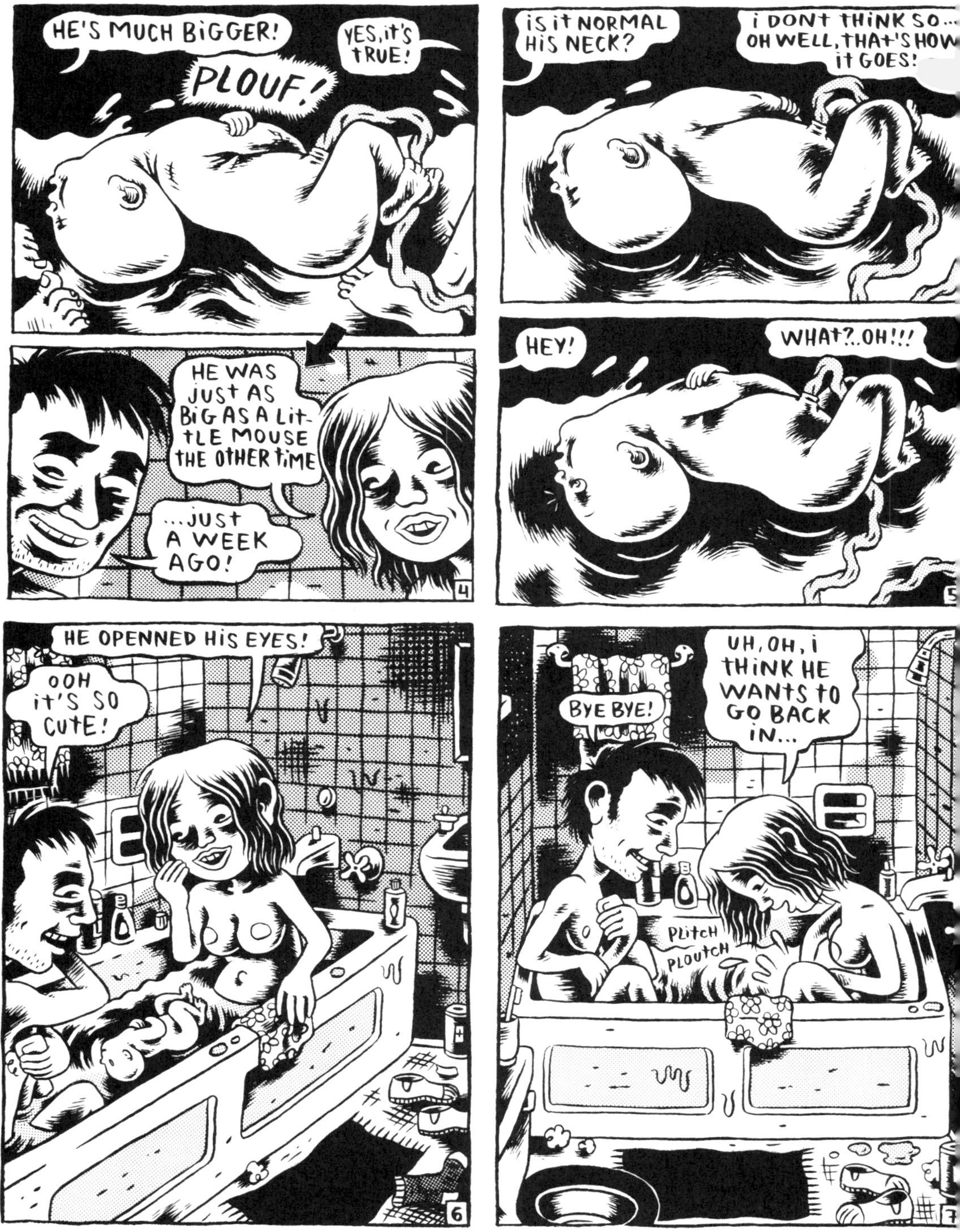
HE'S MUCH BIGGER!
YES, it's TRUE!
PLOUF!
is it NORMAL HIS NECK?
i DONT THINK SO... OH WELL, THAT'S HOW it GOES!
HE WAS JUST AS BIG AS A LIT-TLE MOUSE THE OTHER TIME
...JUST A WEEK AGO!
HEY!
WHAT?..OH!!!
HE OPENNED HIS EYES!
OOH it'S SO CUTE!
BYE BYE!
UH, OH, i THINK HE WANTS TO GO BACK IN...
PLITCH
PLOUTCH

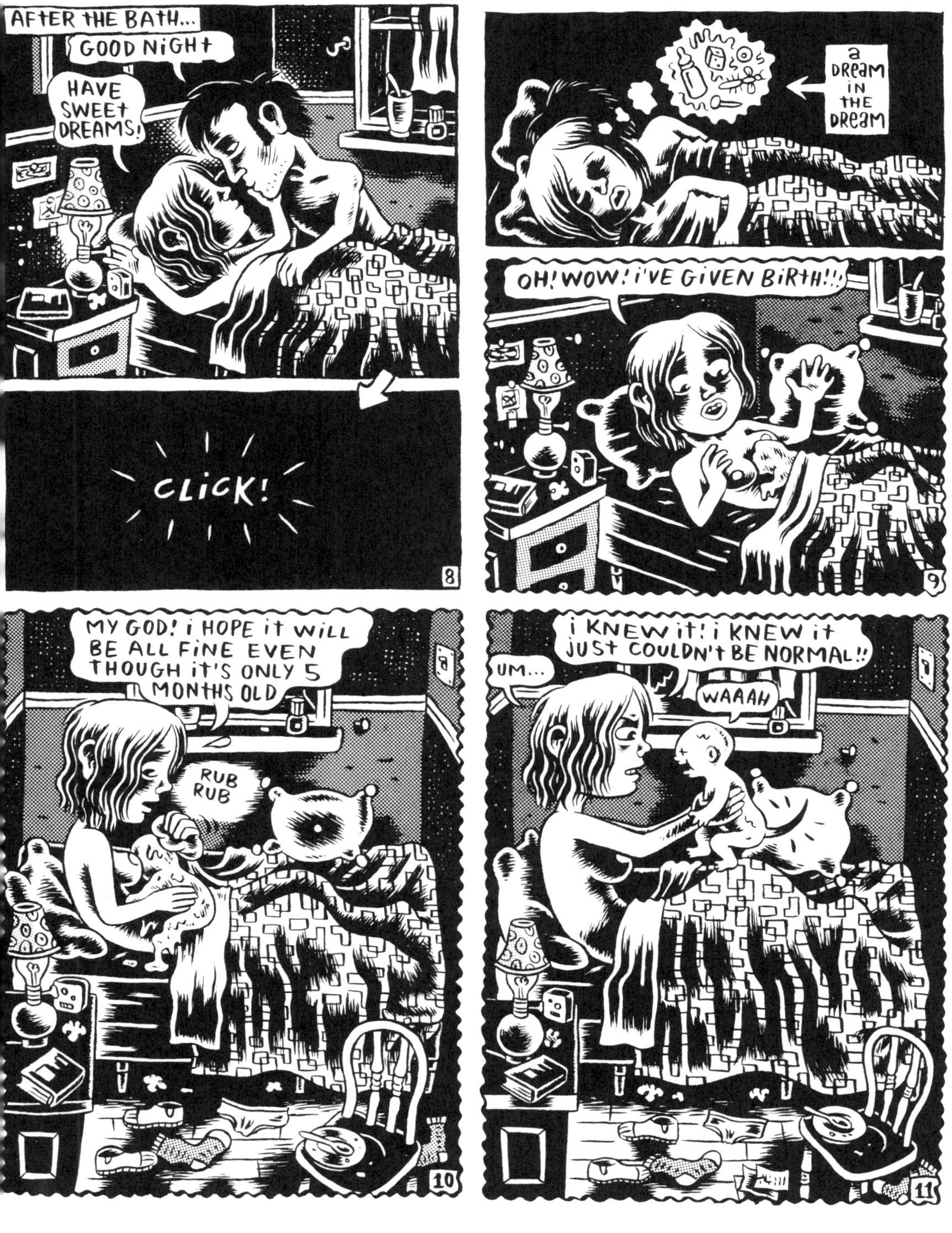
AFTER THE BATH...
GOOD NIGHT
HAVE SWEET DREAMS!
CLICK!
8
a DREAM IN THE DREAM
OH! WOW! i'VE GIVEN BIRTH!!!
9
MY GOD! i HOPE iT WILL BE ALL FiNE EVEN THOUGH iT'S ONLY 5 MONTHS OLD
RUB RUB
10
i KNEW iT! i KNEW iT JUST COULDN'T BE NORMAL!!
UM...
WAAAH
11

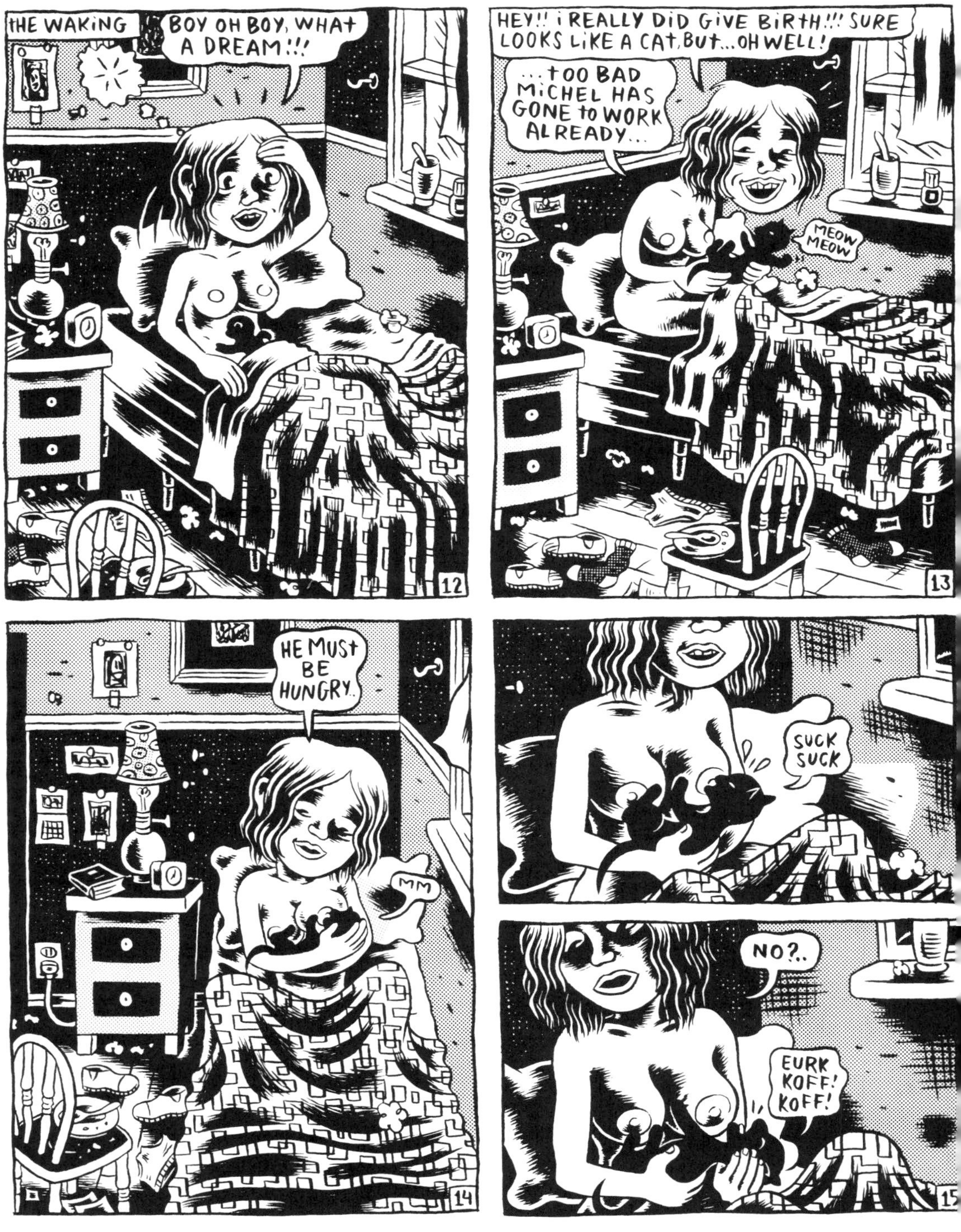
THE WAKING
BOY OH BOY, WHAT A DREAM!!!
12
HEY!! I REALLY DID GIVE BIRTH!!! SURE LOOKS LIKE A CAT, BUT... OH WELL!
...TOO BAD MICHEL HAS GONE TO WORK ALREADY...
MEOW MEOW
13
HE MUST BE HUNGRY..
MM
14
SUCK SUCK
NO?..
EURK KOFF! KOFF!
15

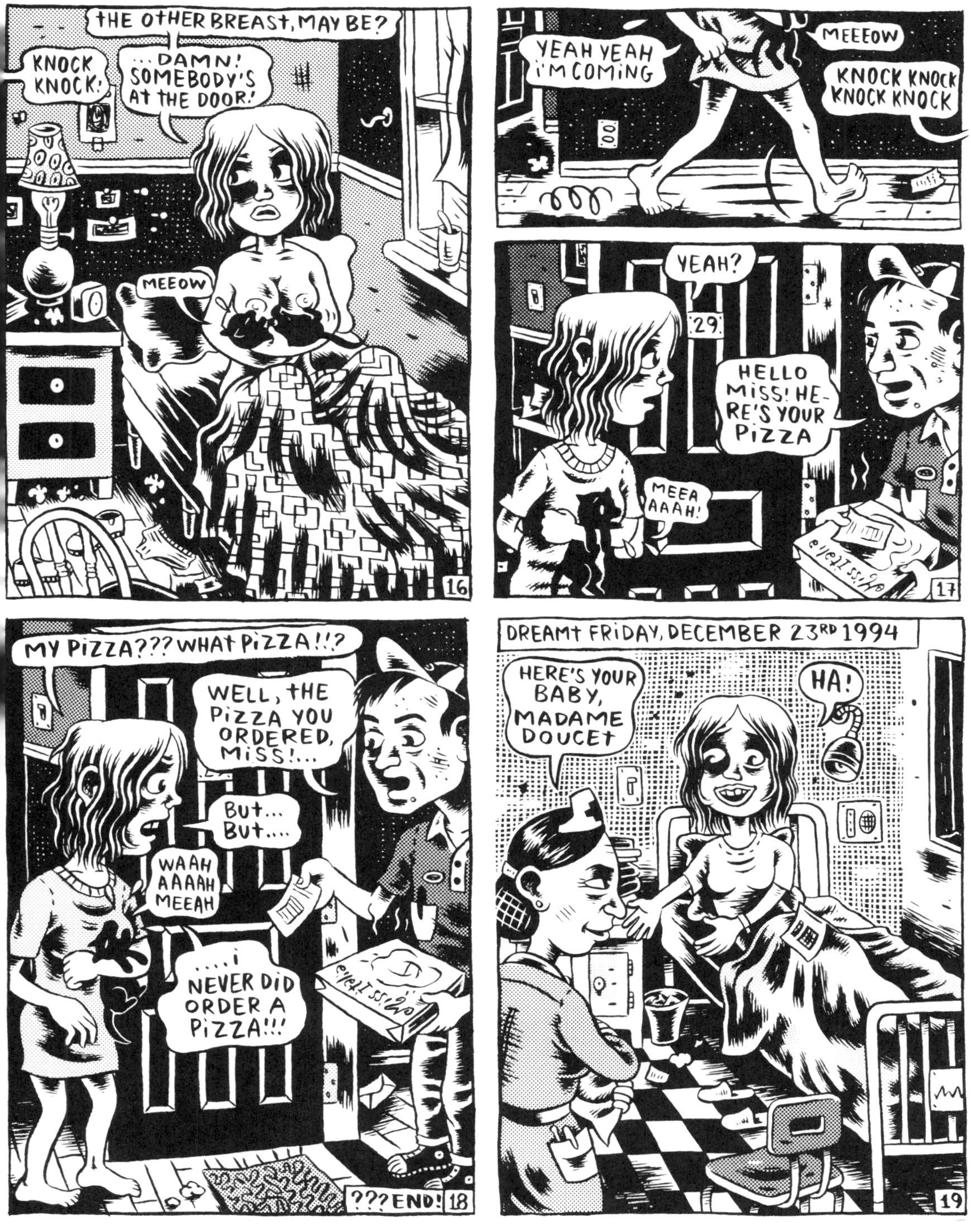
THE OTHER BREAST, MAY BE?
KNOCK KNOCK!
...DAMN! SOMEBODY'S AT THE DOOR!
MEEOW
16
YEAH YEAH I'M COMING
MEEEOW
KNOCK KNOCK KNOCK KNOCK
YEAH?
29
HELLO MISS! HERE'S YOUR PIZZA
MEEA AAAH!
17
MY PIZZA??? WHAT PIZZA!!?
WELL, THE PIZZA YOU ORDERED, MISS!...
But... But....
WAAH AAAAH MEEAH
....I NEVER DID ORDER A PIZZA!!!
???END! 18
DREAMT FRIDAY, DECEMBER 23RD 1994
HERE'S YOUR BABY, MADAME DOUCET
HA!
19

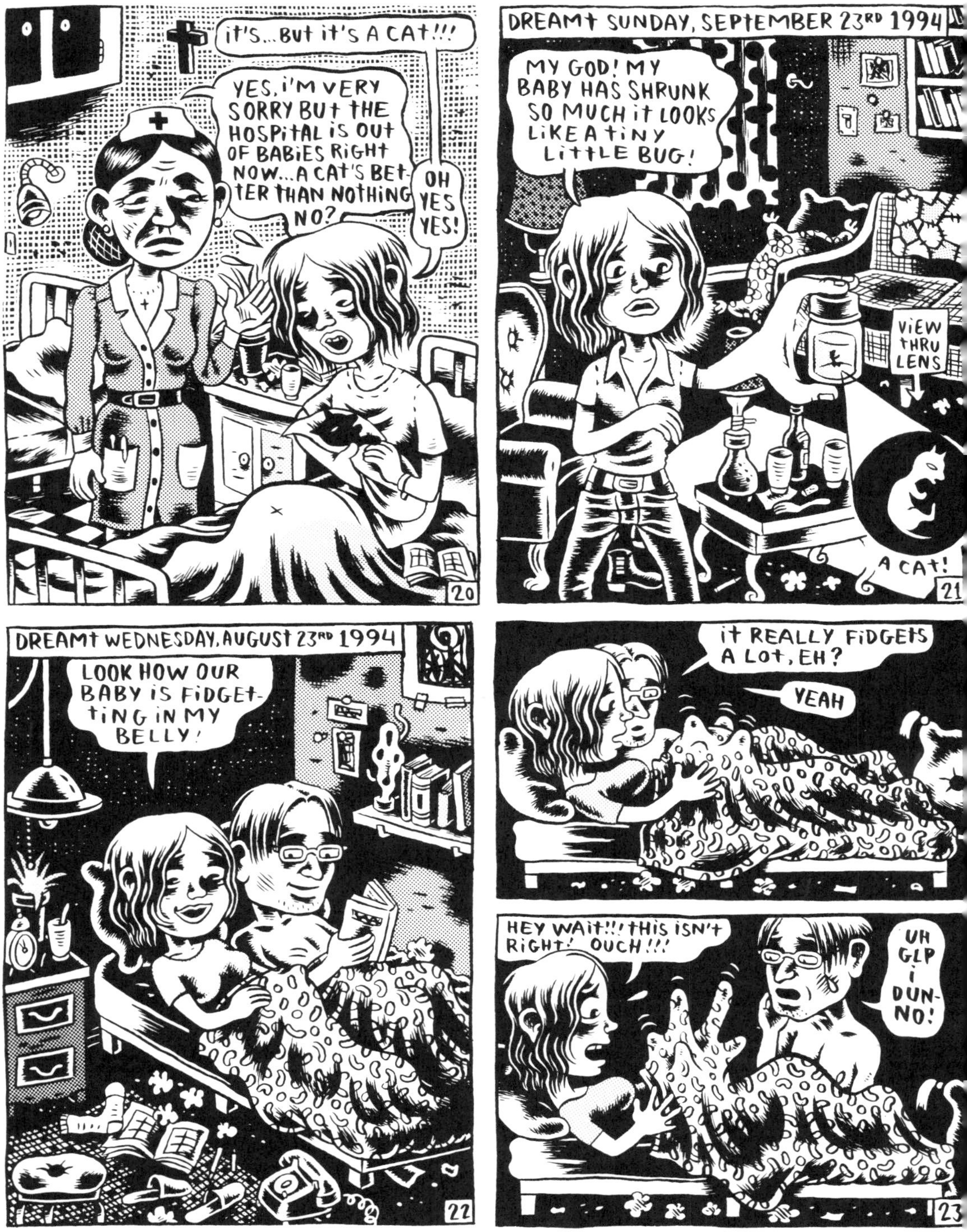

IT'S...BUT IT'S A CAT!!!
YES, I'M VERY SORRY BUT THE HOSPITAL IS OUT OF BABIES RIGHT NOW...A CAT'S BETTER THAN NOTHING NO?
OH YES YES!
20
DREAMT SUNDAY, SEPTEMBER 23RD 1994
MY GOD! MY BABY HAS SHRUNK SO MUCH IT LOOKS LIKE A TINY LITTLE BUG!
VIEW THRU LENS
A CAT!
21
DREAMT WEDNESDAY, AUGUST 23RD 1994
LOOK HOW OUR BABY IS FIDGETTING IN MY BELLY!
22
IT REALLY FIDGETS A LOT, EH?
YEAH
HEY WAIT!!! THIS ISN'T RIGHT! OUCH!!!
UH GLP I DUNNO!
23

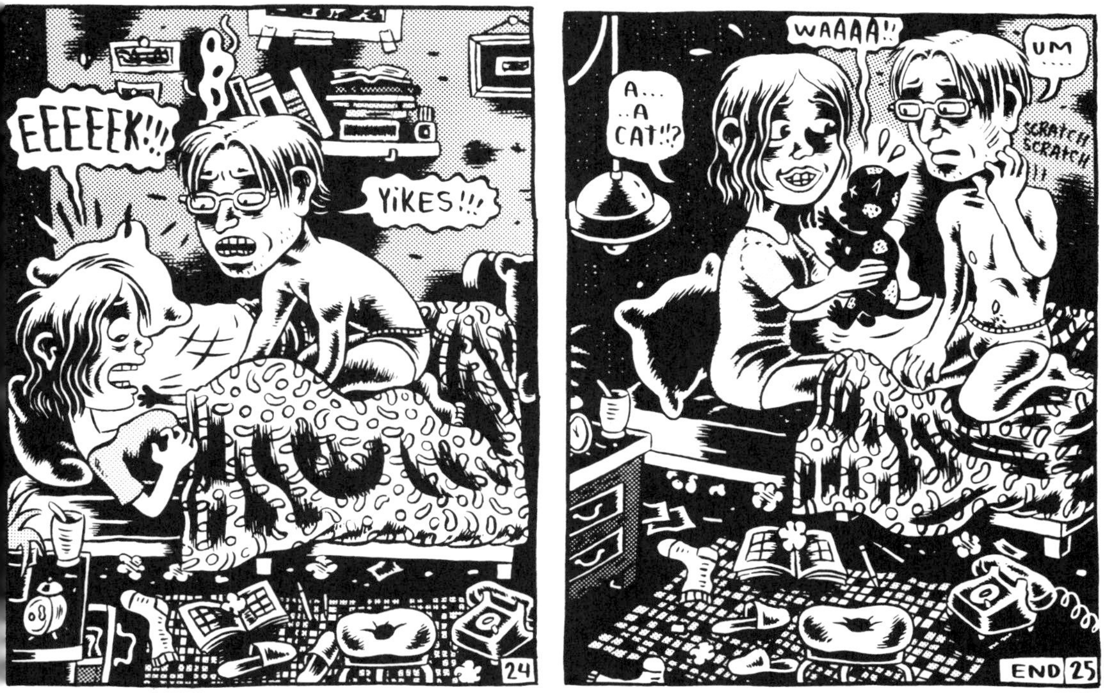
EEEEEK!!!
YIKES!!!
24
WAAAA!!
A...
..A
CAT!!?
UM
....
SCRATCH
SCRATCH
END
25

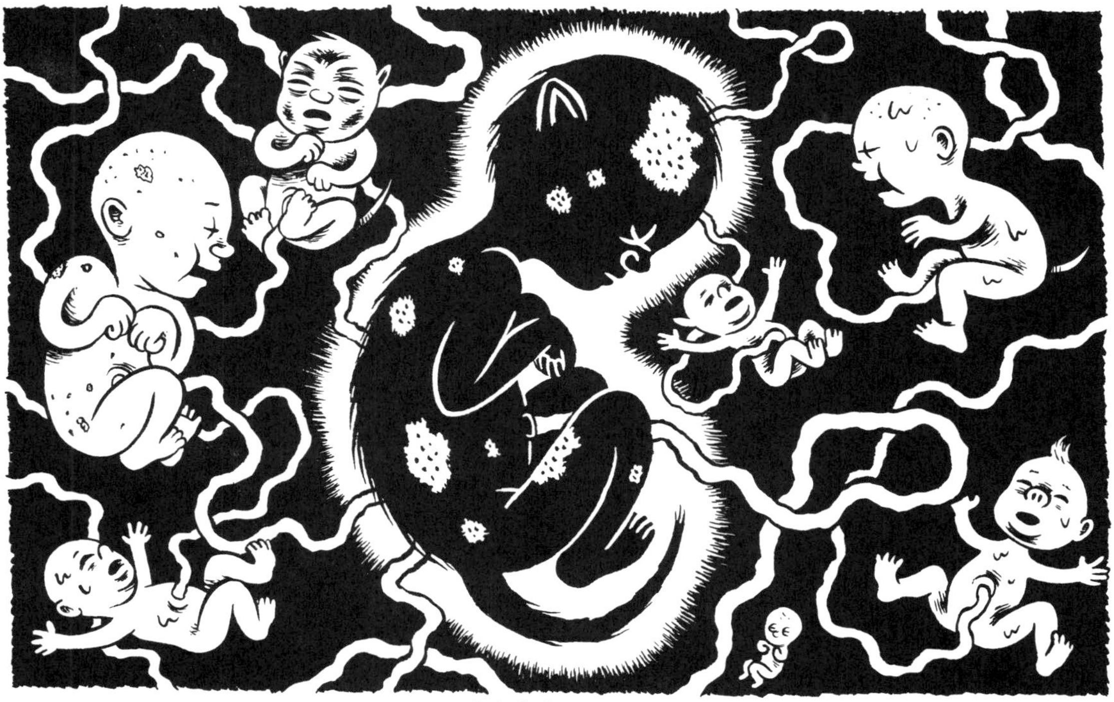

MAMAN!

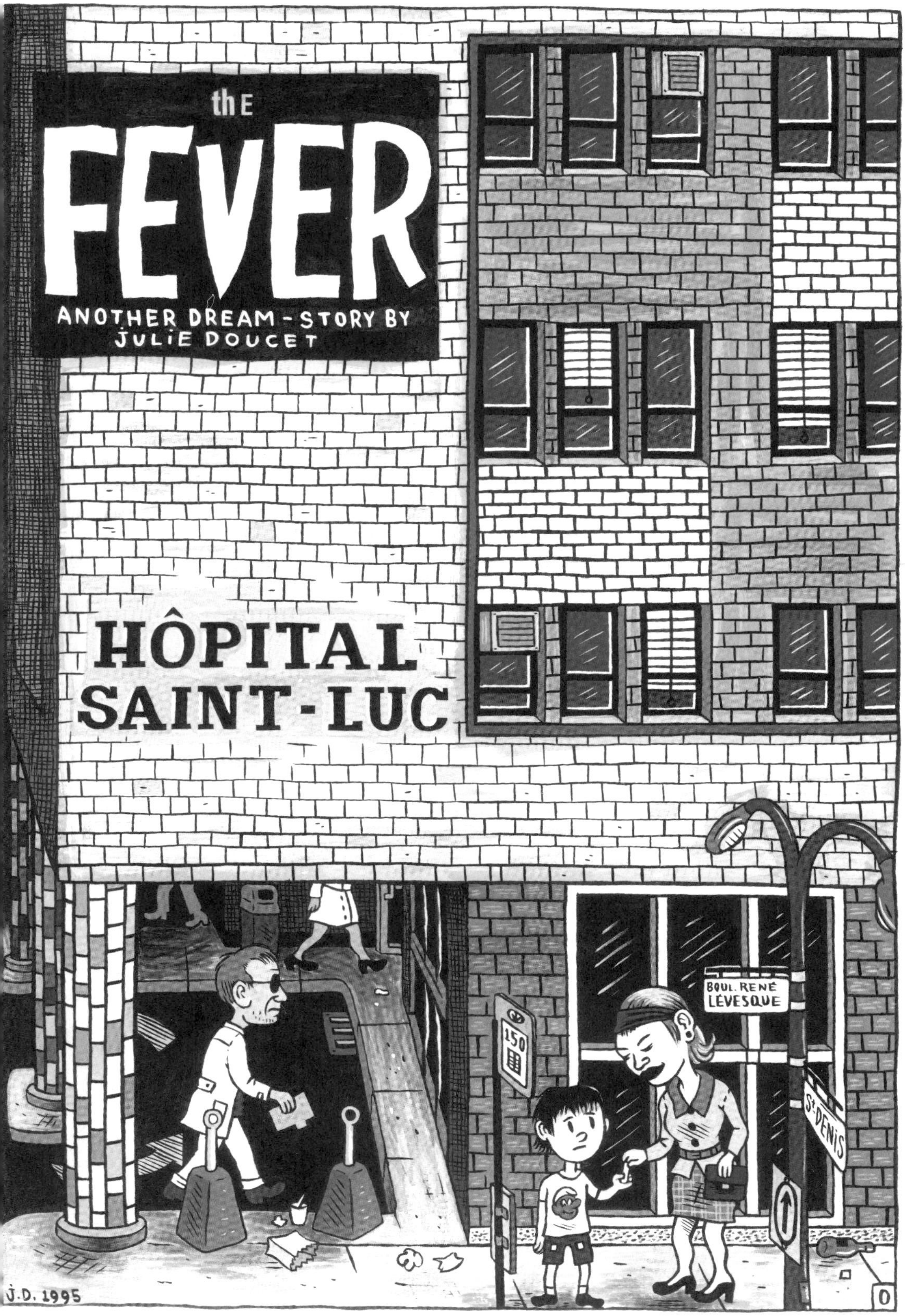

thE
FEVER
ANOTHER DREAM-STORY BY
JULIE DOUCET
HÔPITAL
SAINT-LUC
BOUL. RENÉ
LÉVESQUE
150
St-DENIS
J.D. 1995
0

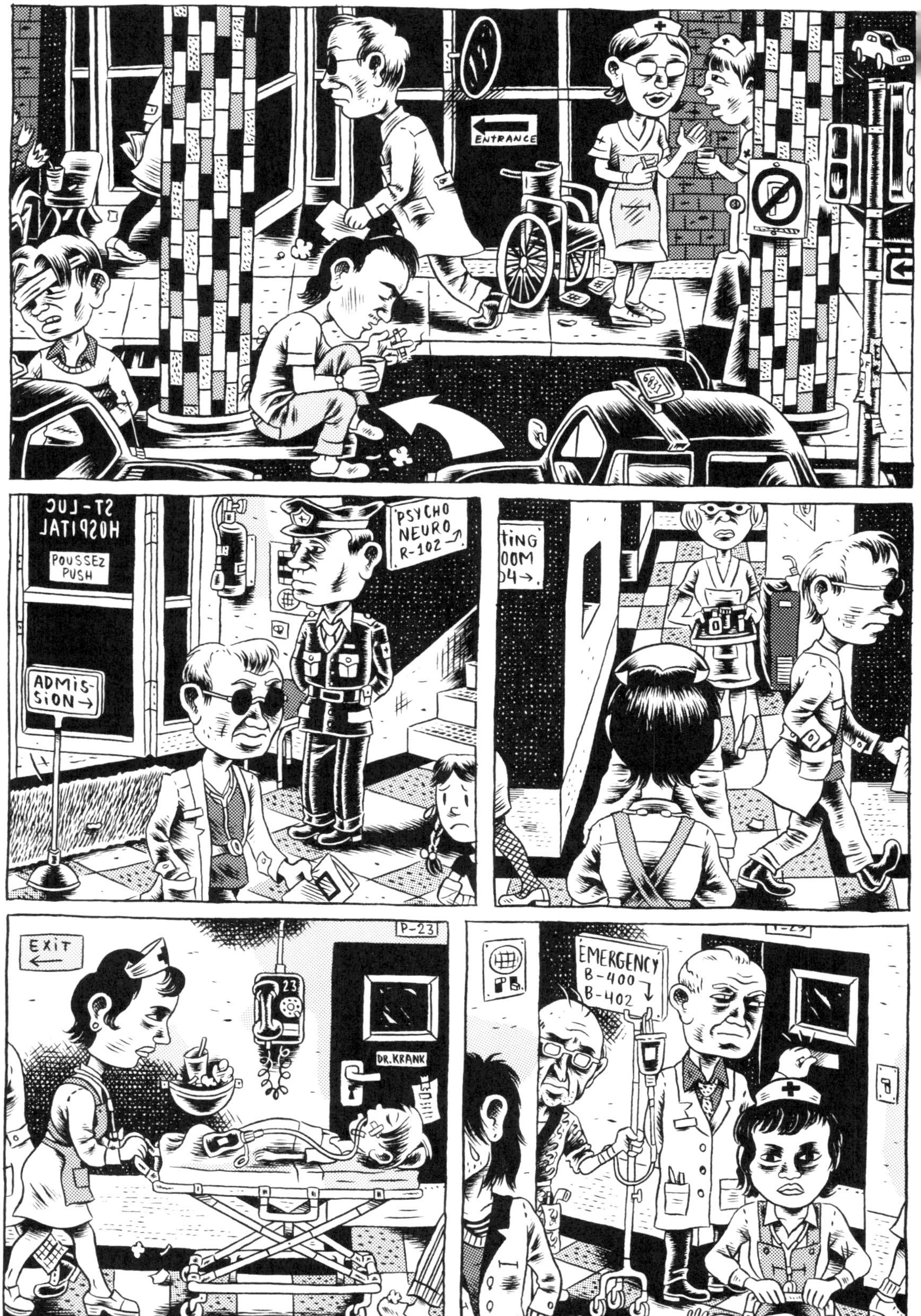
ENTRANCE
6831
ST-LUC
HOSPITAL
POUSSEZ
PUSH
ADMIS-
SION →
PSYCHO
NEURO
R-102
TING
OOM
04 →
EXIT
P-23
23
DR. KRANK
EMERGENCY
B-400
B-402
PB.

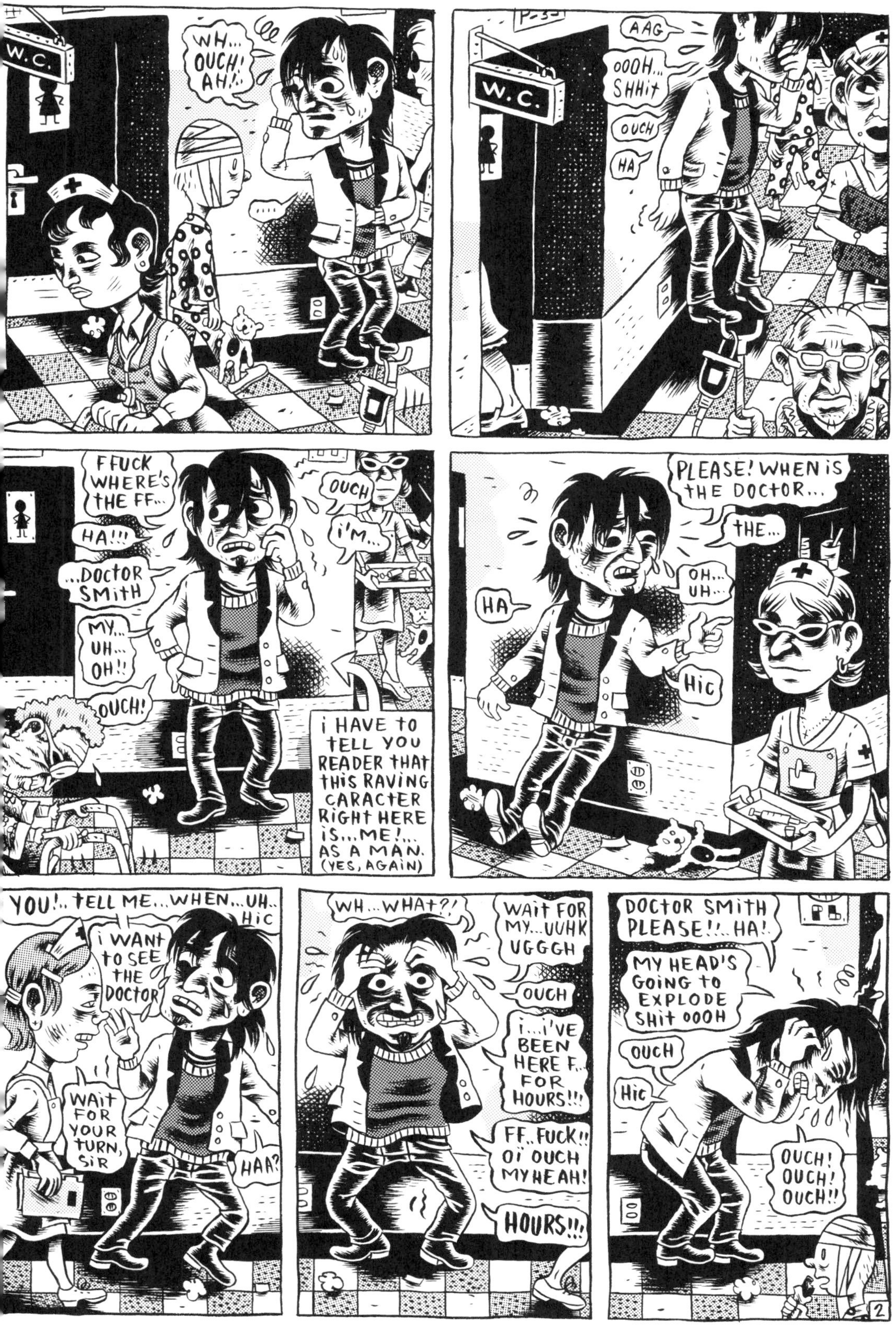
W.C.
WH... OUCH! AH!..
....
AAG
W.C.
OOOH... SHHit
OUCH
HA
FFUCK WHERE'S THE FF...
HA!!!
...DOCTOR SMitH
MY... UH... OH!!
OUCH!
OUCH
i'M...
i HAVE TO tELL YOU READER tHAt tHiS RAViNG CARACtER RiGHt HERE iS...ME!... AS A MAN. (YES, AGAiN)
PLEASE! WHEN iS tHE DOCtOR...
tHE...
HA
OH... UH...
Hic
YOU!.. tELL ME...WHEN...UH.. Hic
i WANt tO SEE tHE DOCtOR
WAit FOR YOUR tURN, SiR
HAA?
WH...WHAt?!
WAit FOR MY...UUHK UGGGH
OUCH
i...i'VE BEEN HERE F... FOR HOURS!!!
FF.. FUCK!! Oi OUCH MY HEAH!
HOURS!!!
DOCtOR SMitH PLEASE!!..HA!
MY HEAD'S GOiNG tO EXPLODE SHit OOOH
OUCH
Hic
OUCH! OUCH! OUCH!!

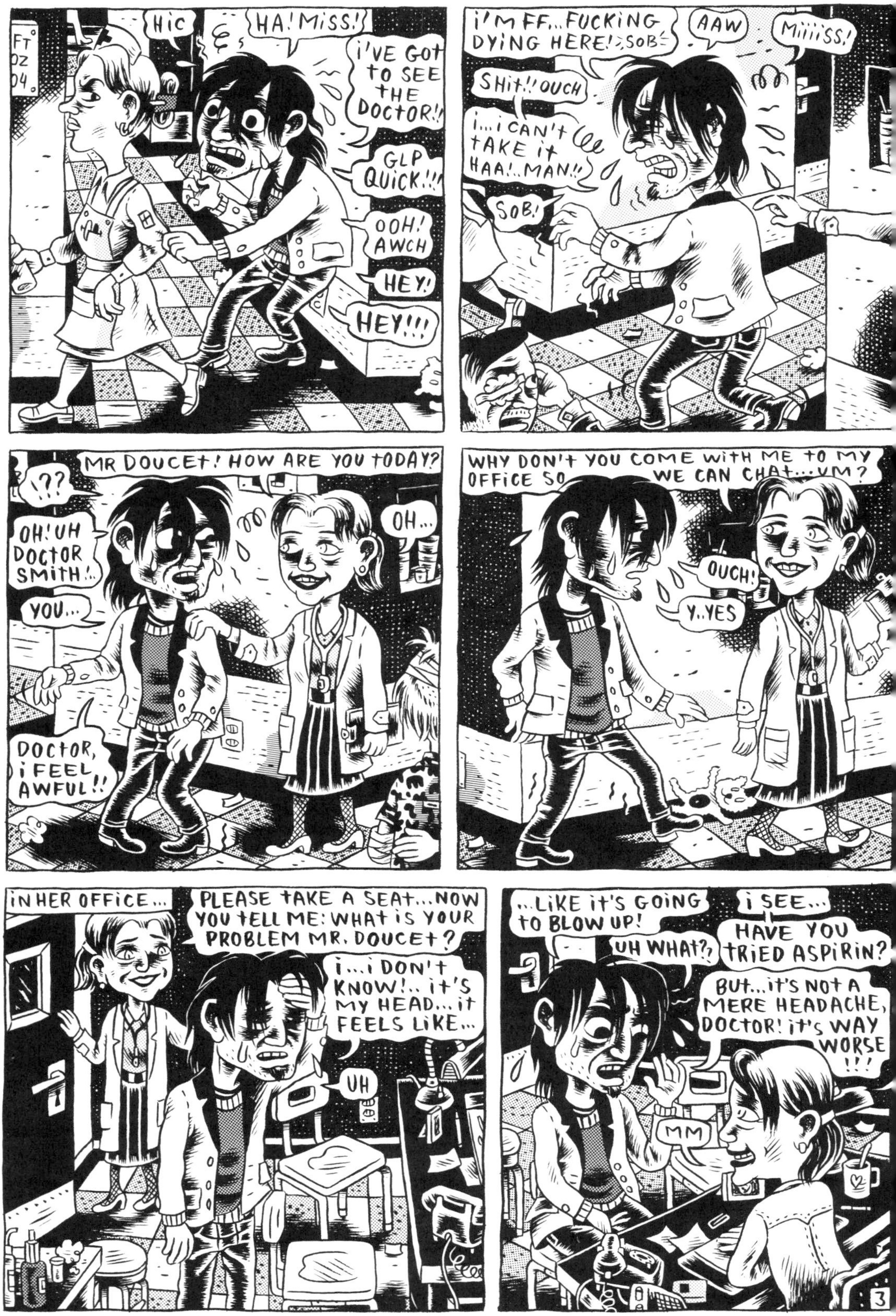
HIC
HA! MISS!
I'VE GOT TO SEE THE DOCTOR!!
GLP QUICK!!!
OOH! AWCH
HEY!
HEY!!!
I'M FF... FUCKING DYING HERE! SOB
AAW
MIIIISS!
SHIT!! OUCH
I... I CAN'T TAKE IT HAA!.. MAN!!
SOB!
MR DOUCET! HOW ARE YOU TODAY?
!??
OH...
OH! UH DOCTOR SMITH!..
YOU...
DOCTOR, I FEEL AWFUL!!
WHY DON'T YOU COME WITH ME TO MY OFFICE SO WE CAN CHAT... UM?
OUCH!
Y.. YES
IN HER OFFICE...
PLEASE TAKE A SEAT... NOW YOU TELL ME: WHAT IS YOUR PROBLEM MR. DOUCET?
I... I DON'T KNOW!.. IT'S MY HEAD... IT FEELS LIKE...
UH
...LIKE IT'S GOING TO BLOW UP!
I SEE...
UH WHAT?
HAVE YOU TRIED ASPIRIN?
BUT... IT'S NOT A MERE HEADACHE, DOCTOR! IT'S WAY WORSE!!!
MM

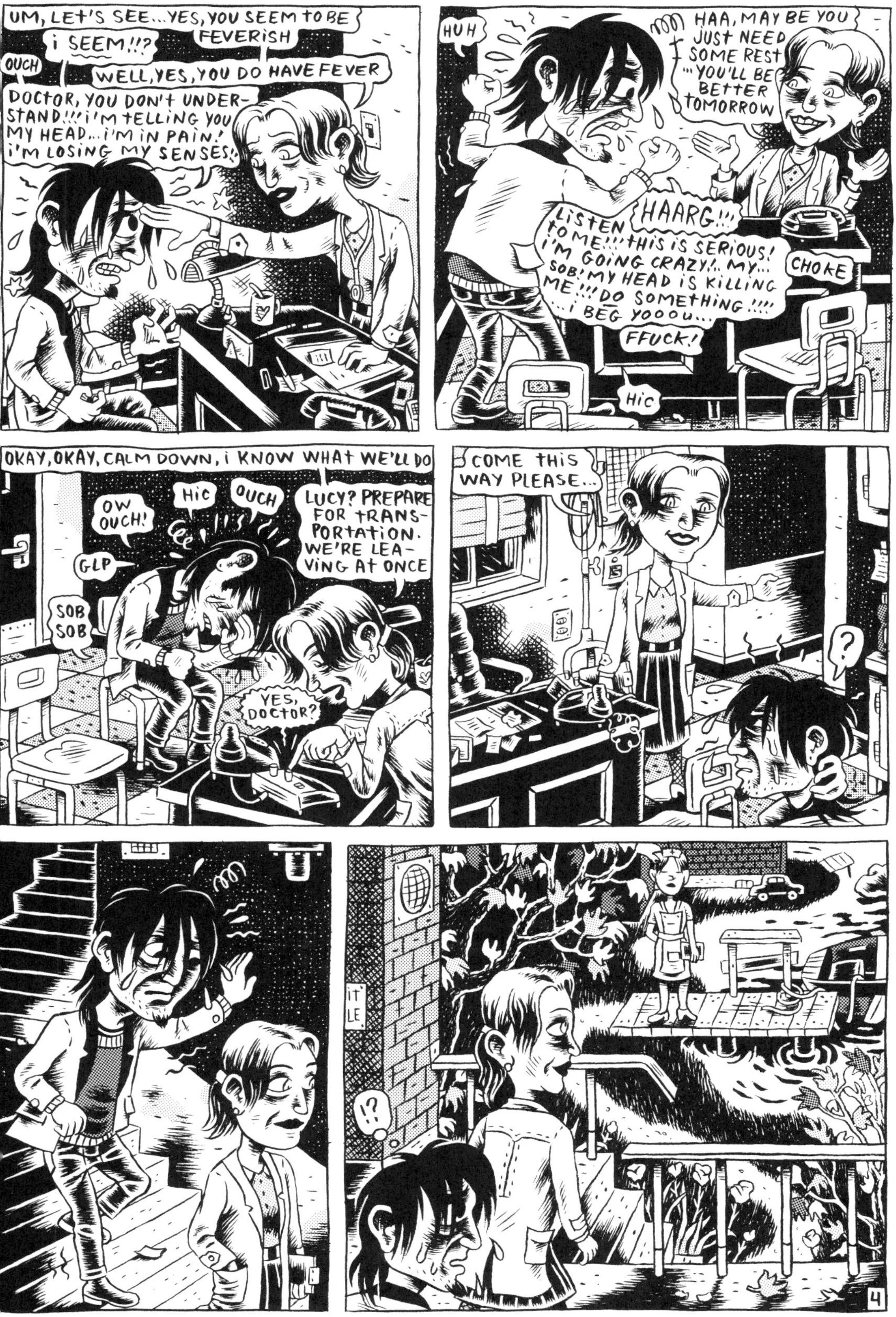
UM, LET'S SEE... YES, YOU SEEM TO BE FEVERISH
i SEEM!!?
WELL, YES, YOU DO HAVE FEVER
OUCH
DOCTOR, YOU DON'T UNDERSTAND!!! i'M TELLING YOU MY HEAD... i'M IN PAIN! i'M LOSING MY SENSES!
HUH
HAA, MAYBE YOU JUST NEED SOME REST ...YOU'LL BE BETTER TOMORROW
HAARG!!!
LISTEN TO ME!!! THIS IS SERIOUS! I'M GOING CRAZY!.. MY... SOB! MY HEAD IS KILLING ME!!! DO SOMETHING!!!! ...i BEG YOOOU...
CHOKE
FFUCK!
HIC
OKAY, OKAY, CALM DOWN, i KNOW WHAT WE'LL DO
OW OUCH!
HIC
OUCH
GLP
SOB SOB
LUCY? PREPARE FOR TRANSPORTATION. WE'RE LEAVING AT ONCE
YES, DOCTOR?
COME THIS WAY PLEASE...
?
!?

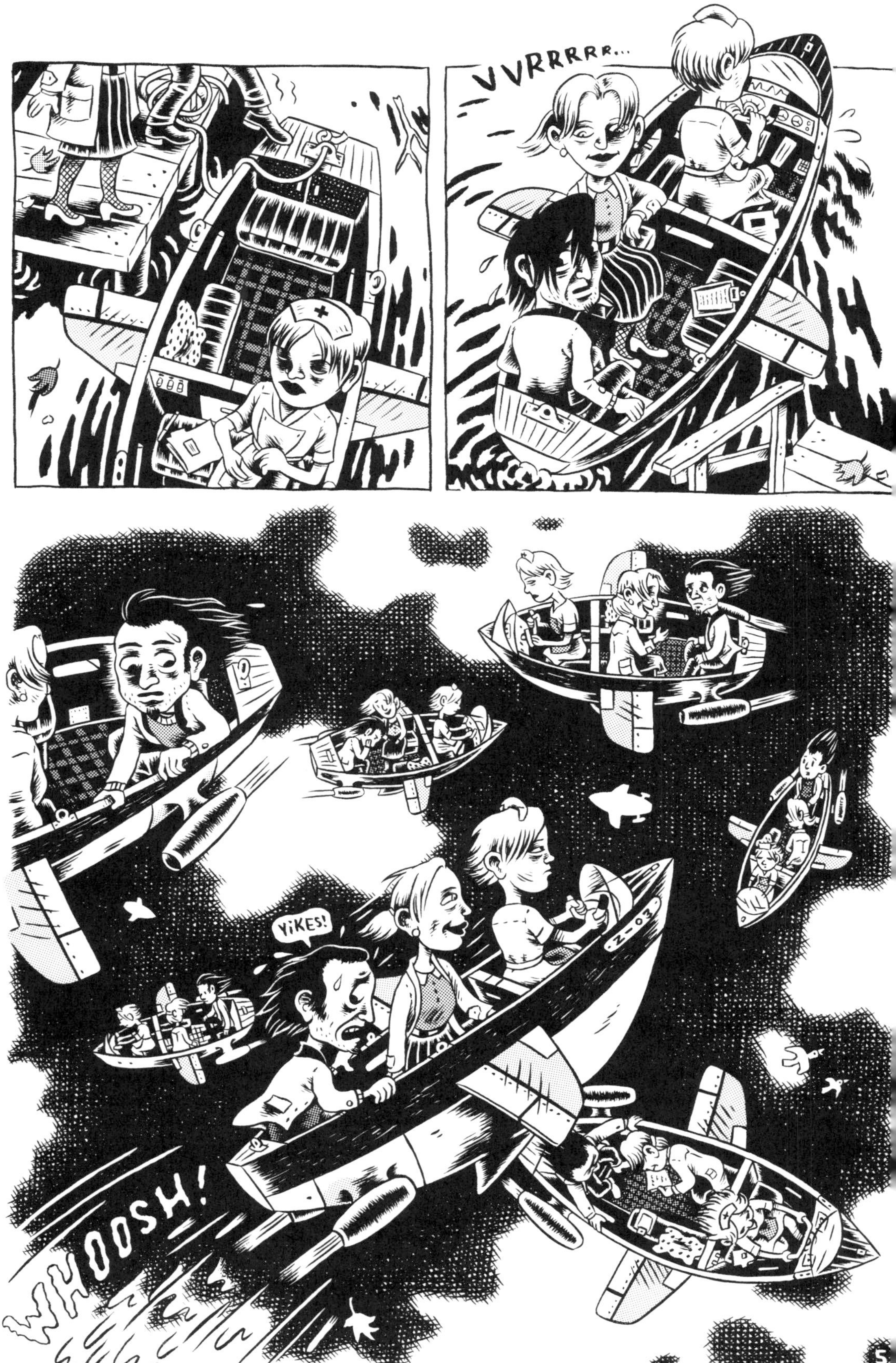
VVRRRRR...
YIKES!
WHOOSH!

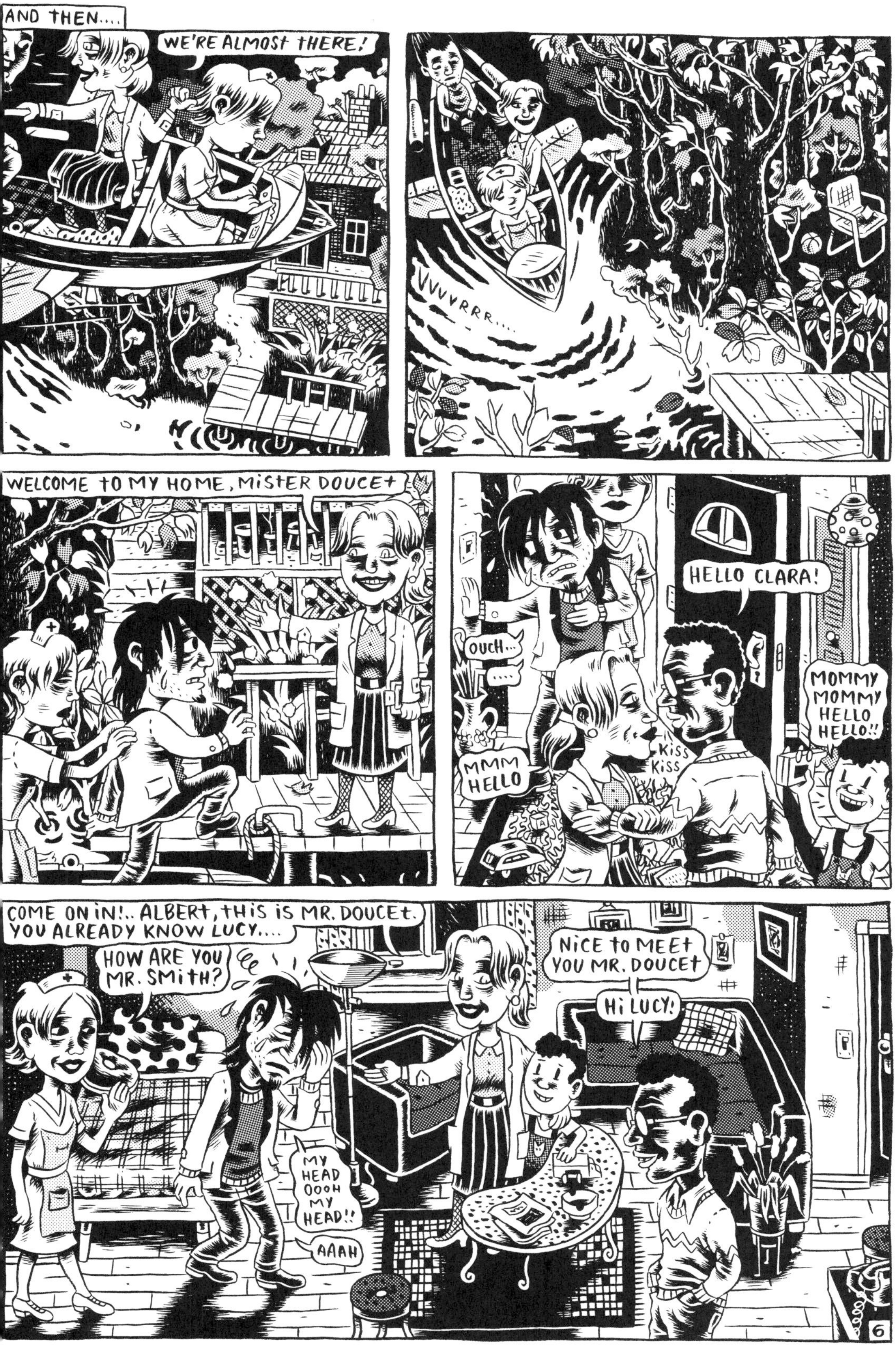
AND THEN....
WE'RE ALMOST THERE!
VVVVRRR....
WELCOME TO MY HOME, MISTER DOUCET
HELLO CLARA!
OUCH...
.....
MOMMY MOMMY HELLO HELLO!!
MMM HELLO
KISS KISS
COME ON IN!.. ALBERT, THIS IS MR. DOUCET. YOU ALREADY KNOW LUCY....
HOW ARE YOU MR. SMITH?
NICE TO MEET YOU MR. DOUCET
HI LUCY!
MY HEAD OOOH MY HEAD!!
AAAH
6

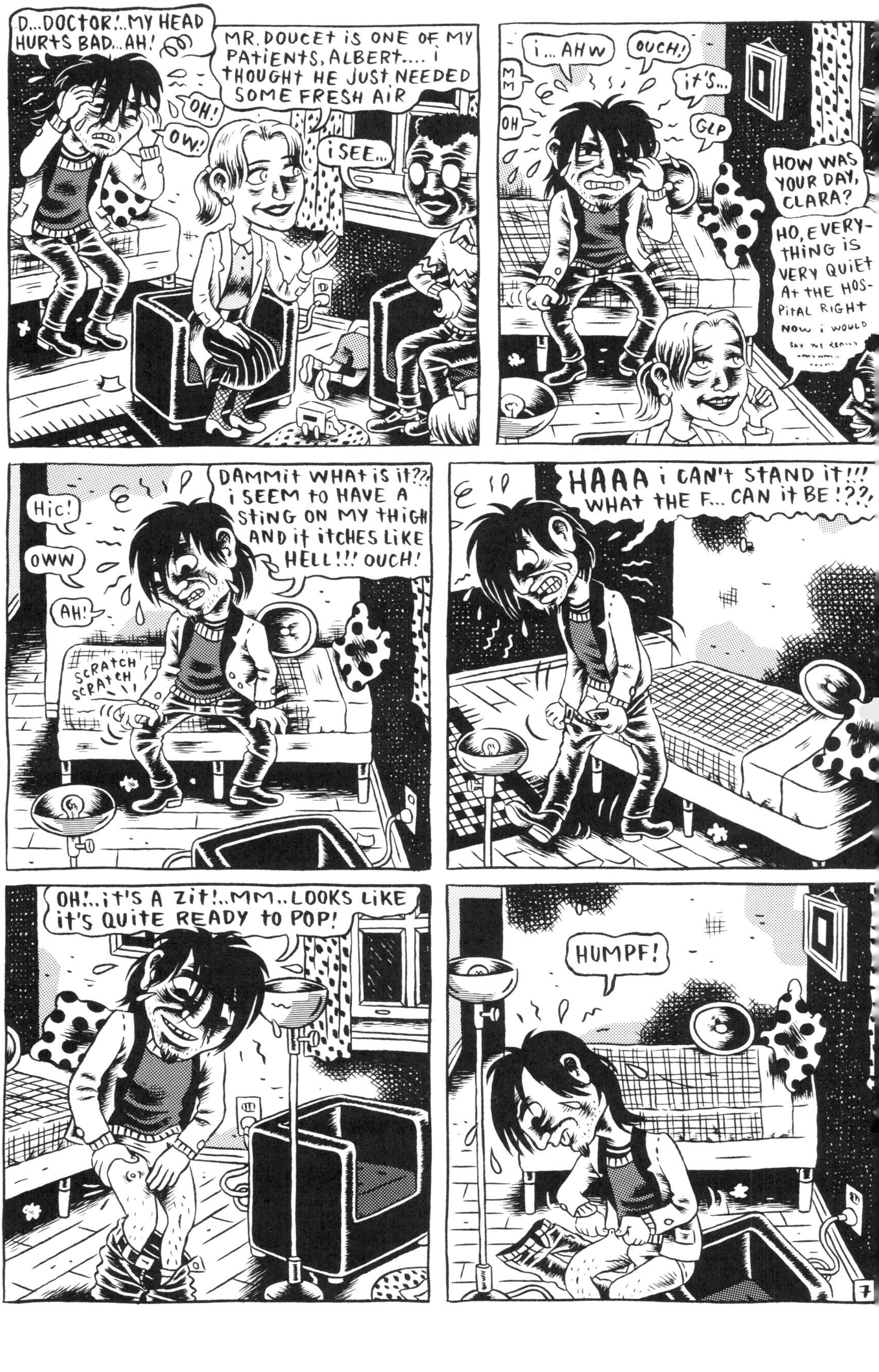

D...DOCTOR!..MY HEAD HURTS BAD...AH!
MR. DOUCET IS ONE OF MY PATIENTS, ALBERT.... I THOUGHT HE JUST NEEDED SOME FRESH AIR
OH!
OW!
I SEE...
I... AHW
OUCH!
IT'S...
MM
OH
GLP
HOW WAS YOUR DAY, CLARA?
HO, EVERYTHING IS VERY QUIET AT THE HOSPITAL RIGHT NOW I WOULD
Hic!
OWW
AH!
DAMMIT WHAT IS IT??? I SEEM TO HAVE A STING ON MY THIGH AND IT ITCHES LIKE HELL!!! OUCH!
SCRATCH SCRATCH
HAAA I CAN'T STAND IT!!! WHAT THE F... CAN IT BE!??
OH!..IT'S A ZIT!..MM..LOOKS LIKE IT'S QUITE READY TO POP!
HUMPF!

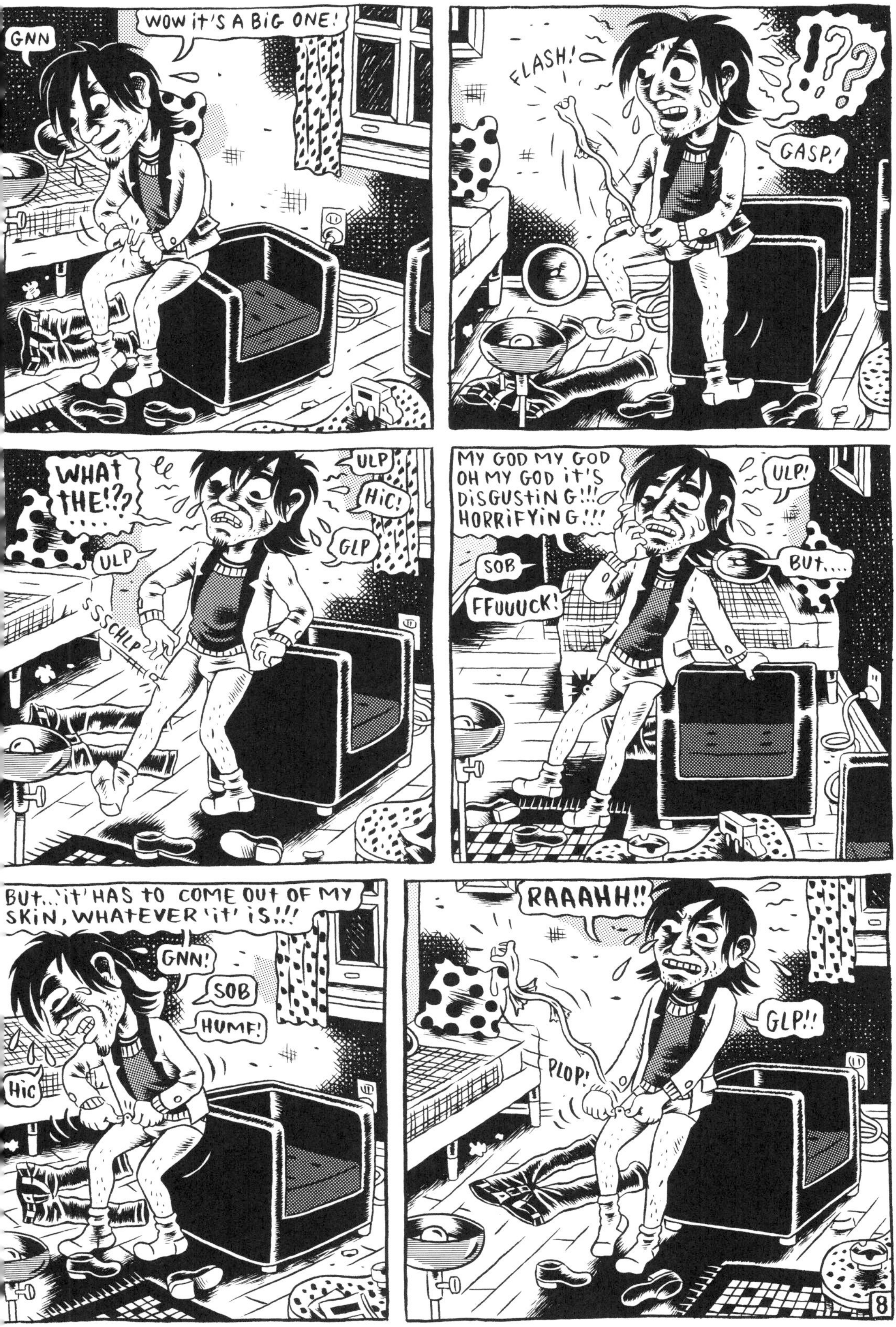
GNN
WOW it'S A BiG ONE!
FLASH!
!??
GASP!
WHAT THE!??
ULP
HiC!
GLP
ULP
SSSCHLP
MY GOD MY GOD OH MY GOD it'S DiSGUSTiNG!!! HORRiFYiNG!!!
ULP!
SOB
BUt....
FFUUUCK!
BUt...'it' HAS tO COME OUt OF MY SKiN, WHAtEVER 'it' iS!!!
GNN!
SOB
HUMF!
HiC
RAAAHH!!
GLP!!
PLOP!
8

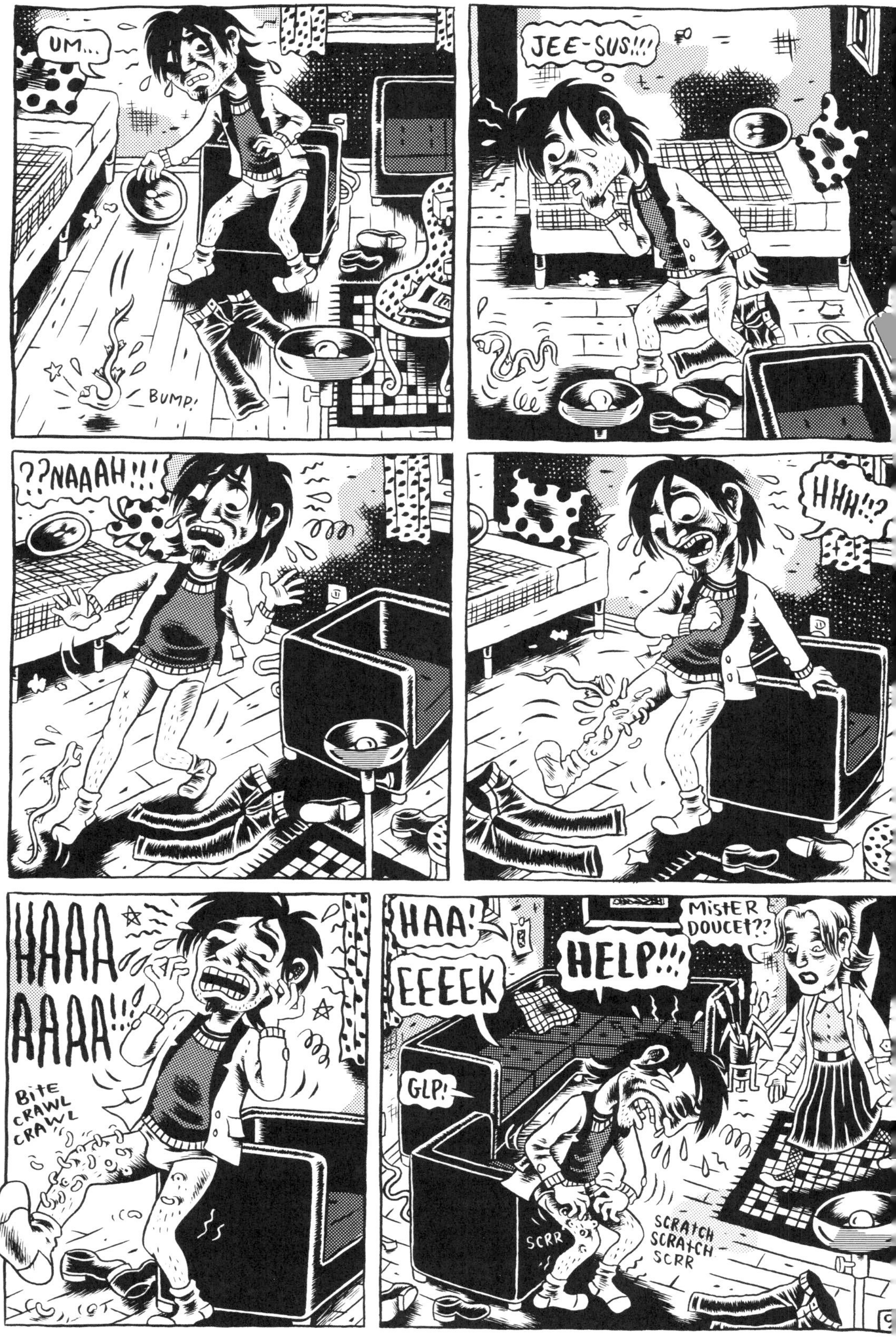
UM...
BUMP!
JEE-SUS!!!
??NAAAH!!!
HHH!!?
HAAA AAAA!!!
BITE
CRAWL
CRAWL
HAA!
EEEEK
HELP!!!
MISTER DOUCET??
GLP!
SCRR
SCRATCH
SCRATCH
SCRR

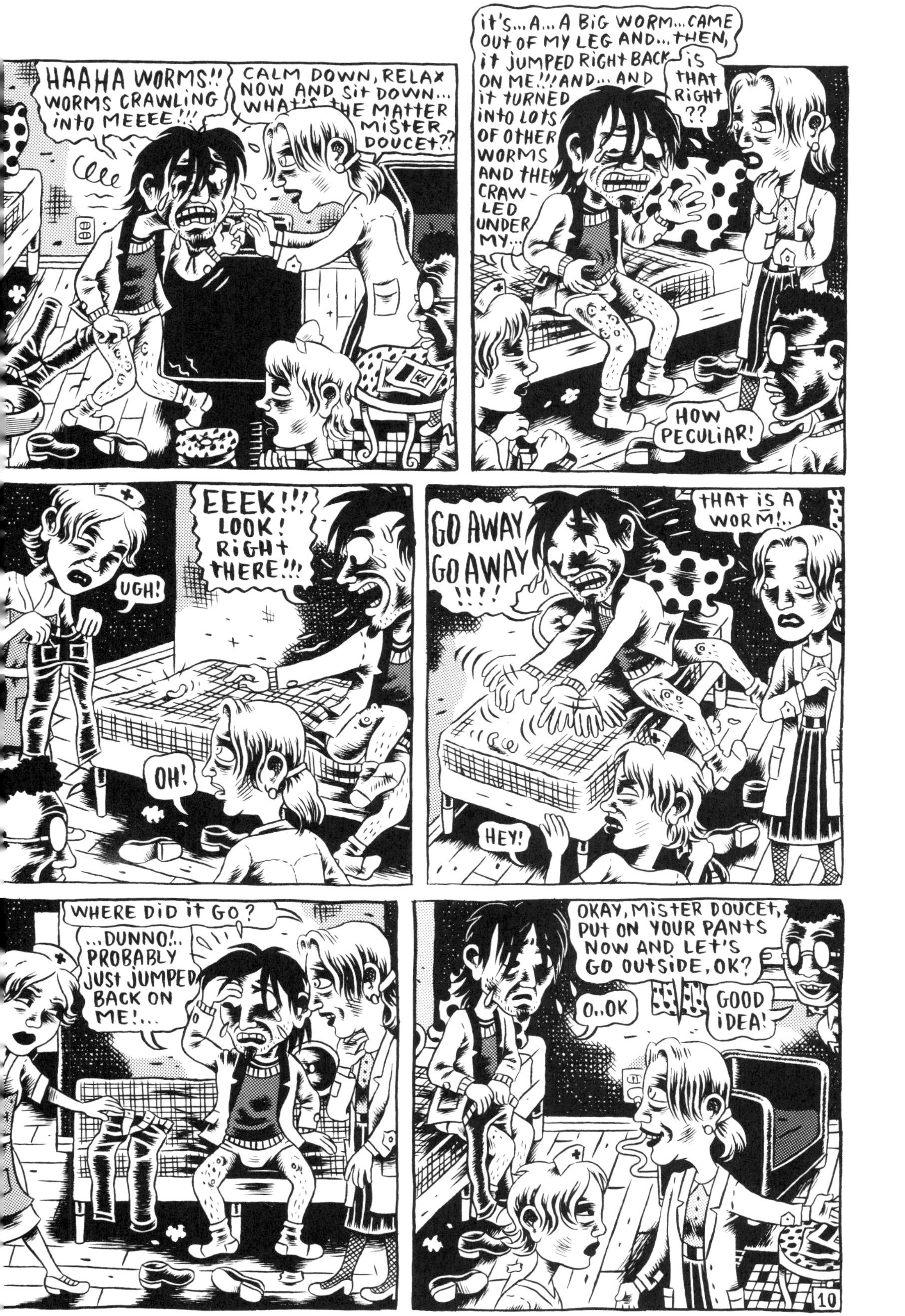
HAAHA WORMS!! WORMS CRAWLING iNTO MEEEE!!!
CALM DOWN, RELAX NOW AND SiT DOWN... WHAT'S THE MATTER MiSTER DOUCET??
iT'S... A... A BiG WORM... CAME OUT OF MY LEG AND... THEN, iT JUMPED RiGHT BACK ON ME!!! AND... AND iT TURNED iNTO LOTS OF OTHER WORMS AND THE CRAW-LED UNDER MY...
iS THAT RiGHT ??
HOW PECULiAR!
UGH!
EEEK!!! LOOK! RiGHT THERE!!!
OH!
GO AWAY GO AWAY !!!!
THAT iS A WORM!..
HEY!
WHERE DiD iT GO?
...DUNNO!.. PROBABLY JUST JUMPED BACK ON ME!...
OKAY, MiSTER DOUCET, PUT ON YOUR PANTS NOW AND LET'S GO OUTSiDE, OK?
O..OK
GOOD iDEA!
10

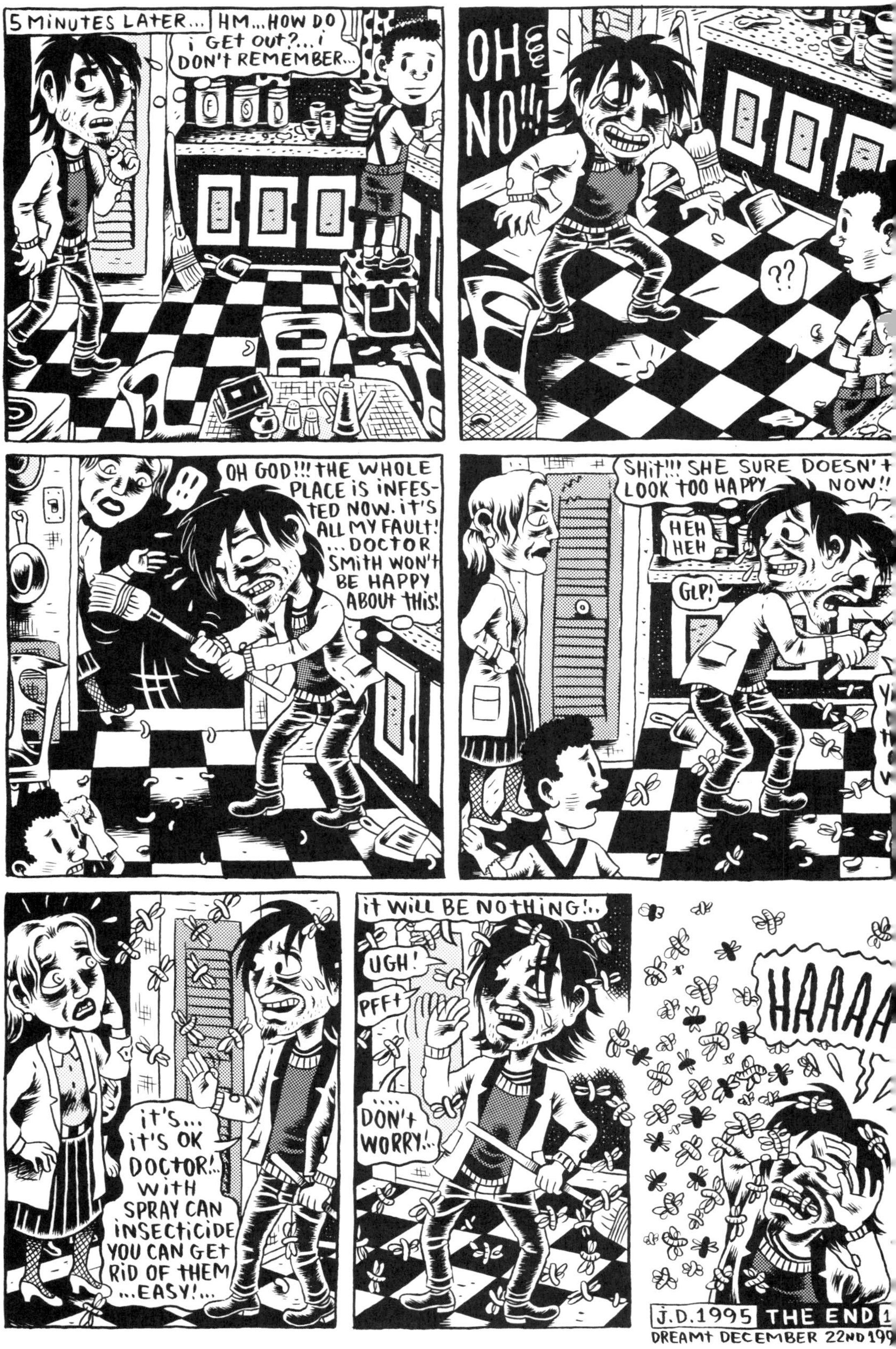
5 MINUTES LATER...
HM...HOW DO i GET OUT?...i DON'T REMEMBER...
OH NO!!!
??
!
OH GOD!!! THE WHOLE PLACE IS INFESTED NOW. iT'S ALL MY FAULT! ...DOCTOR SMITH WON'T BE HAPPY ABOUT THIS!
SHIT!!! SHE SURE DOESN'T LOOK TOO HAPPY NOW!!
HEH HEH
GLP!
iT'S... iT'S OK DOCTOR!... WiTH SPRAY CAN iNSECTiCiDE YOU CAN GET RiD OF THEM ...EASY!...
iT WiLL BE NOTHiNG!..
UGH!
PFFT
.... DON'T WORRY!..
HAAAA
J.D. 1995
THE END
DREAMT DECEMBER 22ND 199

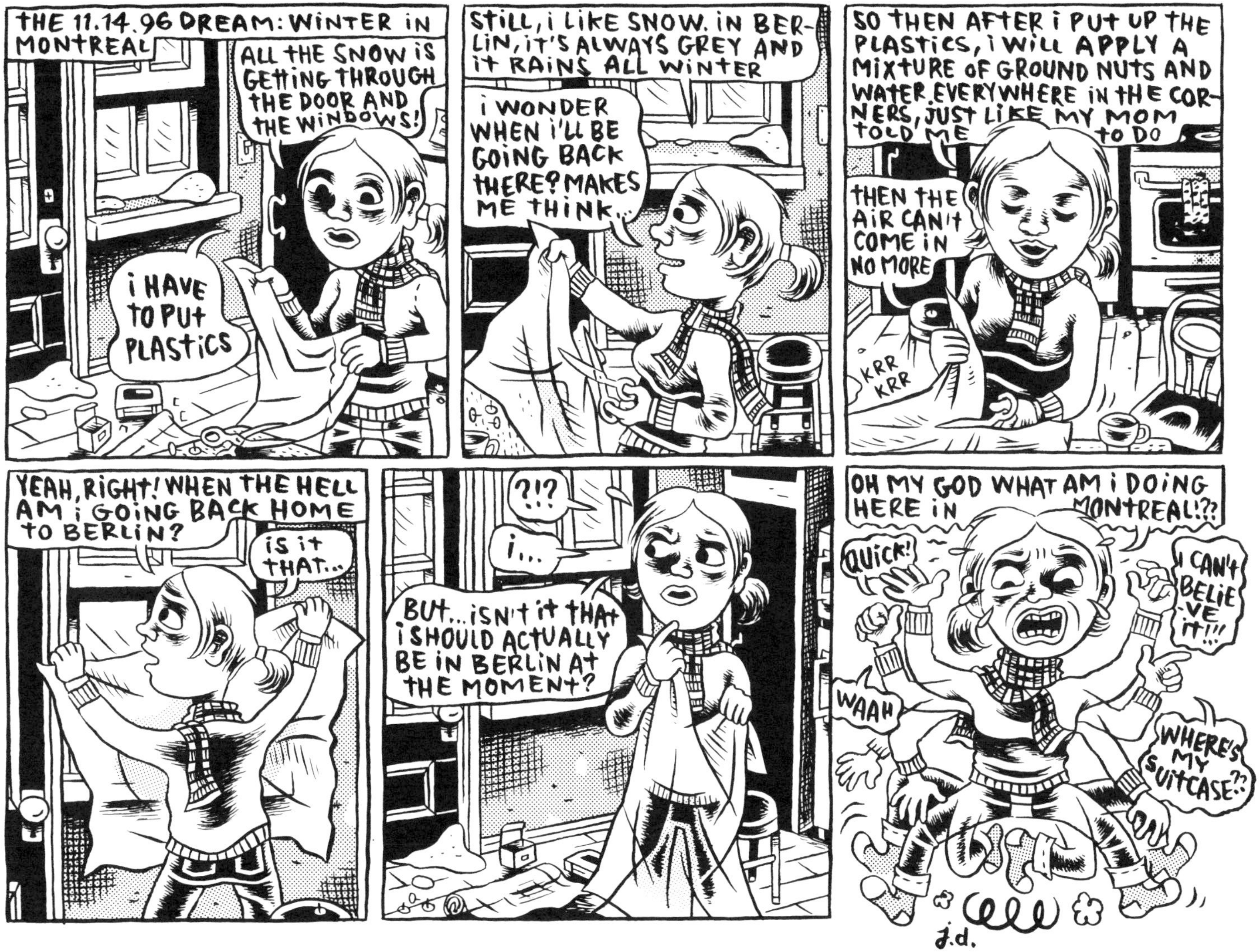
THE 11.14.96 DREAM: WINTER IN MONTREAL
ALL THE SNOW IS GETTING THROUGH THE DOOR AND THE WINDOWS!
I HAVE TO PUT PLASTICS
STILL, I LIKE SNOW. IN BERLIN, IT'S ALWAYS GREY AND IT RAINS ALL WINTER
I WONDER WHEN I'LL BE GOING BACK THERE? MAKES ME THINK...
SO THEN AFTER I PUT UP THE PLASTICS, I WILL APPLY A MIXTURE OF GROUND NUTS AND WATER EVERYWHERE IN THE CORNERS, JUST LIKE MY MOM TOLD ME TO DO
THEN THE AIR CAN'T COME IN NO MORE
KRR KRR
YEAH, RIGHT! WHEN THE HELL AM I GOING BACK HOME TO BERLIN?
IS IT THAT...
?!?
I...
BUT... ISN'T IT THAT I SHOULD ACTUALLY BE IN BERLIN AT THE MOMENT?
OH MY GOD WHAT AM I DOING HERE IN MONTREAL!??
QUICK!
I CAN'T BELIEVE IT!!!
WAAH
WHERE'S MY SUITCASE??
J.D.

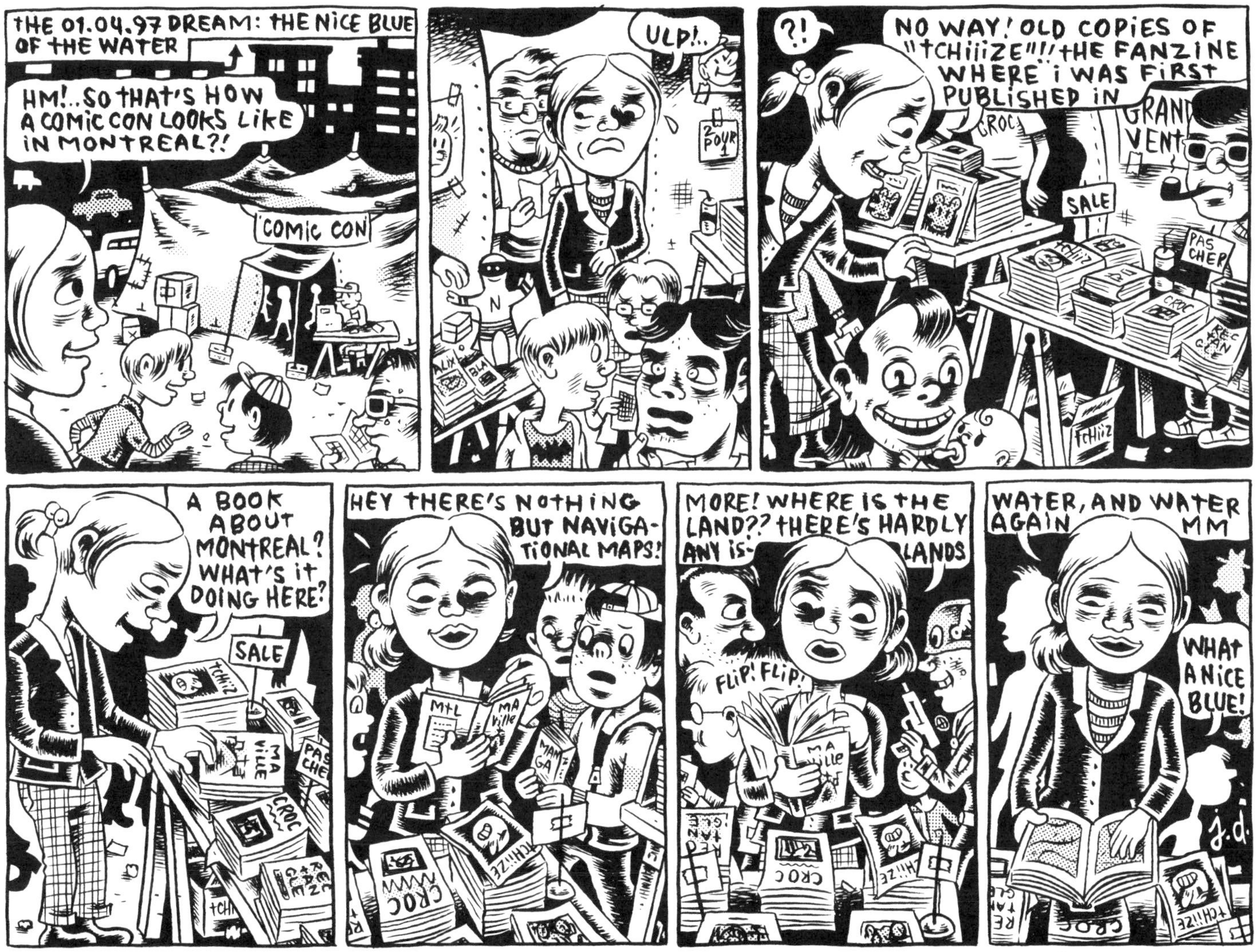
THE 01.04.97 DREAM: THE NICE BLUE OF THE WATER
HM!.. SO THAT'S HOW A COMIC CON LOOKS LIKE IN MONTREAL?!
COMIC CON
ULP!..
2 POUR 1
?!
NO WAY! OLD COPIES OF "TCHIIIZE"!! THE FANZINE WHERE I WAS FIRST PUBLISHED IN
GRAND VENT
SALE
PAS CHER
CROC
TCHIIIZ
A BOOK ABOUT MONTREAL? WHAT'S IT DOING HERE?
SALE
MA VILLE
CROC
HEY THERE'S NOTHING BUT NAVIGA-TIONAL MAPS!
MTL
MA VILLE
MANGA
CROC
TCHIIIZE
MORE! WHERE IS THE LAND?? THERE'S HARDLY ANY IS-LANDS
FLIP! FLIP!
MA VILLE
CROC
WATER, AND WATER AGAIN MM
WHAT A NICE BLUE!
J.D.

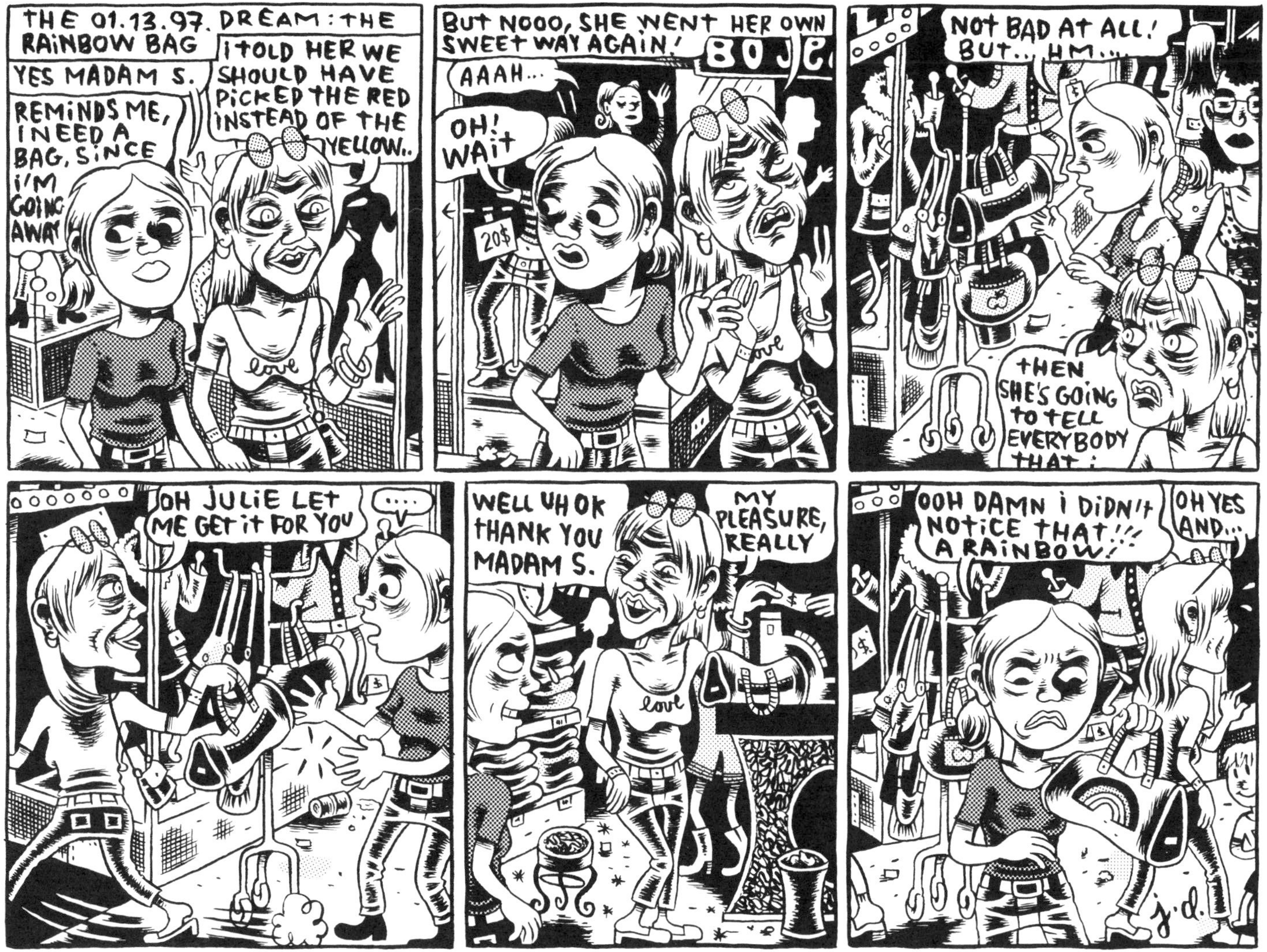
THE 01.13.97. DREAM: THE RAINBOW BAG
YES MADAM S.
REMINDS ME, I NEED A BAG, SINCE I'M GOING AWAY
I TOLD HER WE SHOULD HAVE PICKED THE RED INSTEAD OF THE YELLOW..
BUT NOOO, SHE WENT HER OWN SWEET WAY AGAIN!
AAAH...
OH! WAIT
20$
NOT BAD AT ALL! BUT.. HM...
THEN SHE'S GOING TO TELL EVERYBODY THAT:
OH JULIE LET ME GET IT FOR YOU
....
WELL UH OK THANK YOU MADAM S.
MY PLEASURE, REALLY
OOH DAMN I DIDN'T NOTICE THAT!!! A RAINBOW!!
OH YES AND...
j.d.

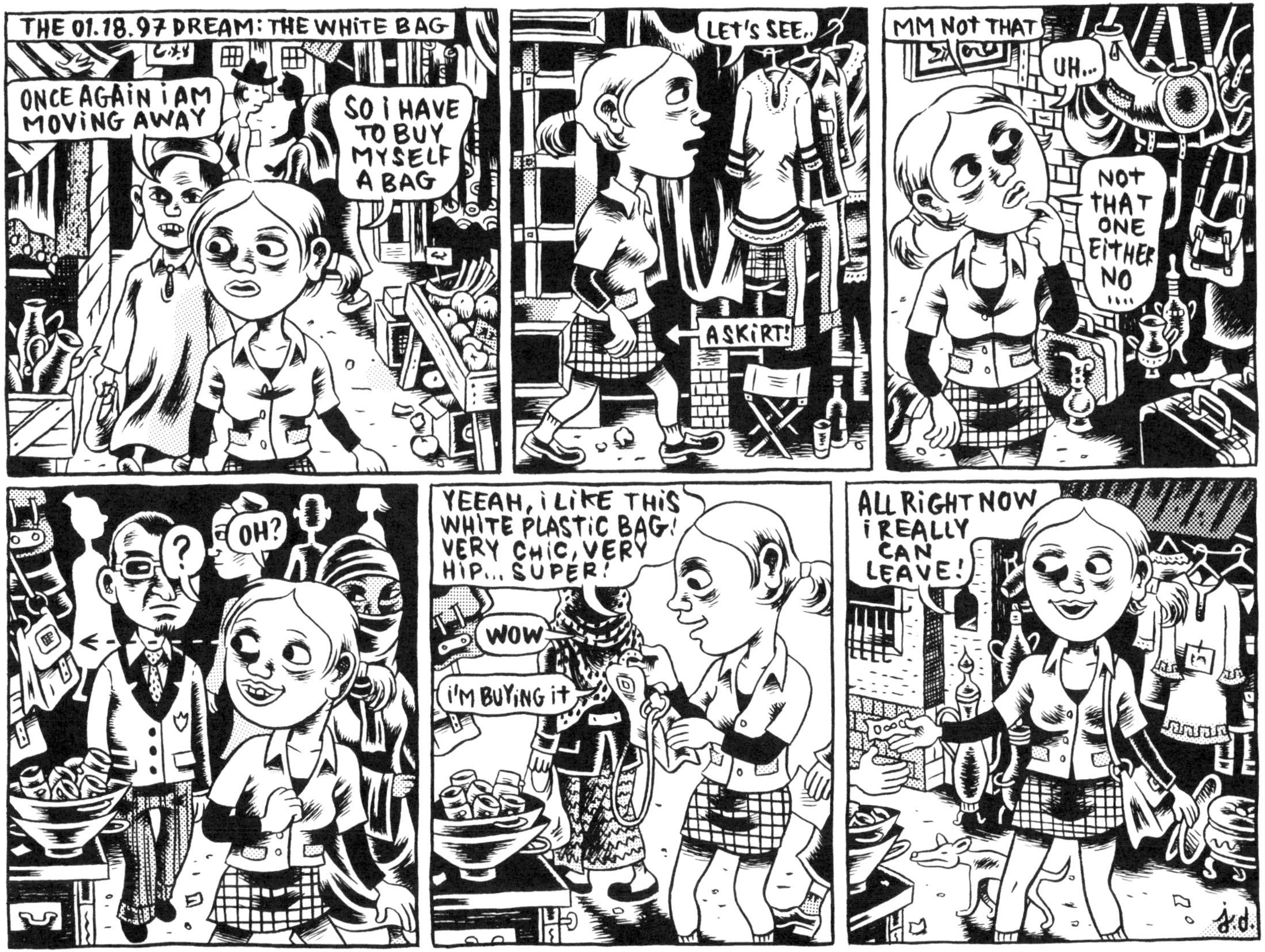
THE 01.18.97 DREAM: THE WHITE BAG
ONCE AGAIN I AM MOVING AWAY
SO I HAVE TO BUY MYSELF A BAG
LET'S SEE..
A SKIRT!
MM NOT THAT
UH...
NOT THAT ONE EITHER NO !!!!
?
OH?
YEEAH, I LIKE THIS WHITE PLASTIC BAG! VERY CHIC, VERY HIP... SUPER!
WOW
I'M BUYING IT
ALL RIGHT NOW I REALLY CAN LEAVE!
J.D.

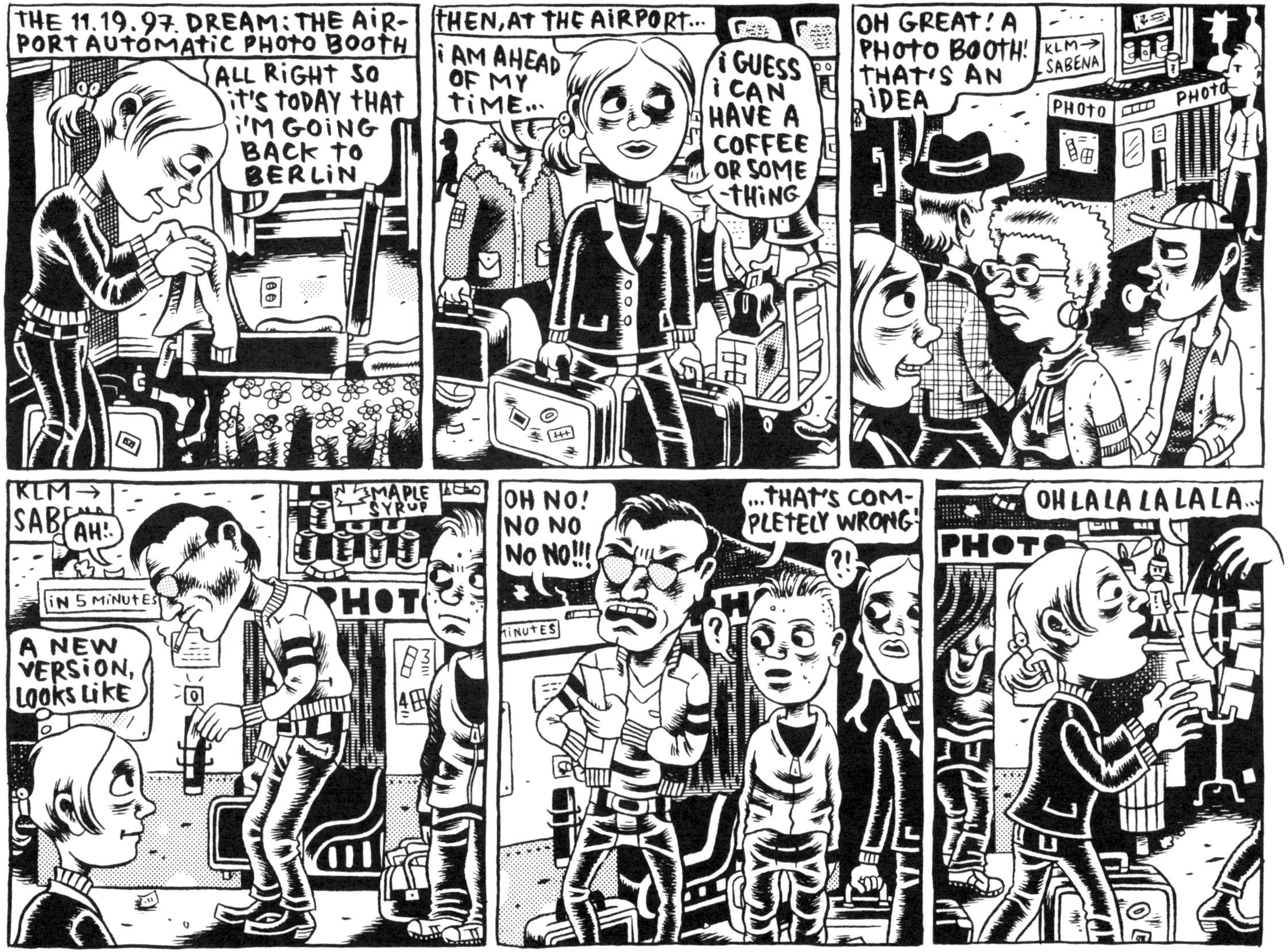
THE 11.19.97. DREAM: THE AIRPORT AUTOMATIC PHOTO BOOTH
ALL RIGHT SO IT'S TODAY THAT I'M GOING BACK TO BERLIN
THEN, AT THE AIRPORT...
I AM AHEAD OF MY TIME...
I GUESS I CAN HAVE A COFFEE OR SOME-THING
OH GREAT! A PHOTO BOOTH! THAT'S AN IDEA
KLM → SABENA
PHOTO
PHOTO
KLM → SAB
AH!
MAPLE SYRUP
IN 5 MINUTES
PHOT
A NEW VERSION, LOOKS LIKE
OH NO! NO NO NO NO!!!
...THAT'S COMPLETELY WRONG!
?!
?
MINUTES
OH LA LA LA LA LA...
PHOTO

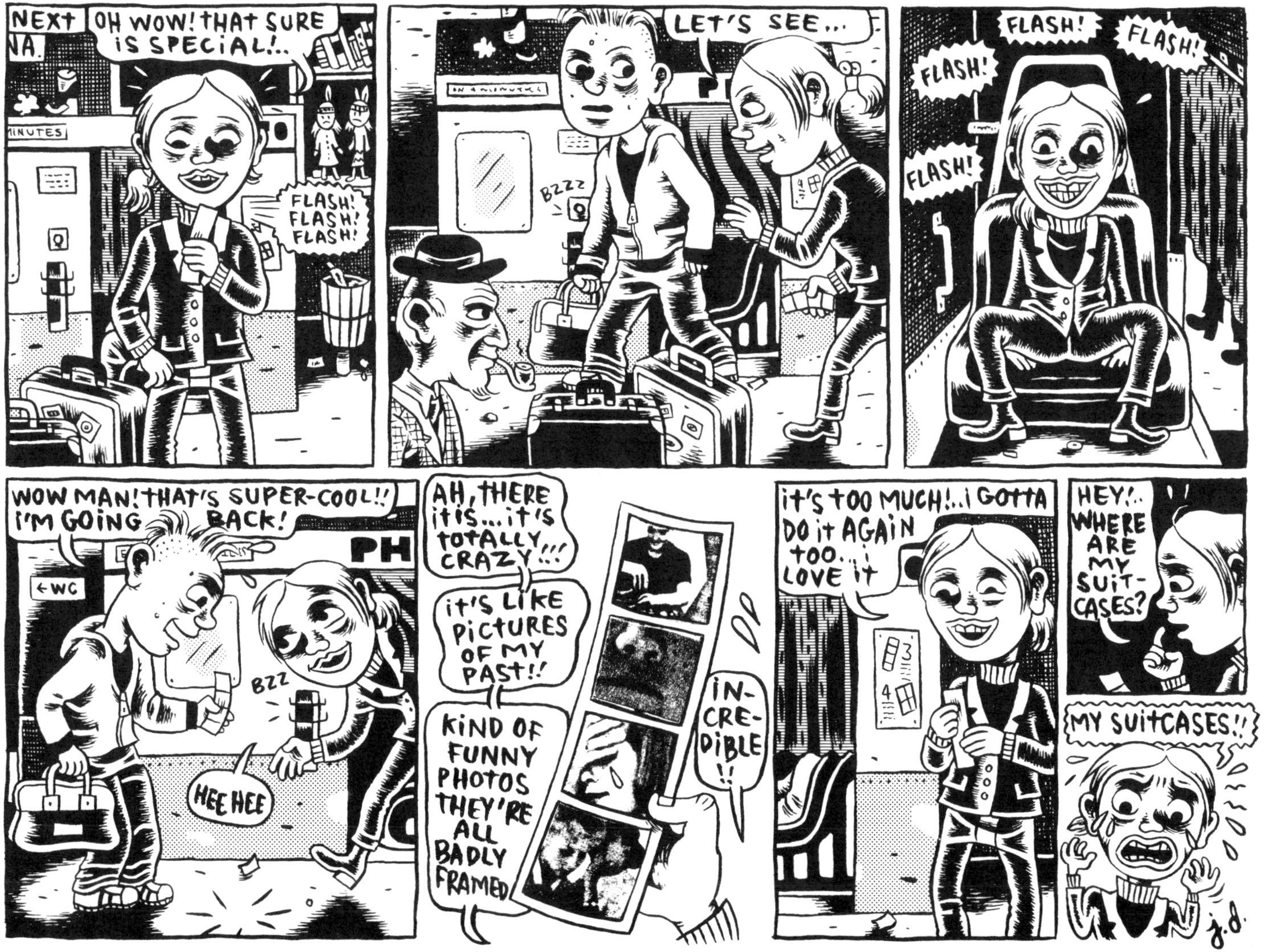
NEXT
NA.
MINUTES
OH WOW! THAT SURE IS SPECIAL!..
FLASH! FLASH! FLASH!
BZZZ
LET'S SEE...
FLASH!
FLASH!
FLASH!
FLASH!
WOW MAN! THAT'S SUPER-COOL!! I'M GOING BACK!
←WC
PH
BZZ
HEE HEE
AH, THERE IT IS... IT'S TOTALLY CRAZY!!!
IT'S LIKE PICTURES OF MY PAST!!
KIND OF FUNNY PHOTOS THEY'RE ALL BADLY FRAMED
IN-CRE-DIBLE !!
IT'S TOO MUCH!.. I GOTTA DO IT AGAIN TOO... I LOVE IT
HEY!.. WHERE ARE MY SUIT-CASES?
MY SUITCASES!!
j.d.

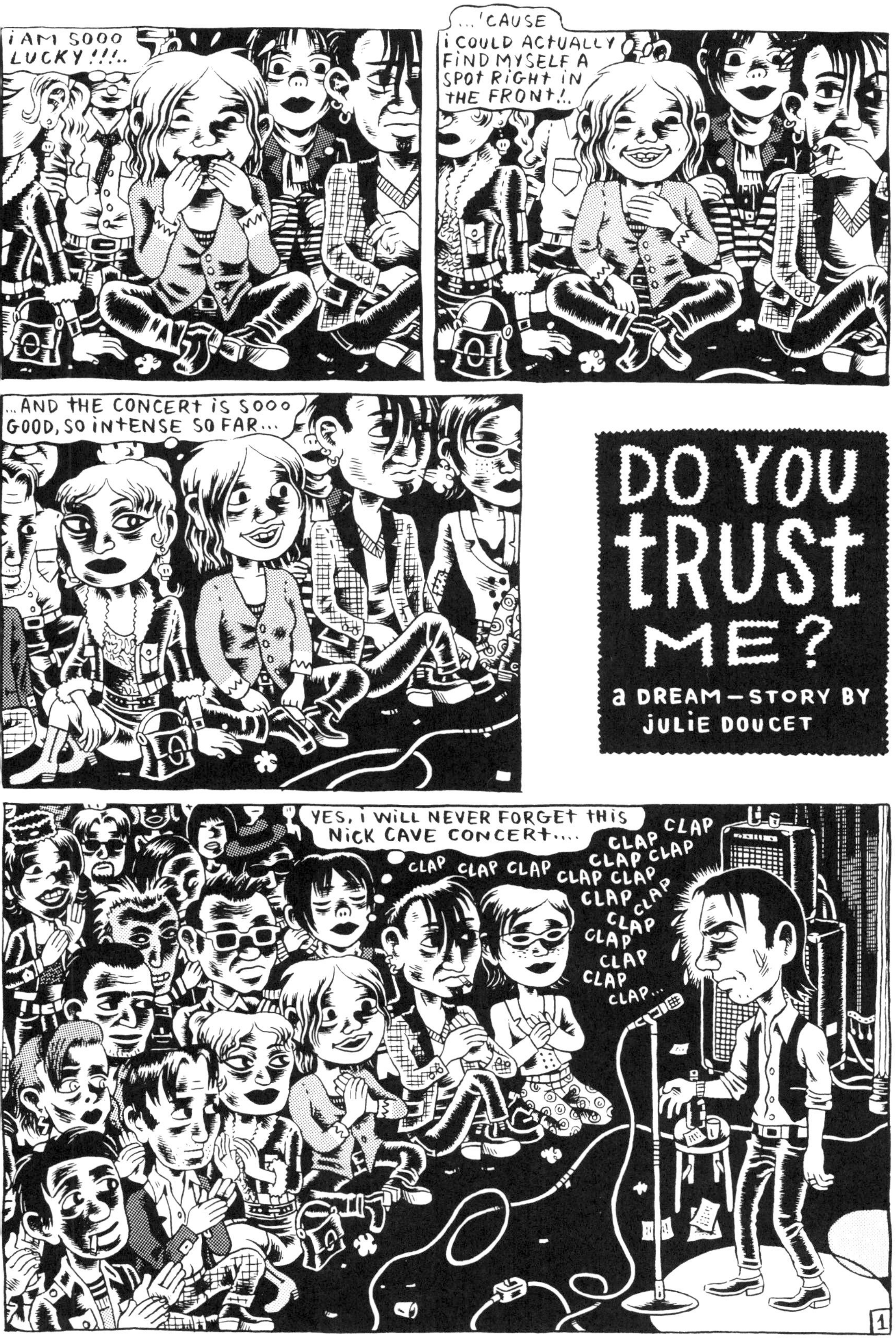
i AM SOOO LUCKY!!!..
...'CAUSE i COULD ACTUALLY FiND MYSELF A SPOT RiGHT iN THE FRONT!..
...AND THE CONCERT iS SOOO GOOD, SO iNTENSE SO FAR...
DO YOU TRUST ME?
a DREAM-STORY BY JULiE DOUCET
YES, i WiLL NEVER FORGET THiS NiCK CAVE CONCERT....
CLAP CLAP CLAP CLAP CLAP CLAP CLAP CLAP CLAP CLAP CLAP CLAP CLAP CLAP CLAP CLAP CLAP...
1

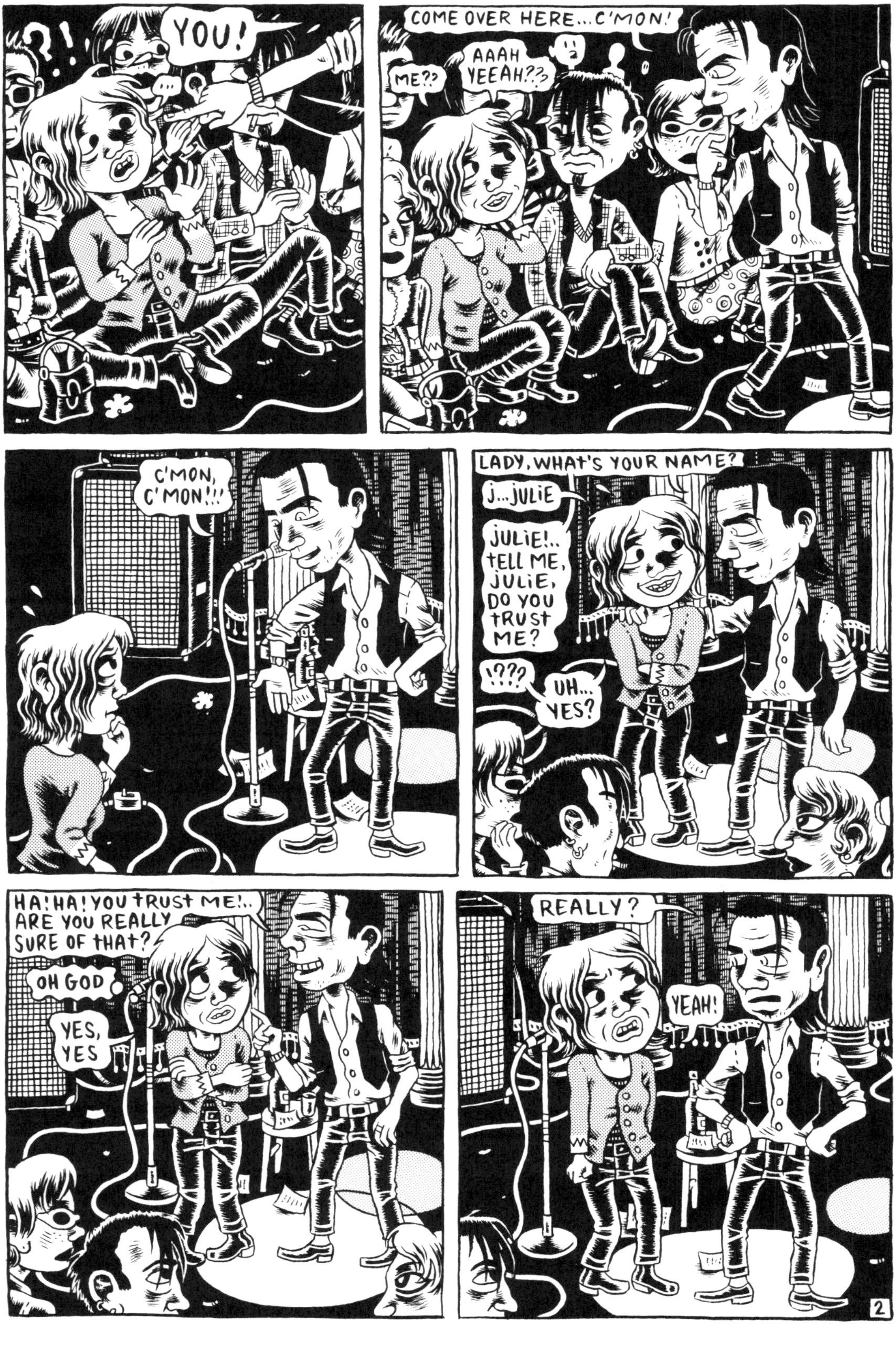
?!
YOU!
...
COME OVER HERE...C'MON!
ME??
AAAH YEEAH???
C'MON, C'MON!!!
LADY, WHAT'S YOUR NAME?
J...JULIE
JULIE!.. TELL ME, JULIE, DO YOU TRUST ME?
!???
UH... YES?
HA! HA! YOU TRUST ME!.. ARE YOU REALLY SURE OF THAT?
OH GOD
YES, YES
REALLY?
YEAH!

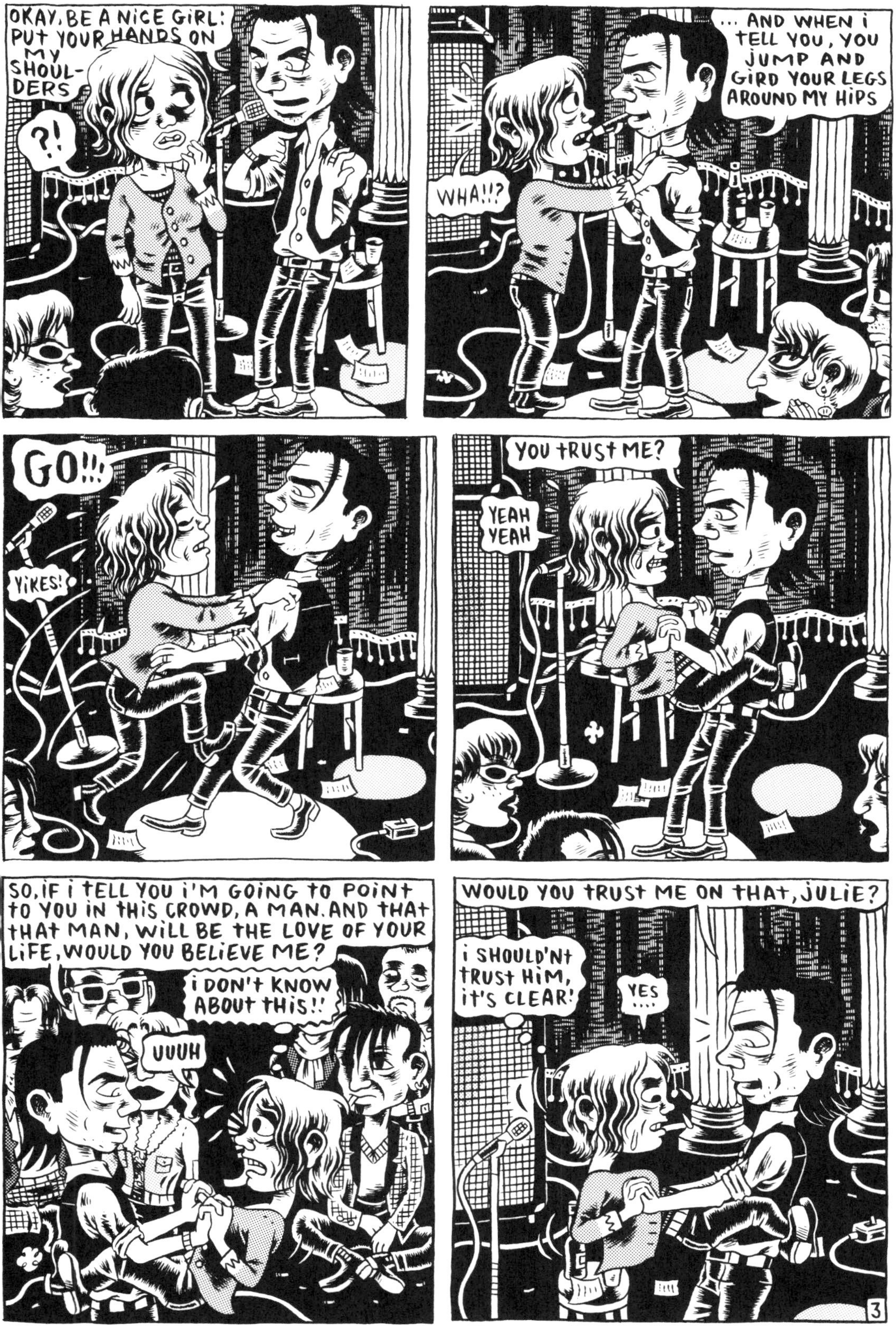

OKAY, BE A NICE GIRL: PUT YOUR HANDS ON MY SHOULDERS
?!
... AND WHEN I TELL YOU, YOU JUMP AND GIRD YOUR LEGS AROUND MY HIPS
WHA!!?
GO!!!
YIKES!
YOU TRUST ME?
YEAH YEAH
SO, IF I TELL YOU I'M GOING TO POINT TO YOU IN THIS CROWD, A MAN. AND THAT THAT MAN, WILL BE THE LOVE OF YOUR LIFE, WOULD YOU BELIEVE ME?
I DON'T KNOW ABOUT THIS!!
UUUH
WOULD YOU TRUST ME ON THAT, JULIE?
I SHOULD'NT TRUST HIM, IT'S CLEAR!
YES ....
3

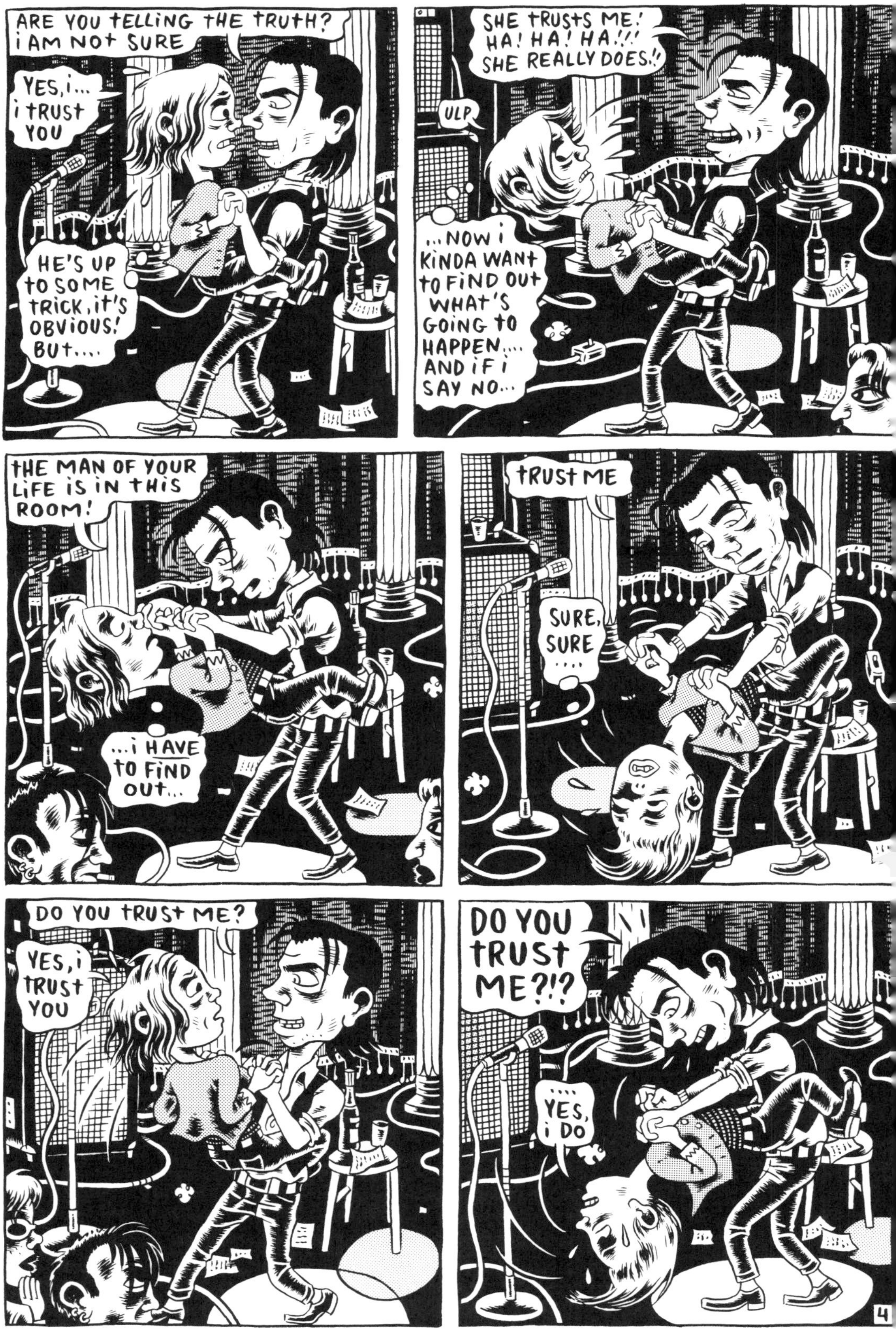
ARE YOU TELLING THE TRUTH? I AM NOT SURE
YES, I... I TRUST YOU
HE'S UP TO SOME TRICK, IT'S OBVIOUS! BUT....
SHE TRUSTS ME! HA! HA! HA!!! SHE REALLY DOES!!
ULP
...NOW I KINDA WANT TO FIND OUT WHAT'S GOING TO HAPPEN.... AND IF I SAY NO...
THE MAN OF YOUR LIFE IS IN THIS ROOM!
...I HAVE TO FIND OUT...
TRUST ME
SURE, SURE ....
DO YOU TRUST ME?
YES, I TRUST YOU
DO YOU TRUST ME?!?
.... YES, I DO

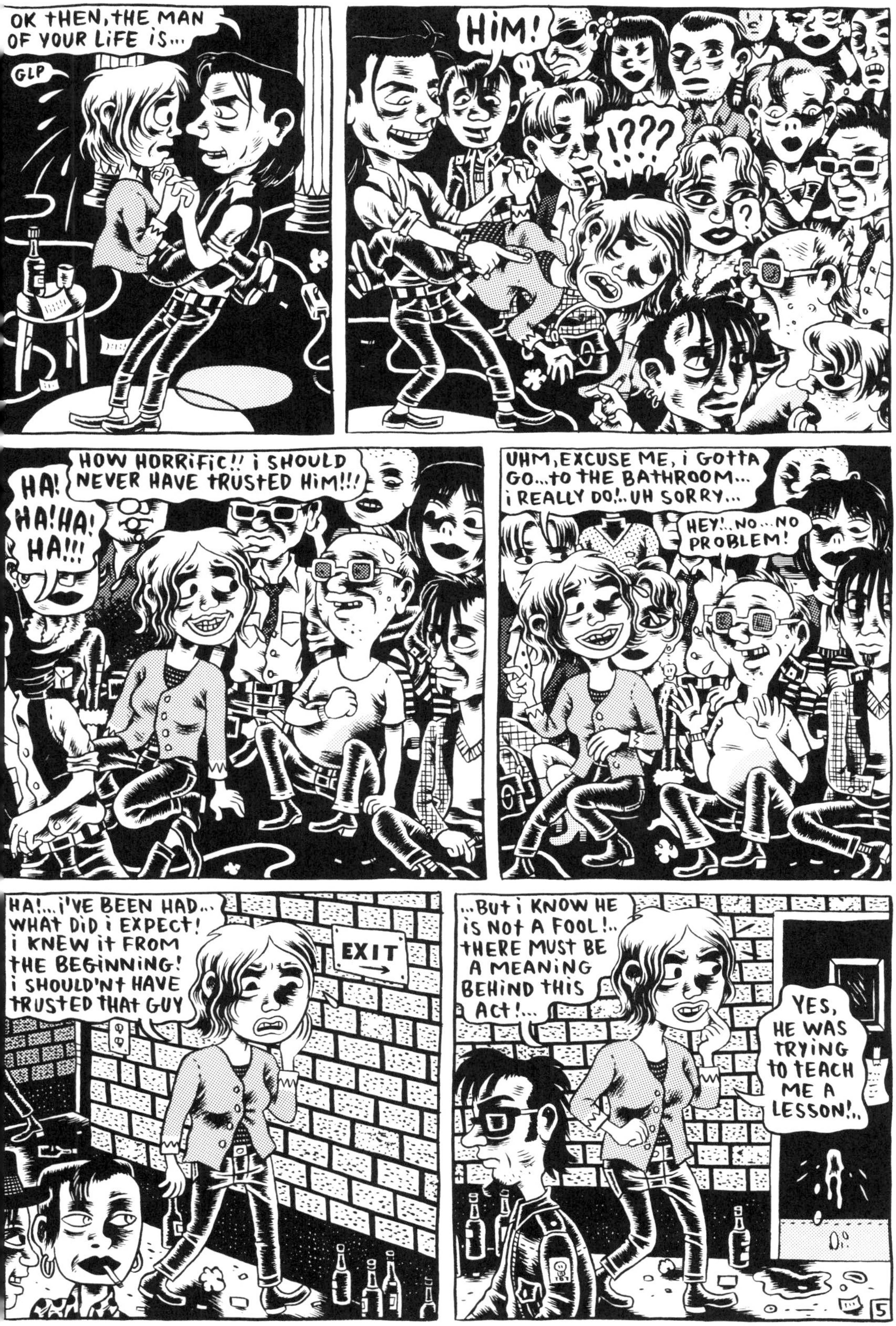
OK THEN, THE MAN OF YOUR LIFE IS...
GLP
HIM!
!???
?
HA! HA! HA! HA!!!
HOW HORRIFIC!! I SHOULD NEVER HAVE TRUSTED HIM!!!
UHM, EXCUSE ME, I GOTTA GO... TO THE BATHROOM... I REALLY DO!.. UH SORRY...
HEY!.. NO... NO PROBLEM!
HA!... I'VE BEEN HAD... WHAT DID I EXPECT! I KNEW IT FROM THE BEGINNING! I SHOULD'NT HAVE TRUSTED THAT GUY
EXIT
...BUT I KNOW HE IS NOT A FOOL!.. THERE MUST BE A MEANING BEHIND THIS ACT!...
YES, HE WAS TRYING TO TEACH ME A LESSON!..
5

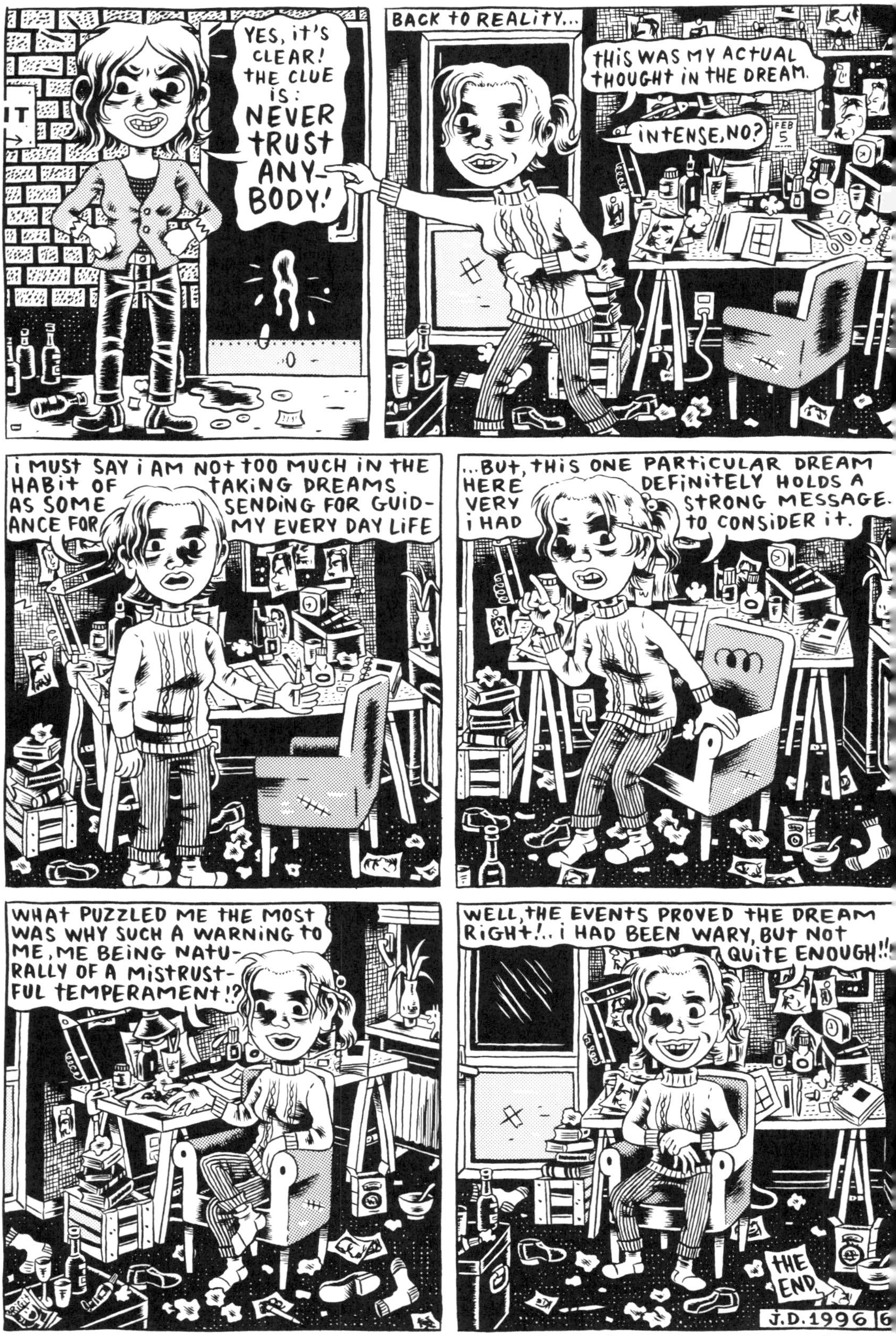
IT
YES, IT'S CLEAR! THE CLUE IS: NEVER TRUST ANY-BODY!
BACK TO REALITY...
THIS WAS MY ACTUAL THOUGHT IN THE DREAM.
INTENSE, NO?
FEB 5
I MUST SAY I AM NOT TOO MUCH IN THE HABIT OF TAKING DREAMS AS SOME SENDING FOR GUID-ANCE FOR MY EVERY DAY LIFE
...BUT, THIS ONE PARTICULAR DREAM HERE DEFINITELY HOLDS A VERY STRONG MESSAGE. I HAD TO CONSIDER IT.
WHAT PUZZLED ME THE MOST WAS WHY SUCH A WARNING TO ME, ME BEING NATU-RALLY OF A MISTRUST-FUL TEMPERAMENT!?
WELL, THE EVENTS PROVED THE DREAM RIGHT!.. I HAD BEEN WARY, BUT NOT QUITE ENOUGH!!
THE END
J.D.1996 6

DReamt july 1995 – DRAWN january 1996

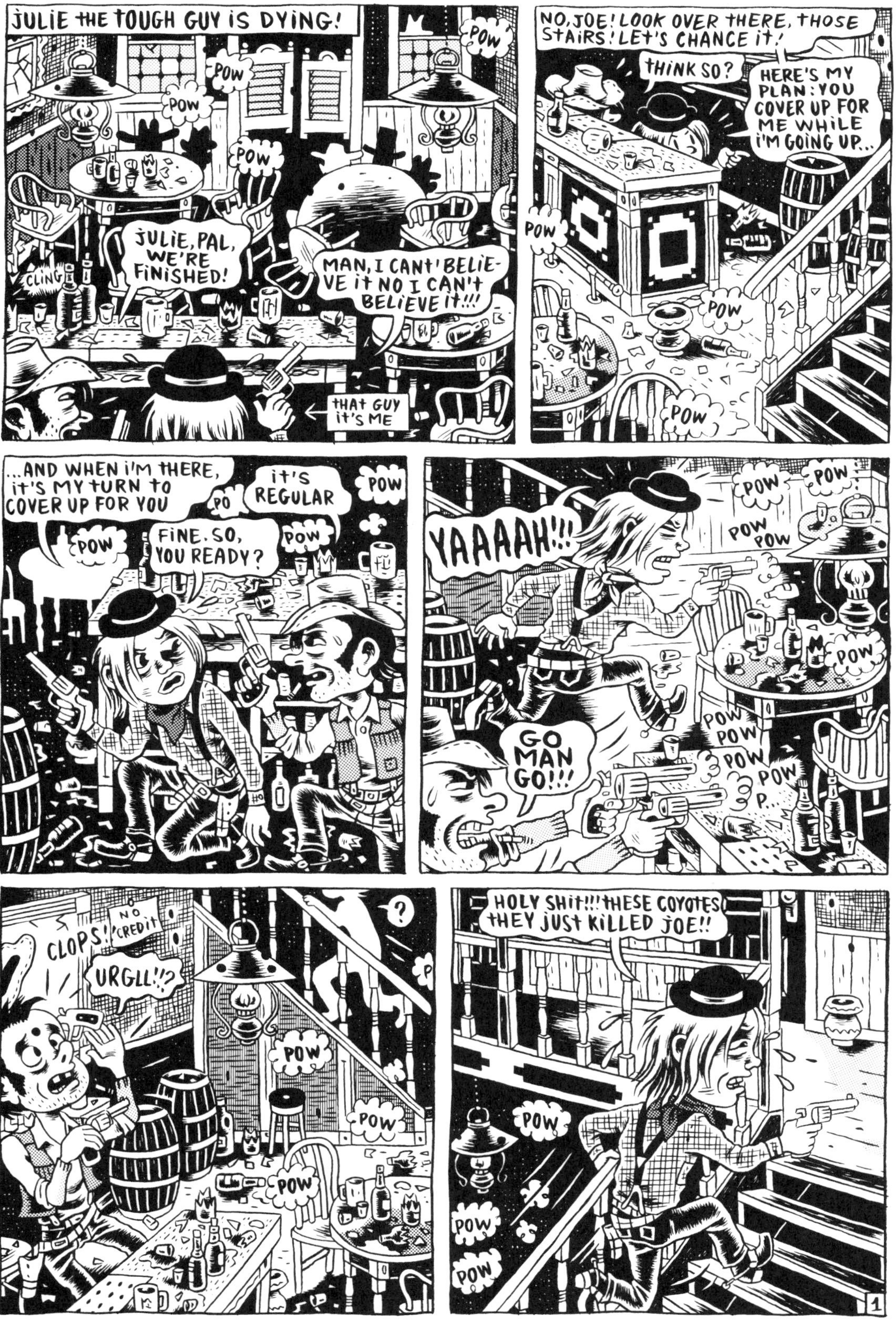
JULIE THE TOUGH GUY IS DYING!
POW
POW
POW
POW
JULIE, PAL, WE'RE FINISHED!
CLING
MAN, I CAN'T BELIEVE IT NO I CAN'T BELIEVE IT!!!
THAT GUY IT'S ME
NO, JOE! LOOK OVER THERE, THOSE STAIRS! LET'S CHANCE IT!
THINK SO?
HERE'S MY PLAN: YOU COVER UP FOR ME WHILE I'M GOING UP...
POW
POW
POW
...AND WHEN I'M THERE, IT'S MY TURN TO COVER UP FOR YOU
PO
IT'S REGULAR
POW
POW
FINE. SO, YOU READY?
POW
YAAAAH!!!
POW
POW
POW POW
POW
GO MAN GO!!!
POW POW POW POW P...
CLOPS!
NO CREDIT
URGLL!?
?
POW
POW
POW
HOLY SHIT!!! THESE COYOTES THEY JUST KILLED JOE!!
POW
POW
POW

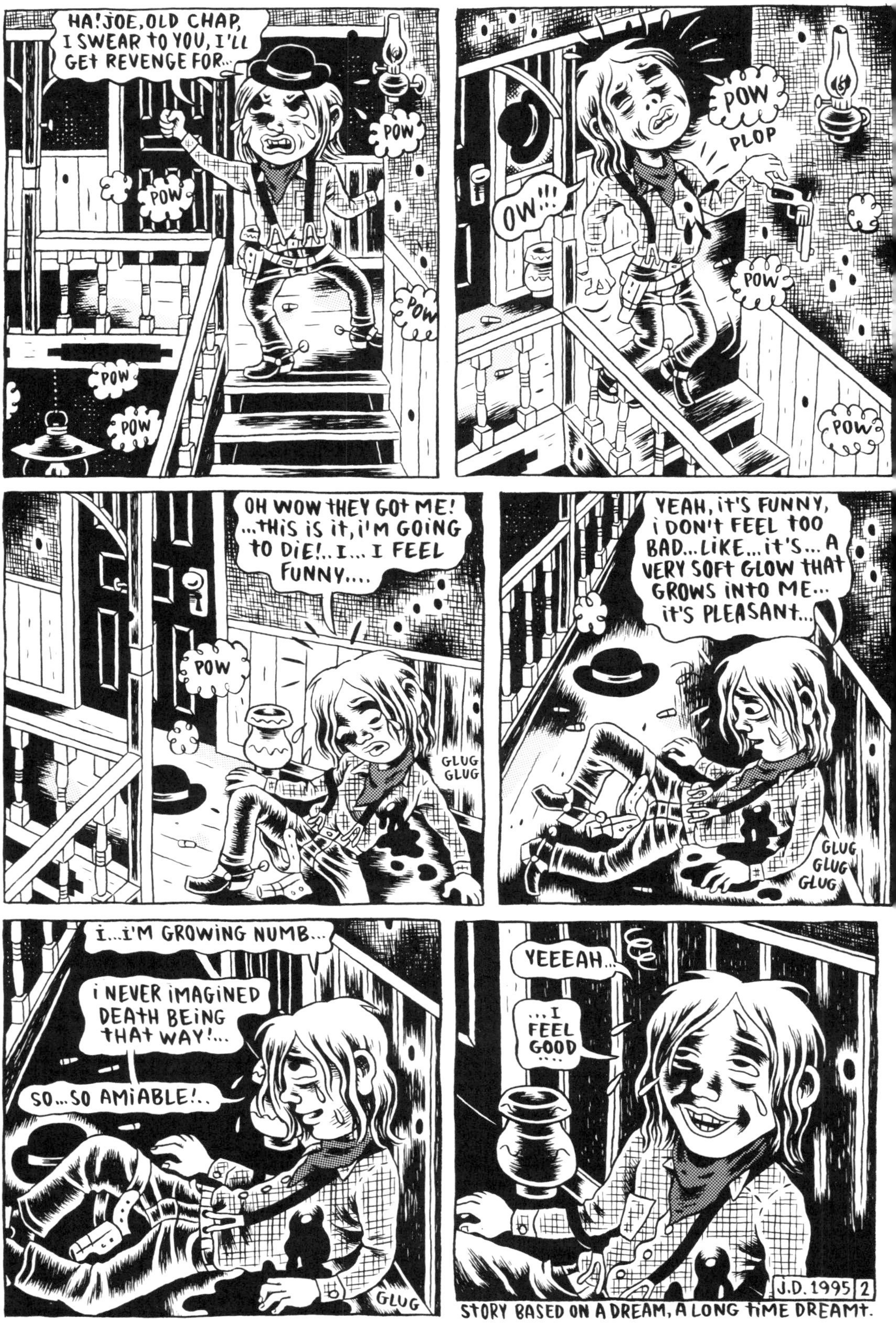
HA! JOE, OLD CHAP, I SWEAR TO YOU, I'LL GET REVENGE FOR...
POW
POW
POW
POW
POW
POW
PLOP
OW!!!
POW
POW
POW
OH WOW THEY GOT ME! ...THIS IS IT, I'M GOING TO DIE!.. I... I FEEL FUNNY....
POW
GLUG GLUG
YEAH, IT'S FUNNY, I DON'T FEEL TOO BAD... LIKE... IT'S... A VERY SOFT GLOW THAT GROWS INTO ME... IT'S PLEASANT...
GLUG GLUG GLUG
I... I'M GROWING NUMB...
I NEVER IMAGINED DEATH BEING THAT WAY!...
SO... SO AMIABLE!..
GLUG
YEEEAH...
...I FEEL GOOD....
J.D. 1995 2
STORY BASED ON A DREAM, A LONG TIME DREAMT.

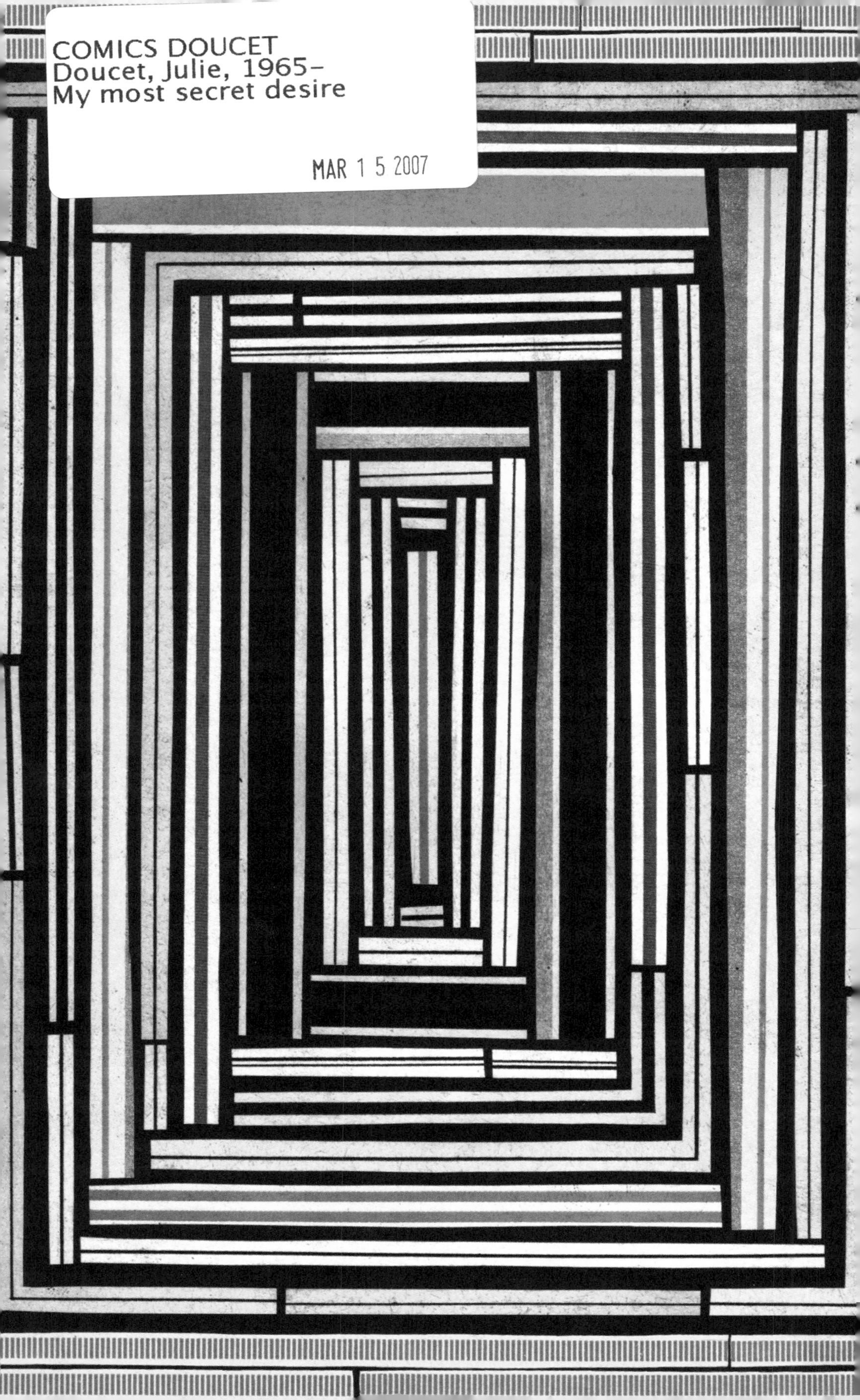